BAKING SUBSTITUTIONS

THE A-Z OF COMMON, UNIQUE, AND HARD-TO-FIND INGREDIENTS

Jean B. MacLeod

MacLeod How-To Books

Baking Substitutions: The A-Z of Common, Unique, and Hard-to-Find Ingredients

ISBN-13: 9780997446449

To the memory of Ian,
with love

CONTENTS

INGREDIENT SUBSTITUTIONS

A

AÇAI (South American antioxidant-rich berry) – 3.5 ounces frozen pulp/puree
- 1/2 to 3/4 cup dried Chilean wineberries/maqui berries, soaked in liquid for 30 minutes (higher in antioxidants)
- 1 cup fresh or frozen wild blueberries (lower in antioxidants)
- 1 cup fresh, or 1/2 cup dried, blue Oregon grapes/*Mahonia aquifolium/Berberis aquifolium* (lower in antioxidants; much tarter; press fresh berries through a food mill to remove large seeds)
- 1 cup fresh silverberries/*Elaeagnus umbellata* or *E. multiflora* (lower in antioxidants; higher in vitamin C and lycopene; press through a food mill to remove large seeds)

AÇAI JUICE (antioxidant-rich juice) – 1 cup
- 2 tablespoons freeze-dried açai powder mixed with 1 cup water
- 2 tablespoons maqui berry powder mixed with 1 cup water (higher in antioxidants)
- 1 cup 100% blueberry juice, preferably fresh-pressed (lower in antioxidants)
- 2 tablespoons freeze-dried blueberry powder mixed with 1 cup water (lower in antioxidants)

ACIDULATED WATER (anti-browning agent for certain cut fruits and vegetables) – 1 cup
- 1 cup water plus 3/4 teaspoon kosher salt (rinse thoroughly with fresh water after soaking)
- 1 cup water plus 1 teaspoon distilled white vinegar
- 1 cup water plus 2 teaspoons lemon juice

➺ 1 cup water plus small pinch ascorbic acid granules, or 1 (250-mg) pure vitamin C pill crushed to a powder

➺ 1 cup apple juice (for holding prepared apples)

ACITRÓN/BIGNAGA CACTUS (Mexican candied cactus pieces) – 4 ounces

➺ 4 ounces candied pineapple

AGAVE SYRUP/NECTAR, LIGHT OR DARK – 1 cup

➺ 7/8 cup grade A dark, robust maple syrup plus 1 tablespoon water

➺ 1 cup palm honey/syrup, heavy/rich simple syrup, or Swedish light syrup/ljus sirap

➺ 3/4 cup mild-flavored liquid honey, such as acacia or clove, plus 2 tablespoons water

➺ 1 cup birch syrup, yacon syrup, coconut nectar, or Jerusalem artichoke syrup

AGRUMATO-LEMON OIL (Italian citrus oil) See LEMON-OLIVE OIL

ALLSPICE, JAMAICAN/PIMENTO BERRIES, DRIED – 1 teaspoon ground

➺ 1 teaspoon ground Mexican or Central American allspice (larger berries; less aromatic)

➺ Scant 1/2 teaspoon each ground cloves and cinnamon plus scant 1/4 teaspoon ground nutmeg

➺ 1/2 teaspoon ground cinnamon plus 1/8 teaspoon ground cloves

ALMOND BUTTER – 1 cup

➺ 1 cup coconut butter, cashew butter, peanut butter, or tahini
Make Your Own Grind 2 cups roasted almonds with 1/2 teaspoon sea salt (optional) in a food processor until reduced to a paste, about 10 minutes, scraping down the sides of the bowl as needed. Transfer to a sterilized jar and store in the refrigerator; it will last for up to 4 weeks.

ALMOND EXTRACT – 1 teaspoon
- ⇨ 2 drops bitter almond oil
- ⇨ 1 teaspoon amaretto extract
- ⇨ 2 tablespoons almond-flavored liqueur (reduce liquid in the recipe by 2 tablespoons)

ALMOND FLOUR, TOASTED – 1 cup
Make Your Own Spread 1 cup almond flour on a baking sheet and toast in a preheated 350°F oven until golden, 6 to 7 minutes.

ALMOND LIQUEUR/ALMOND-FLAVORED SPIRIT (such as amaretto, crème d'amande, or ratafia) – 1 tablespoon for cooking
- ⇨ 1/4 teaspoon almond extract plus 1 tablespoon vodka or water

ALMOND MEAL – 1 cup
- ⇨ 1 cup almond flour/powder (finer texture; more expensive)
- ⇨ 1 cup hazelnut or chestnut flour
- ⇨ 1 cup pumpkin seed or sunflower seed meal (denser texture; best for cookies and muffins)

Make Your Own Grind 1 1/2 cups sliced or slivered almonds in a blender or food processor until mealy (add a teaspoon or more of sugar or flour from the recipe to avoid oiliness or freeze the almonds before grinding). Alternatively, grind the almonds in batches in a spice/coffee grinder, then strain and regrind any large pieces. Store, refrigerated, in an airtight container; it will keep for up to 6 months.

ALMOND MILK – 1 cup
- ⇨ 7/8 cup purified water plus 1/8 cup smooth raw almond butter, processed in a blender or food processor until smooth
- ⇨ 1 cup unsweetened hazelnut, walnut, or soy milk

Make Your Own Soak 1 to 2 cups freshly blanched raw almonds in water to cover for 10 to 12 hours; drain, rinse, and then blend with 4 cups water until smooth, 3 to 4 minutes. Strain through a nutmilk bag or cheesecloth-lined sieve, pressing firmly on the pulp to extract all the liquid. Keep refrigerated and shake before using. It will keep for up to 5 days. (For a thinner milk, increase water to 5 cups; for a more nutritious milk, blend the almonds with fresh coconut water.)

ALMOND PASTE – 1 cup
Make Your Own Pulse 1 cup finely ground blanched almonds, 3/4 cup granulated sugar, 2 tablespoons water, and 1/2 teaspoon pure almond extract in a food processor until a paste forms, and then knead until smooth. It will keep, well-wrapped, for up to 1 month in the refrigerator, or up to 1 year in the freezer.

ALMOND SYRUP/ORZATA (Greek sweetener) – 1 tablespoon
☞ 1 tablespoon orgeat syrup

ALMONDS, MARCONA ROASTED (soft flat Spanish almonds) – 1 pound
☞ 1 pound California blanched almonds, soaked in salted water for 8 to 12 hours; drained, tossed with 1 tablespoon olive oil, then toasted at 300°F until dry, 10 to 15 minutes, stirring halfway through
☞ 1 pound oven-roasted almonds, such as Blue Diamond

ALMONDS, SWEET – 1 cup shelled
☞ 1 cup shelled and skinned hazelnuts

AMARANTH FLOUR – 1 cup
☞ 1 cup brown rice flour
☞ 1 cup sorghum flour
☞ 1 cup light-colored teff flour

AMMONIUM BICARBONATE/AMMONIUM CARBONATE/ HARTSHORN/BAKER'S AMMONIA (leavening agent) – 1 teaspoon finely crushed
☞ 1 teaspoon cream of tartar
☞ 1 teaspoon single-acting, aluminum-free baking powder
☞ 1 1/4 teaspoons baking soda

ANISE EXTRACT – 1 teaspoon
- 1 1/2 tablespoons anise seeds, ground in a mortar or a spice/coffee grinder
- 2 teaspoons ground anise seeds
- 1/8 teaspoon anise oil

ANISE LIQUEUR/ANISE-FLAVORED SPIRIT (such as ouzo, pastis, sambuca, xtabentún, or other unsweetened anise-flavored spirit) – 1 tablespoon for cooking
- 1 tablespoon vodka plus 1 teaspoon ground anise seeds
- 1/2 teaspoon anise extract plus 2 teaspoons water

ANISE SEEDS – 1 teaspoon
- 2 whole star anise pods, crushed or coarsely ground, or 1 1/2 teaspoons broken pieces
- 1/4 teaspoon anise extract
- 1 1/4 teaspoons fennel or caraway seeds

APPELSTROOP (thick Dutch syrup) – 1 cup
- 4 cups fresh apple juice, simmered until reduced to 1 cup, 45 to 60 minutes
- 1 cup *keukenstroop*, molasses, or strong honey

APPLE BRANDY/APPLEJACK (such as Calvados or Laird's) – 2 tablespoons
- 1 tablespoon each apple juice concentrate and brandy
- 2 tablespoons hard cider

APPLE CIDER – 1 cup
- 3/4 cup apple juice and 1/4 cup unsweetened applesauce

APPLE PIE SPICE – 1 tablespoon
- 2 teaspoons ground cinnamon, 1/2 teaspoon ground nutmeg, and 1/2 teaspoon ground ginger (or a pinch of allspice)

APPLES, FRESH – 1 pound
- ⇨ 1 pound pears or Asian pears (add lemon juice for tartness)
- ⇨ 1 pound quinces (tarter flavor; for cooking and jam; rich in pectin)
- ⇨ 1 pound crab apples or unsprayed hawthorne fruits/thorn apples/ *Crataegus* species (use for cooking, especially combined with other fruits for jams and sauces; tarter flavor; rich in pectin)

APRICOTS, FRESH – 1 pound
- ⇨ 1 pound fresh apriums (yellowish-white hybrid; three-quarters apricot and one-quarter plum)
- ⇨ 1 pound fresh plumcots (clingstone hybrid; one-half plum and one-half apricot)
- ⇨ 1 cup dried apricots, soaked in boiling water 1 hour, then drained and blotted dry
- ⇨ 1 cup dried quandongs, soaked in boiling water until softened (tarter flavor; use for jams, pies, or sauces)
- ⇨ 1 pound ripe wild plums/*Prunus americana*, scalded and peeled (light orange-yellow flesh; similar in taste to apricots but stronger; use in jam)

AREPA FLOUR/MASAREPA/HARINA PAN (Latin American precooked white cornmeal) – 1 cup
- ⇨ 1 cup masa harina
- ⇨ 1 cup quick-cooking corn grits
- ⇨ 1 cup extra-fine-grind cornmeal, preferably white

ARGAN OIL (Moroccan golden-colored unrefined oil) – 1 cup
- ⇨ 1/2 cup each extra-virgin olive oil and peanut oil
- ⇨ 1 cup peanut oil, hazelnut oil, or walnut oil

ARONIA BERRY/BLACK CHOKEBERRY, FRESH OR FROZEN – 1 cup
- ⇨ 1 cup fresh or frozen cranberries or blueberries (fewer antioxidants)

ARONIA/CHOKEBERRY JUICE, FRESH OR FROZEN – 1 cup
- ⇨ 1 cup cranberry or pomegranate juice

ARROPE (Spanish grape syrup) *See GRAPE MOLASSES/MUST SYRUP*

ARROWROOT POWDER (thickening agent producing a clear appearance) – 2 teaspoons
- ⇨ 1 tablespoon tapioca starch; or 2 1/2 teaspoons small tapioca pearls, ground until powdery (will have a clear appearance)
- ⇨ 1 1/2 tablespoons kudzu powder (will have a clear appearance)
- ⇨ 1 1/2 tablespoons low- or no-sugar needed fruit pectin (will have a clear appearance)
- ⇨ 1 1/2 teaspoons cornstarch (will have a cloudy, translucent appearance)
- ⇨ 1 1/4 teaspoons potato starch (will have a cloudy, translucent appearance; do not boil)
- ⇨ 2 teaspoons coconut flour (will have a cloudy, translucent appearance and slightly sweet taste)
- ⇨ 1 tablespoon all-purpose or quick-mixing flour (cook at least 5 more minutes after thickened; will have an opaque appearance)

ASCORBIC ACID CRYSTALS (water-soluble vitamin C; used for preventing browning of certain fruits and vegetables) – 1 teaspoon (3,000 milligrams)
- ⇨ 6 (500-mg) ascorbic acid tablets (granulated vitamin C), crushed to a powder with a spoon or dissolved in water
- ⇨ 1 tablespoon citric acid powder (found in the canning section of the supermarket)

ASCORBIC ACID POWDER (vitamin C powder for strengthening gluten in whole-grain bread dough) – 1/8 teaspoon
- ⇨ 1 tablespoon lemon juice

ASHTAR (Lebanese clotted cream) *See CREAM, CLOTTED*

ASIAN PEAR/KOREAN PEAR/JAPANESE PEAR – 1 medium
- ⇨ 2 crisp pears, such as Bosc

ATE (Mexican concentrated fruit paste) *See GUAVA PASTE; QUINCE PASTE*

ATTA/PATENT DURA FLOUR/CHAPATI FLOUR (Indian extra-fine soft whole-wheat flour) – 1 cup *See also BESAN; MAIDA*
- ⇨ 1 cup whole-wheat pastry flour, sifted
- ⇨ 1/2 cup each white whole-wheat flour and maida (Indian soft white flour), sifted
- ⇨ 2/3 cup all-purpose flour and 1/3 cup finely ground whole-wheat flour, sifted before measuring to remove any coarse flakes

B

BACON – 2 ounces (1 thick slice or 2 to 3 medium/thin slices)

- 2 to 3 slices lower-sodium pork or turkey bacon (less salt)
- 2 ounces bacon ends (less expensive)
- 2 to 3 small slices smoked ham or Canadian bacon (less fat; drier)
- 2 to 3 slices *pancetta affumicata*
- 2 to 3 slices plain slab pancetta/*tesa*, rigatino pancetta, or *prosciutto crudo* (unsmoked)
- 2 to 3 slices duck prosciutto or duck pastrami (less fat; drier)
- 1 thick slice smoky tempeh bacon, such as Fakin' Bacon; soy bacon, such as Lightlife Smart Bacon; or any smoke-seasoned prebaked tofu (less fat; moister)
- 3 or more applewood smoked dulse strips, baked at 250°F until lightly toasted, 4 to 7 minutes; or fried in an oiled skillet over medium heat until crisp, 15 to 20 seconds each side
- Chicken skin from a cooked chicken, seasoned with salt and fried in a dry skillet over medium heat until crispy, or baked in a preheated 350°F degree oven until brown and crisp
- 2 to 3 tablespoons real bacon bits, coconut bacon pieces, or any imitation vegan bacon-flavored bits (for flavoring)
- A sprinkling of bacon salt (for flavoring only; reduce the salt in the recipe accordingly)

BACON BITS – 1/4 cup

- 1/4 cup imitation (vegan) bacon bits
- 1/4 cup crumbled smoked tempeh
- 1/4 cup dry-roasted tamari sunflower seeds
- Kiri kombu/sea vegetable, fried in 350°F oil until crisp, 1 to 2 minutes, and then crumbled (measure after crumbling)

BAKER'S AMMONIA See *AMMONIUM BICARBONATE/BAKER'S AMMONIA*

BAKER'S CARAMEL/CARAMEL COLOR (dry, powdered non-sweet coloring agent) – 1 teaspoon

- ⇨ 1 teaspoon gravy browner, such as Gravy Master or Kitchen Bouquet
- ⇨ 1 tablespoon extra-strong coffee

Make Your Own Melt 1/4 cup granulated sugar over low heat, stirring constantly, until very dark brown, about 3 minutes; cool completely, about 10 minutes, before slowly stirring in 1/4 cup hot water. Use 1 to 2 teaspoons in place of baker's caramel. Store in a tightly covered container at room temperature; it will keep for up to 3 months.

BAKEWELL CREAM (New England pyrophosphate leavening agent usually combined with baking soda) – 1 teaspoon

- ⇨ 1 teaspoon cream of tartar (to replace 1 teaspoon Bakewell Cream)
- ⇨ 1 teaspoon baking powder (reduce the baking soda in the recipe by 1/2 teaspoon)

BAKING MIX/ALL-PURPOSE BISCUIT MIX – 1 cup

Make Your Own Whisk together 1 cup flour (all-purpose, cake, or pastry), 1 1/2 teaspoons baking powder, and 1/2 teaspoon salt, then cut in 2 tablespoons chilled vegetable shortening.

BAKING POWDER, DOUBLE ACTING (leavening agent) – 1 teaspoon

- ⇨ 1 1/4 teaspoons sodium-free baking powder containing monocalcium phosphate, potato starch, and potassium bicarbonate, such as Hain's Featherweight
- ⇨ 1/2 teaspoon cream of tartar and 1/4 teaspoon baking soda (bake the batter immediately after mixing; not for batter being refrigerated or frozen before baking)
- ⇨ 1/4 teaspoon baking soda plus 1/2 cup well-shaken buttermilk to replace sweet milk or other fluid called for in the recipe (bake the batter immediately after mixing; not for batter being refrigerated or frozen before baking)

☞ 1 teaspoon baker's ammonia/ammonium bicarbonate (for super crisp cookies and crackers only)

☞ Beat egg whites separately and fold them into the batter (for recipes using eggs and baking powder)

BAKING SODA/SODIUM BICARBONATE (leavening agent) – 1/4 teaspoon

☞ 1/4 teaspoon potassium bicarbonate for a low-sodium alternative (add toward the end of mixing and avoid overbeating)

☞ 1/2 teaspoon calcium carbonate–based baking soda, such as Energ-G (for a sodium-free alternative)

☞ 1 teaspoon double-acting baking powder plus replace buttermilk or other acidic liquid in the recipe with sweet milk

BANANA FLOUR/PISANG STARCH (Filipino plantain flour) – 1 tablespoon for thickening

☞ 2 teaspoons arrowroot powder

☞ 1 tablespoon superfine sweet rice flour/glutinous rice flour, such as Mochiko or Erawan brand

BARBERRIES, DRIED/ZERESHK (Persian sour cooking fruit) – 1 cup

☞ 1 cup coarsely chopped dried cranberries or sour/tart cherries

☞ 1 cup dried currants (red or Zante)

BARLEY FLOUR – 1 cup

☞ 2/3 cup whole hulled/pot barley, whole hull-less barley, or pearl barley, ground in batches in a spice/coffee grinder until powdery (For Tibetan roasted barley flour/tsampa, or Ecuadorian toasted barley flour/máchica, toast the barley in a dry skillet until golden, about 4 minutes, then cool before grinding.)

☞ 1 cup whole-wheat, whole spelt, or light/white rye flour

BARLEY MALT SYRUP, PLAIN (non-diastatic liquid grain sweetener) – 1 tablespoon

☞ 1 tablespoon non-diastatic barley malt powder

- ⇨ 2 teaspoons diastatic barley malt powder
- ⇨ 1 tablespoon wheat malt syrup
- ⇨ 1 tablespoon Chinese brown rice syrup/*yinnie*
- ⇨ 1 tablespoon honey
- ⇨ 1 tablespoon dark brown sugar
- ⇨ 2 teaspoons mild unsulphured molasses

BARLEY RUSKS/PAXIMADIA/PAXIMATHIA (Cretan and Greek rusk bread)

- ⇨ Italian wheat or barley rusks/*friselle* or Dutch dry rusks/*beschuit*
- ⇨ Zwieback
- ⇨ Friganies (for crushing)

Make Your Own Place 1/2- or 1-inch-thick slices of barley, whole-wheat, or country bread (or halved Kaiser rolls or ciabatta) on a baking sheet and dry in the oven with the pilot light on (or on the lowest setting) until golden and dry, 2 or more hours. Let cool in the oven overnight, then store airtight.

BASIL SALT

Make Your Own Layer fresh basil leaves in kosher salt in a small container (make sure the salt completely covers the leaves); seal and leave several days for the salt to develop flavor.

Or

Pulse 1 or 2 cups fresh basil leaves and 1/2 cup kosher salt in a food processor until combined; spread on a baking sheet and dry at 160°F, 30 to 40 minutes, stirring halfway through. Cool, then pulse again to a fine powder. (For a coarser product, dry the leaves first, pulverize to a powder, then stir into the salt.)

BAY LEAF POWDER – 1 teaspoon

- ⇨ 8 to 10 dried Turkish bay leaves, stem and spines removed, pulverized in a spice/coffee grinder (add a little raw rice, if necessary, to help the grinding process)

BEAU MONDE SEASONING – 1 teaspoon
- 1/2 teaspoon each onion powder and celery salt
- 1 teaspoon seasoning salt

BEAUMONT (French semisoft cheese) – 1 ounce
- 1 ounce Muenster, Reblochon, Saint-Nectaire, Tamié, or Taleggio

BEE BALM/BERGAMOT (mint-family herb) – 1 tablespoon chopped fresh leaves
- 1 tablespoon chopped fresh oregano

BEECH MUSHROOM/BROWN BEECH/PIOPPINI/SHIMEJI – 7 ounces
- 7 ounces golden enoki, oyster, or small cremini mushrooms

BEER – 1 cup, for baking
- 1 cup porter, stout, or other slightly bitter dark ale (for braised meat dishes)
- 1 cup light beer (3% alcohol), low-alcohol beer (less than 2% alcohol), near beer (0.5% alcohol), or non-alcoholic beer (lowest in calories)
- 1 cup gluten-free beer, such as Bard's, Green's, New Grist, or Redbridge; or vegan lager beer
- 1 cup hard cider (gluten-free)
- 1 cup wine (regular or nonalcoholic)
- 1 cup beef or chicken stock
- Small amount beer extract powder (for rubs and blends)

BESAN/GRAM FLOUR/CHANNA FLOUR/FARINE DE POIS CHICHES (Indian chickpea flour) – 1 cup See also CHICKPEA FLOUR; CHICKPEA FLOUR, TOASTED
- 1 cup coarse chickpea flour/*jada besan*, ground to a powder
- 1 cup stone-ground garbanzo bean flour or garbanzo–fava bean flour blend
- 1 cup Italian chickpea flour/*farine de ceci*, such as Bartolini or Lucini Italia (finer texture)
- 2/3 cup fine-grind cornmeal plus 1/3 cup all-purpose flour (for coating fried chicken or seafood)

Make Your Own Toast 3/4 cup dried chickpeas/Bengal gram in a dry skillet over medium heat for 3 minutes, stirring constantly. Cool, grind to a powder in a spice/coffee grinder, then sieve to remove the husks.

BICARBONATE OF SODA/BREAD SODA See BAKING SODA

BIRCH SYRUP – 1 cup
- 1 cup maple syrup
- 1 1/3 cups brown sugar plus 1/4 cup water

BISCUIT MIX See BAKING MIX/ALL-PURPOSE BISCUIT MIX

BISCUITS (topping for a pot pie) – 6 small
Make Your Own Stir 1 cup sour cream (or 3/4 cup heavy cream) into 1 cup self-rising flour and 1 teaspoon sugar until just mixed. Pat into a rectangle, divide into 6 squares and bake on an ungreased baking sheet in a preheated 475°F oven until golden brown, 10 to 15 minutes. See FLOUR, SELF-RISING
Or
Stir 1/2 cup soymilk or almond milk and 1/4 cup extra-virgin olive oil into 1 cup self-rising flour and 1 teaspoon sugar until just mixed. Spoon dough in 6 places onto an ungreased baking sheet and bake in a preheated 450°F oven until golden brown, 10 to 12 minutes.

BITTER ALMOND OIL See OIL OF BITTER ALMONDS

BITTER ORANGE See ORANGE, SOUR/BITTER/SEVILLE

BLACKBERRIES (black or dark purple berries) – 1 cup
- 1 cup boysenberries (purplish-red; larger and slightly sweeter; cross between blackberry, loganberry, and raspberry)
- 1 cup nectarberries (larger and sweeter; cross between blackberry and boysenberry)
- 1 cup loganberries (purplish-red; sweeter and tarter; cross between Pacific dewberry and raspberry)

- ☞ 1 cup tayberries (bright deep purple; sweeter; cross between blackberry and raspberry)
- ☞ 1 cup marionberries (dark red to black; larger and sweeter; cross between Chelahem blackberry and olallieberry)
- ☞ 1 cup olallieberries (dark purple; larger and sweeter; cross between youngberry and loganberry)
- ☞ 1 cup youngberries (dark red; smaller and tarter; cross between blackberry, raspberry, and dewberry)
- ☞ 1 cup dewberries (smaller and juicier) or Pacific/California dewberries (larger)
- ☞ 1 cup raspberries (preferably black caps; smaller, softer, and sweeter)
- ☞ 1 cup mulberries, black or red/*Morus nigra/M. rubra* (purplish-black; larger, denser, and less tart)
- ☞ 1 cup cloudberries/*Rubus chamaemorus* (amber; smaller, juicier, and tarter)

BLACK CURRANT JUICE – 1 cup
- ☞ 1 cup 100% pure pomegranate juice

BLACK CURRANT VINEGAR – 1 tablespoon
- ☞ 1 tablespoon red wine vinegar plus a few drops of black currant liqueur, such as crème de cassis
- ☞ 1 tablespoon raspberry vinegar

BLACK FOOD COLORING – few drops
- ☞ Few drops squid or cuttlefish ink

BLUEBERRIES, CULTIVATED, AND WILD BLUEBERRIES/VACCINIUM OVALIFOLIUM – 1 cup
- ☞ 1 cup bilberries/whortleberries/*Vaccinium myrtillus* (dark blue or black; smaller and tarter)
- ☞ 1 cup cascade/blue bilberries/*Vaccinium deliciosum* (smaller and juicier)
- ☞ 1 cup black huckleberries/*Vaccinium membranaceum* (thicker skin; tarter; crunchier seeds)

⇨ 1 cup haskap berries/honeyberries/*Lonicera caerulea* (blue-purple; smaller and tarter; seedless)

⇨ 1 cup salal berries/*Gaultheria shallon* (dark blue; seedy and juicy; blueberry/blackberry taste)

⇨ 1 cup juneberries/serviceberries/sarvisberries/*Amelanchier alnifolia* (purple-black; harder seeds; some berries more tart than others; cook to soften the seeds before adding to muffin batter)

⇨ 1 cup black crowberries/*Empetrum nigrum* (tart with several seeds; freeze overnight to improve flavor; use in cobblers and jam)

BOURSAULT (triple-crème cheese) – 1 ounce
⇨ 1 ounce Brie, Bouche d'affinois, Brillat-Savarin, Delice de Bourogne, Excelsior, Explorateur, Largo, La Tur, Lucullus, Mt. Tam, Italian Piedmont, Pierre Robert, or Saint-André

BOURSIN (seasoned triple-crème cheese) – 1 ounce
⇨ 1 ounce Alouette, Rondelé, or Tartare

⇨ 1 ounce herbed cream cheese plus a little butter

⇨ 1 ounce creamed cream cheese plus a little white wine, minced garlic, dried thyme, and coarsely ground black pepper

BOYSENBERRIES – 1 cup
⇨ 1 cup nectarberries (larger and sweeter; cross between blackberry and boysenberry)

⇨ 1 cup loganberries (redder color; cross between blackberry and red raspberry)

⇨ 1 cup blackberries (tarter; larger seeds)

⇨ 1 cup olallieberries (larger and sweeter; cross between loganberry and youngberry)

BRAN *See OAT BRAN; WHEAT BRAN, UNPROCESSED/MILLERS BRAN*

BRANDY – 1 tablespoon for cooking
⇨ 1 tablespoon rum, hard cider, unsweetened apple juice, or brewed coffee

☞ 1/2 teaspoon imitation brandy, rum, or bourbon extract plus 2 1/2 teaspoons vodka or water

BRANDY EXTRACT – 1 teaspoon
☞ 2 tablespoons brandy or rum; reduce the liquid in the recipe by 2 tablespoons

BRAZIL NUT MILK – 4 cups
Make Your Own Soak 1 cup raw Brazil nuts in water to cover 4 hours. Drain, rinse, then blend with 4 cups water until smooth, about 4 minutes. Strain through a nutmilk bag or cheesecloth-lined sieve, pressing firmly on the pulp to extract all the liquid. Keep refrigerated and shake before using; it should keep for up to 5 days.

BREAD, STALE (dried bread for breadcrumbs, pudding, strata, or stuffing) – 1 pound
☞ 1 pound fresh bread slices, spread on a tray or baking sheet and left to dry at room temperature, 6 to 8 hours
☞ 1 pound fresh bread slices, baked at 250°F until slightly dried, 15 to 20 minutes, or longer for thoroughly dried

BREADCRUMBS, FRESH (filler/binding agent) – 1 cup
☞ 1 cup coarsely grated frozen bread or rolls (grate on the large holes of a box grater; for sliced bread, grate 3 or 4 halved pieces at a time)
☞ 1 cup unsweetened cornbread or corn muffin crumbs
☞ 1 cup instant mashed potato flakes, coarsely ground in a blender
☞ 1 cup rolled oats, coarsely ground in a blender
☞ 1 cup quick-cooking/instant couscous, soaked in water 5 minutes; or fine-ground bulgur (grind #1), simmered 5 minutes

BREADCRUMBS, ITALIAN-STYLE SEASONED – 1 heaping cup
☞ 1 cup dry breadcrumbs plus 2 tablespoons grated Parmesan cheese, 1 tablespoon dried parsley, and 1 tablespoon Italian seasoning
☞ 1 1/4 cups seasoned croutons or seasoned Melba toast, crushed or ground

BREADING/COATING MIX – 1 generous cup

- 1 cup flour, dry breadcrumbs, or ground toasted oats, plus 2 to 3 tablespoons grated Parmesan cheese and 1/2 teaspoon each salt, paprika, and crushed dried herbs (optional)
- 3 ounces (about 26) savory or cheese crackers, crushed or ground
- 4 ounces (2 cups) canned fried onions plus a pinch of salt (optional), crushed or ground
- 2 cups whole-grain flake or bran cereal, finely crushed
- 3 to 4 cups cornflakes (4 ounces), lightly crushed
- 2 to 3 cups flavored croutons, spicy tortilla chips, flavored pita chips, fish-shaped crackers, or nonsalted light-colored potato chips, crushed or ground and then measured
- 1 cup packaged biscuit mix plus 1 tablespoon seasoning dry rub or spice blend, such as Italian, Cajun, Creole, Poultry, Greek, or herbs de Provence

BREADING/COATING MIX, GLUTEN-FREE – 1 cup (about)

- 1 cup rice or potato flour seasoned with grated Parmesan (or nutritional yeast), garlic salt, paprika, and dried parsley (Alternatively, replace some of the rice or potato flour with whole-grain soy flour, which inhibits fat absorption.)
- 1 cup finely ground fresh gluten-free bread crumbs, toasted in a preheated 425°F oven until golden brown, 5 to 7 minutes, then seasoned with grated Parmesan, 1 scant teaspoon cornstarch, plus a pinch each of onion powder and Italian seasoning
- 1 cup almond meal, coconut flour, golden flaxseed meal, finely chopped walnuts or hazelnuts, fine cornmeal, rice bran, or instant mashed potato flakes
- 3 cups cornflakes or plain potato chips, or 2 cups puffed/crisped rice or corn cereal, crushed with a rolling pin
- 2 cups cold unsalted plain popcorn (preferably hot-air popped), ground in small batches in a blender or food processor until powdery
- 1 or 2 puffed rice cakes (white or brown), broken up and ground in a blender or food processor

⇨ 1 1/2 to 2 cups gluten-free corn chips, pulsed in a food processor until the mixture resembles coarse meal

BRIE (French soft-ripened smooth cheese) – 1 ounce
⇨ 1 ounce American-style Brie (firmer, longer lasting) or Appalachian (thicker; square-shaped)
⇨ 1 ounce Bouche d'affinois, Camembert, Chevru, Coulommiers, Caprice des Dieux (double-crème), Crema Dania (double-crème), Dunbarra, Humboldt Fog (chèvre), Le Petit Créme, Le Fougerus, or Sharpham

BRIK PASTRY/FEUILLES DE BRIK/MALSUSQA/WARKA/OUARKA (North African and Middle Eastern tissue-thin sheets of pastry dough) – 1 pound
⇨ 1 pound thawed frozen phyllo/filo dough or strudel dough brushed with oil (for baking; less sturdy)
⇨ 1 pound country-style phyllo dough/horiatiko (thicker and easier to work with)
⇨ 8 ounces frozen puff pastry sheets, brushed with oil (for baking; not for frying)
⇨ 1 pound fresh or thawed frozen yufka dough, lumpia wrappers, or rice-flour spring-roll wrappers (for frying)

BROWN RICE FLOUR See FLOUR, RICE, BROWN

BROWN RICE SYRUP/YINNIE (Chinese naturally processed sweetener) – 1 cup
⇨ 3/4 cup mild-flavored liquid honey or maple syrup plus 2 tablespoons water
⇨ 1 cup agave syrup/nectar or coconut nectar

BROWN SUGAR See SUGAR, DARK BROWN; SUGAR, LIGHT BROWN

BROWN SUGAR SYRUP/KURO MITSU (Japanese sweetener) – 1 cup
⇨ 1 1/3 cups (firmly packed) brown sugar, a pinch of salt, and 1/2 cup boiling water, simmered until syrupy and reduced to 1 cup

BUCKWHEAT FLOUR *See FLOUR, BUCKWHEAT*

BUDDHA'S HAND/FINGERED CITRON – 1
- 1 fresh etrog citron or pomelo
- 2 large thick-skinned lemons

BUTTER REPLACEMENT, FAT-FREE – 1/2 cup, for baking
- 1/2 cup thick, unsweetened applesauce, well drained (for spice cake)
- 1/2 cup prune puree (for chocolate cake)
- 1/2 cup mashed bananas (for muffins)

BUTTER, BRITTANY (cooking butter containing sea salt crystals) – 2 ounces (1/4 cup)
- 2 ounces softened unsalted European butter plus 2 teaspoons coarse sea salt, thoroughly combined

BUTTER, CLARIFIED – 4 ounces (1/2 cup)
- 1/2 cup pure ghee/*usli ghee*, vegetable-oil ghee/*vanaspati ghee*, light sesame oil, macadamia nut oil, or refined coconut oil
- 1/2 cup nonhydrogenated solid vegetable shortening (or rendered leaf lard) plus a few drops toasted sesame oil (or hazelnut oil) for the taste
- 5 ounces unsalted butter (lower smoke point; be careful not to overheat)

Make Your Own Slowly heat 5 ounces unsalted butter in a small saucepan until melted (or microwave for 2 minutes on High in a loosely covered large microwave-safe bowl); let sit until the milk solids settle, about 30 minutes, then gently pour the butter into a container, and leave the milky residue behind.

BUTTER, CULTURED – 4 ounces (1/2 cup)
- Homemade butter made with 1 cup heavy cream (not ultra-pasteurized) and 1/2 cup crème fraîche instead of all heavy cream

BUTTER, EUROPEAN-STYLE/HIGH FAT (82 to 84% butterfat) – 4 ounces (1/2 cup)

- ⇨ 1/2 cup plus 2 teaspoons North American–style butter; reduce the liquid in the recipe by 1 tablespoon

BUTTER, FRESH – 8 ounces (1 cup/2 sticks)

- ⇨ 8 ounces (1 cup) canned butter, such as Red Feather (expensive)
- ⇨ 4 ounces (1 cup) powdered butter plus 1 cup water
- ⇨ 8 ounces (1 cup) vegan margarine containing 80% fat, such as Earth Balance (reduce the salt in the recipe by 1/2 teaspoon if the recipe calls for unsalted butter)
- ⇨ 6 ounces (3/4 cup) plus 2 tablespoons butter-flavored shortening, or nonhydrogenated vegetable shortening, such as organic palm shortening, or lard, preferably rendered leaf lard (for pie crusts and biscuits)
- ⇨ 5 ounces (3/4 cup) plus 2 tablespoons chicken fat (for sautéing aromatics, roasting root vegetables, and frying eggs)
- ⇨ 8 ounces (1 cup) European-style/high-fat butter (for buttercream, croissants, puff pastry, or shortbread; increase the baking time for all-butter pie crust; for cookies, reduce the butter by 2 teaspoons if critical to the recipe)
- ⇨ 18 ounces (1 1/2 cups) pure whipped butter (for cakes and cookies that require creaming the butter and sugar together)
- ⇨ 5 1/2 ounces (3/4 cup) plus 2 tablespoons refined coconut oil (for drop cookies, brownies, muffins, and sweet breads)
- ⇨ 5 3/4 ounces (3/4 cup) plus 2 tablespoons coconut butter (for frostings)
- ⇨ 6 fluid ounces (3/4 cup) mild olive oil, macadamia nut oil, or cold-pressed canola or safflower oil plus 1/4 cup water (for drop cookies not cutout cookies, brownies, muffins, and sweet breads)
- ⇨ 7.7 ounces (1 cup) unsalted soy butter (does not melt but can be used for pastry)
- ⇨ 1 cup pureed avocado (for sweet breads and brownies; reduce the oven temperature by 25% and increase the baking time)

☞ 1/2 cup mild-tasting vegetable oil plus 1/2 cup thick unsweetened applesauce that has been drained for 15 minutes (for lowfat quick breads; avoid overmixing and reduce the baking time slightly)

Make Your Own Blend or whip 2 cups heavy cream (not ultra-pasteurized) until butter forms, 5 to 8 minutes; strain, rinse in cold water until clear, then knead or press to extract the remaining buttermilk. Store, refrigerated, up to 3 weeks.

BUTTER, SALTED – 8 ounces (1 cup/2 sticks)

☞ 8 ounces unsalted butter plus increase salt in the recipe by 1/2 teaspoon

BUTTER, SOFT SPREAD – 1 cup

Make Your Own Beat 4 ounces (1/2 cup/1 stick) unsalted butter until creamy, then slowly beat in 1/2 cup grapeseed or canola oil; pour into an airtight container and keep refrigerated. Alternatively, pulse the oil and butter in a blender, then pour into a container; it will harden when chilled. (Light or mild-tasting olive oil can be used but extra-virgin olive oil can turn bitter when whipped; for salted spread, use salted butter plus 1/4 teaspoon fine sea salt.)

BUTTER, SOFT SPREAD, REDUCED FAT – 1 pound

Make Your Own Beat 8 ounces (1 cup/2 sticks) room-temperature butter until creamy, then slowly beat in 1 cup chilled evaporated milk. Transfer to an airtight container and keep refrigerated.

BUTTER, WHIPPED – 1 cup

☞ 2/3 cup firm butter, beaten until light and fluffy

BUTTER-FLAVORED GRANULES – 1 tablespoon

☞ 4 tablespoons (2 ounces/1/4 cup/1/2 stick) salted or unsalted butter

BUTTERMILK STARTER CULTURE, DIRECT SET – 1 packet (1/2 teaspoon)

☞ 1/4 cup cultured buttermilk

BUTTERMILK, CULTURED (2% butterfat) – 1 cup

⇨ 1/4 cup buttermilk powder added to dry ingredients, plus 1 cup water as liquid component (less acidic than fresh; less efficient for yeast dough)

⇨ 1 cup minus 1 tablespoon room-temperature lowfat milk plus 1 tablespoon distilled white vinegar or cider vinegar (or lemon juice), left 10 minutes until thickened (for baking)

⇨ 1 cup lowfat milk (or 1/2 cup each full-fat milk and water) plus 1 1/2 teaspoons cream of tartar (mix cream of tartar with dry ingredients before adding milk)

⇨ 1 (8-ounce) bottle cow or goat yogurt drink

⇨ 1 cup kefir (slightly alcoholic due to fermentation)

⇨ 1 cup Bulgarian buttermilk (thicker and more tart)

⇨ 1/2 cup plain full-fat yogurt whisked with 1/2 cup water until smooth

⇨ 1/2 cup plain lowfat yogurt whisked with 1/2 cup lowfat milk until smooth

⇨ 2/3 cup plain nonfat yogurt whisked with 1/3 cup full-fat or lowfat milk until smooth

⇨ 1 cup plain homemade yogurt (thicker)

⇨ 1 cup whey (thinner)

BUTTERMILK, EUROPEAN-STYLE – 1 cup

⇨ 3/4 cup cultured buttermilk whisked with 1/4 cup plain full-fat yogurt until smooth

BUTTERMILK, LACTOSE-FREE – 1 cup, for baking

⇨ 1 cup soy, rice, or almond milk plus 2 teaspoons lemon juice (or cider vinegar) left until slightly thickened, about 10 minutes (if using rice milk, reduce the amount in recipes by up to 25%; rice-based buttermilk will be thin)

⇨ 1 cup plain dairy-free yogurt plus 1 tablespoon lemon juice (or distilled white or cider vinegar) left, undisturbed, 5 to 10 minutes

⇨ 1 cup water plus 1 tablespoon lemon juice or vinegar

C

CACAO NIBS *See COCOA NIBS*

CACAO POWDER, RAW (unprocessed cocoa) – 1/4 cup
- 1/4 cup cocoa nibs, pulverized to a fine powder
- 3 to 4 tablespoons natural cocoa powder (less potent)

CACIOCAVALLO (Southern Italian cow's milk cheese) – 1 ounce
- 1 ounce scamorza or Italian provolone

CACIOCAVALLO, SMOKED – 1 ounce
- 1 ounce smoked mozzarella/*mozzarella affumicata*, smoked provolone, or smoked scamorza
- 1 ounce Polish Kurplanka (lightly smoked with garlic)

CAKE GLAZE – 1 cup *See also FRUIT GLAZE*
- 1 cup store-bought frosting plus a little liquid (water, milk, cream) heated in a small pan over low heat, stirring constantly, until liquid enough to pour

CALAMONDIN/KALAMANSI/LIMAU KETSURI (Southeast Asian citrus fruit) – 1
- 3 large kumquats or mandarinquats
- 2 or 3 fully ripe (yellowing) Key limes
- 1 small blood orange or sour Valencia orange

CANAPÉ BASES/CASES/SHELLS (small edible items for holding hot or cold toppings)
- Sturdy flat commercial chips (bagel, black bean, cassava, gluten-free, lentil, multigrain, pita, rice, tortilla, or vegetable)

☞ Mini buckwheat blini/*oladyi*/*binchiki*, thin silver-dollar pancakes, mini oatcakes, thin mini cornmeal cakes, thin mini biscuit halves, or tiny pastry shells

☞ Lavash crisps (pieces of crisp lavash, recrisped in the oven or microwave, then cooled and broken into pieces)

☞ Mini poppadoms (plain uncooked mini poppadoms/pappadams, toasted or fried until blistered and crisp)

☞ Polenta rounds (chilled prepared polenta cut into rounds, lightly coated with melted butter or cooking spray, and broiled or fried until lightly browned, about 5 minutes each side)

☞ Polenta cups (warm prepared polenta spooned into greased mini muffin cups, an indentation made in the top center of each cup, then chilled until set)

☞ Pumpernickel/rye triangles (pumpernickel or rye cocktail bread cut into triangles; or unsliced pumpkin or rye bread thinly sliced, then cut into triangles

☞ Egg bread squares (1/4-inch-thick brioche slices cut into 2-inch squares and fried in butter)

☞ French bread crisps (thinly sliced French flute or ficelle baked in a preheated 400°F oven until crisp, 4 to 5 minutes, then cooled)

☞ Crostini (day-old baguettes cut in 1/2-inch-thick slices, brushed with olive oil, then baked at 350°F until lightly golden, about 10 minutes)

☞ Bread cups (thin slices of crustless bread cut into rounds, brushed lightly with olive oil, pressed into mini muffin cups, and baked in a preheated 350°F oven until crisp, about 10 minutes; for crunchier croustades, thinly roll out the bread)

☞ Mini toasts (thinly sliced crustless bread brushed lightly with olive oil, cut into 1- to 1 1/2-inch squares, and baked at 400°F until golden, about 5 minutes)

☞ Biscuit bowls (thinly rolled out biscuit dough pressed over the back of mini muffin cups to form bowl shapes; baked at 450°F until lightly browned, 7 to 9 minutes; cooled on the cups; then removed)

☞ Wonton cups (small wonton wrappers pressed into greased mini muffin pans (or draped over inverted muffin cups), sprayed with cooking spray and baked at 350°F until brown and crisp, 4 to 6 minutes)

- Mini pizzette (thinly rolled out pizzette dough cut into small rounds and baked at 400°F until lightly browned, about 10 minutes)
- Phyllo shells (frozen prepared mini shells baked in a preheated 350°F oven until crisp, 3 to 5 minutes or buttered phyllo sheets cut into 2-inch squares, layered in greased mini muffin pans and baked at 350°F until crisp, 6 to 8 minutes)
- Puff pastry squares (puff pastry cut into small squares, brushed with olive oil, and baked at 375°F for 15 minutes)
- Whole-wheat crackers (whole-wheat pie dough rolled thin, cut into rounds, squares, or diamonds and baked at 375°F until golden brown, about 15 minutes)
- Pâte à choux cases (pâte à choux dough thinly spread in greased mini muffin cups and baked at 350°F until golden brown, about 14 minutes; or small baked cream puff shells, halved and hollowed out)
- Waffle rounds (frozen mini waffles toasted in the oven to a golden brown)

CANDIED FRUIT/GLACÉ FRUIT – 1 cup
- 1 cup Italian spiced fruits/*mostarda di Cremona,* drained from the syrup
- 1 cup dried apricots, blueberries, cherries, cranberries, dates, figs, nectarines, peaches, pears, persimmons, or pineapple chunks (chopped if large)

CANELA See CINNAMON, GROUND *(Ceylon, Sri Lanka, Mexican, canela)*

CANE SUGAR, RAW/UNREFINED See SUGAR, DEMERARA; SUGAR, TURBINADO CANE

CANE SYRUP/INVERT SYRUP (Caribbean and Creole strong-flavored sweetener) – 1 cup
- 1 1/4 cups granulated sugar and 1/3 cup water simmered over medium heat until syrupy
- 1 cup plain barley malt syrup or dark corn syrup

☞ 1/2 cup each molasses and light-colored corn syrup

CANE SYRUP/INVERT SYRUP, DARK (strong-flavored dark sweetener) – 1 cup
  ☞ 1 cup sorghum syrup, unsulphured molasses, or treacle

CANOLA OIL/RAPESEED OIL (neutral-flavored oil) – 1 cup
  ☞ 1 cup grapeseed, safflower or sunflower oil

CAPE GOOSEBERRIES/CHINESE LANTERNS/GOLDEN BERRIES/ GROUND CHERRIES – 1 cup fresh or dried
  ☞ 1 cup gooseberries (for fresh; more tart)
  ☞ 1 cup dried cranberries (for dried)

CAPPUCCINO PASTE (flavoring agent for frozen desserts and pastries) – 1 tablespoon
  ☞ 1 tablespoon espresso or coffee paste
  ☞ 3 1/2 tablespoons instant espresso powder mixed with enough heavy cream to form a thick paste

CARAMEL COLORING See BAKER'S CARAMEL/CARAMEL COLOR

CARAMEL PASTE/DULCE DE LECHE/DOCE DE LEITE/AREQUIPE/ MANJAR – 1 cup
  Make Your Own Heat 14-ounces (1 can) sweetened condensed milk, uncovered, in a double boiler over low heat until golden, 2 to 3 hours, replacing water as needed (it will thicken on cooling).
  Or
  Simmer 1 cup firmly packed dark brown sugar, 1/3 cup butter, and 1/4 cup heavy cream (or evaporated milk) until slightly thickened; remove from heat and add 1 teaspoon vanilla extract.

CARAMEL SYRUP/NUOC MAU (Vietnamese sweetener) – 1 teaspoon
  ☞ 1 1/2 teaspoons granulated sugar

CARAWAY SEEDS – 1 tablespoon
- 1 tablespoon anise, fennel, or dill seeds

CARDAMOM PODS, BLACK/BROWN -– 1 tablespoon
- 1 tablespoon Chinese cardamom/*Amomum globosum* (less expensive; more pungent)
- 2 or 3 whole cloves

CARDAMOM PODS, GREEN OR WHITE – 1 tablespoon
- 1 teaspoon ground cardamom
- 1 tablespoon Ethiopian koreima/*Aframomum korarima* (less expensive; more camphor overtones)

CARDAMOM SEEDS, GREEN OR WHITE, GROUND – 1 teaspoon
- Seeds from 6 to 8 green or white cardamom pods, finely ground with a mortar and pestle
- 1 or 2 drops Elaichi essence (Indian cardamom seed essence)
- 3 drops cardamom extract
- 3/4 teaspoon ground cinnamon plus 1/4 teaspoon finely grated lemon zest
- 1/2 teaspoon each ground cloves and nutmeg (or cinnamon)

CASHEW BUTTER – 1 cup
- 1 cup smooth, natural peanut butter (less sweet)

Make Your Own Process 2 cups whole roasted, unsalted cashews and 1/4 teaspoon sea salt in a food processor until reduced to a paste, 6 to 10 minutes, scraping down the sides of the bowl and adding a little oil if needed. Store in a sterilized jar in the refrigerator; it will last for up to 4 weeks.

CASHEW CREAM – 1 to 1 1/4 cups
Make Your Own Soak 1 cup whole raw unsalted cashews in 2 cups water for 4 to 8 hours; drain and rinse, then blend with 1/2 cup water until completely smooth; strain if necessary. For a faster procedure, soak 1 cup cashew pieces in 1/2 cup boiling water 30 minutes. For a thicker,

richer cream use 1/3 cup water and 1/4 cup refined coconut oil. For a thinner, pourable cream use 1 1/2 cups water. Store, refrigerated, for up to 4 days, or freeze for up to 6 months.
Or
Soak 1/3 cup whole raw unsalted cashews in 2/3 cup water for 4 to 8 hours; drain and rinse, then blend with 2/3 cup unsweetened soy milk until completely smooth; strain if necessary. Store, refrigerated, for up to 4 days or freeze for up to 6 months.

CASHEW MILK – 3 to 4 cups
Make Your Own Soak 1 cup whole raw unsalted cashews in water to cover for 4 to 8 hours; drain and rinse, then blend with 4 cups warm water until smooth, 3 to 4 minutes. Strain in a nutmilk bag or cheesecloth-lined sieve, pressing firmly on the pulp to extract all the liquid. Store in a sterilized jar in the refrigerator; it should keep for up to 4 days; shake before using.

CASHEWS – 1 cup
- 1 cup macadamia nuts or pine nuts (more expensive)
- 1 cup almonds (less soft)

CASSAVA FLOUR/YUCA MEAL/MANIOC MEAL – 1 cup
- 1 cup almond flour, chickpea flour, or rice flour

CASSIA See CINNAMON/CASSIA, GROUND

CASSIA BARK See CINNAMON STICK, INDONESIAN

CASSIA LEAF/CINNAMON LEAF/TEJ PATTA (Indian flavoring agent) – 1 dried leaf
- 1 whole clove or small pinch ground cloves
- 1 small dried Turkish bay leaf and a few grains cassia cinnamon

CHANCACA (Latin American unrefined sugar) See PILONCILLO/ PANELA/PANOCHA

CHAPATI FLOUR *See ATTA/PATENT DURA FLOUR/CHAPATI FLOUR*

CHAROLI NUTS/CHIRONGI/CALUMPANG (Indian sweetmeat garnish) – 1 ounce
- 1 ounce slivered blanched almonds
- 1 ounce chopped unsalted pistachios or hazelnuts

CHERRIES, GLACÉ – 1 cup
- 1 cup dried cherries or sweetened dried cranberries

CHERRIES, MARASCHINO, JARRED – 1 cup cherries plus 1 cup liquid
Make Your Own Combine 1 cup fresh pitted cherries, 1 cup vodka, 1/2 cup granulated sugar, and 1/2 teaspoon pure almond extract in a sterilized jar. Place in a cool, dark place for 5 to 6 days, shaking the jar daily. Store, refrigerated, for up to 4 months.

CHERRIES, SOUR/TART, FRESH OR FROZEN (Aleppo, Amarelle, Morello, Montmorency, Natbella, or Early Richmond) – 1 pound (2 cups pitted)
- 1 (24-ounce jar) Morello cherries, drained, or 1 (14- to 16-ounce) can sour cherries, drained
- 1 cup dried pitted Montmorency cherries, soaked in 1 cup boiling water until softened, about 30 minutes (or 6 to 8 hours in cool water)
- 2 cups pitted wild black sweet cherries/*Prunus serotina,* purple-black sandcherries/*Prunus pumila,* red Nanking cherries/*Prunus tomentosa,* or crimson chokecherries/*Prunus virginiana* (smaller; more astringent; best for jams, jellies, syrup, and drying)
- 2 cups pitted dark red cornelian cherries/cornels/*Cornus mas* (huge pits and extremely tart; best for jam, jelly, syrup, or fruit leather)
- 2 cups pitted acerola/Barbados cherry/West Indian cherry (reduce the sugar in the recipe by one-third; best for preserves and cakes)
- 2 1/2 cups pitted fresh sweet cherries or thawed frozen sweet cherries (reduce the sugar in the recipe by one-third; best for cakes, pies, and sauce)

⇨ 2 cups pitted Surinam cherries/Brazilian cherry *pitanga/Eugenia uniflora* (best for jams and jellies)

CHERRY EXTRACT – 1 teaspoon
⇨ 2 to 3 tablespoons cherry juice or liquid from jarred maraschino cherries (sweeter; reduce the liquid in the recipe by 2 to 3 tablespoons)

CHERRY LIQUEUR/CHERRY-FLAVORED SPIRIT (such as Cherry Heering, Cherry Marnier, Cherry Rocher, or Cusenier Heering) – 2 tablespoons
⇨ 2 tablespoons crème de cerise or crème de griotte
⇨ 2 tablespoons cherry schnapps or kirsch (less sweet)
⇨ 1/2 to 1 teaspoon cherry extract plus 2 tablespoons vodka or water

CHESTNUT PURÉE/PUREE DE MARRONS, CANNED – 1 cup
⇨ 1 cup cooked and mashed Japanese white-fleshed sweet potatoes/ *satsuma-imo*

Make Your Own Cover 8 ounces (1 1/4 cups) shelled and peeled chestnuts with water and simmer until very tender, about 1 hour. Drain and process in a food processor or blender until very smooth, adding a tablespoon or two of water if necessary.

CHIA SEEDS/SALBA SEEDS – 2 tablespoons
⇨ 1 1/2 tablespoons chia powder or 2 tablespoons ground flaxseed/ flaxmeal (sprouted or regular)
⇨ 2 tablespoons sesame seeds (lacks omega-3s and gelatinous property)

CHICORY COFFEE See COFFEE, CHICORY

CHICKPEA FLOUR/GARBANZO FLOUR/FARINA DE CECI (20% protein) – 1 cup
⇨ 1 cup Indian *besan*/channa dal flour/gram flour (darker; less finely ground)

⇨ 3/4 to 7/8 cup dried chickpeas ground in batches in a spice/coffee grinder until powdery; sift, then regrind any remaining particles
⇨ 1 cup cold-leached acorn flour, preferably white oak

CHICKPEA FLOUR/GARBANZO FLOUR, TOASTED (South Asian thickening agent) – 1 cup
⇨ 1 cup toasted rice powder

Make Your Own Toast 1 cup chickpea flour in a dry heavy skillet over medium heat until golden, about 10 minutes, stirring constantly; or roast on a baking sheet in a preheated 350°F oven until golden, 12 to 15 minutes, stirring once. Store, tightly sealed, in a cool, dark place.

CHIVE OIL – 1/2 cup
Make Your Own Blanch 1 bunch chives in boiling water for 30 seconds, then dip in ice water; squeeze dry and process in a food processor or blender with 1/2 cup oil and a pinch of salt until combined, about 2 minutes. Store in the refrigerator.

CHIVES, FRESH, FROZEN, OR FREEZE DRIED – 4 ounces
⇨ 4 ounces green parts of scallions or green onions, smashed and cut lengthwise into ribbons
⇨ 4 ounces garlic chives or Chinese garlic stems (more garlicky tasting)
⇨ 4 ounces garlic leaves, slivered (cut leaves sparingly when the plants are no more than 8 inches tall)
⇨ 4 ounces Egyptian walking onion leaves, slivered
⇨ 4 ounces unsprayed wild garlic foliage/shoots/*Allium vineale*

CHOCOLATE CHIPS OR FÈVES, BITTERSWEET OR SEMISWEET (41 to 63% cacao) – 1 cup
⇨ 6 ounces thin chocolate bars (semisweet or bittersweet; regular or dairy-free) cut or broken into pieces a little larger than chocolate chips (will not hold their shape when baked)
⇨ 1 cup carob chips (less flavorful; not for melting)
⇨ 1 cup cocoa nibs (for extra-dark/bittersweet mini chips)
⇨ 2 ounces unsweetened chocolate plus 1/2 cup granulated sugar and 2 tablespoons shortening or vegetable oil (for melting)

☞ 2/3 cup natural unsweetened cocoa powder, 6 tablespoons granulated sugar, and 3 tablespoons shortening or vegetable oil (for melting)

CHOCOLATE CRUMB CRUST See CRUMB CRUST, CHOCOLATE

CHOCOLATE FUDGE TOPPING – 3/4 to 1 cup
Make Your Own Combine 1/2 cup each unsweetened cocoa powder, sugar, and boiling water, plus a pinch of salt; stir over low heat until smooth, about 2 minutes. The sauce hardens upon standing. (For a thinner sauce, use 1/3 cup cocoa powder.)
Or
Heat 1/2 cup heavy cream or evaporated milk and 2 tablespoons corn syrup just until boiling, then pour over 2/3 cup chocolate chips and stir until smooth.

CHOCOLATE LIQUEUR/CHOCOLATE-FLAVORED SPIRIT (such as Godiva, Haagen Dazs, Lejay-Lagoute, or Mozart) – 1 tablespoon for cooking
☞ 1 tablespoon crème de cacao or chocolate syrup (reduce the sugar in the recipe by 1 1/2 teaspoons)

CHOCOLATE MINT SAUCE – 1 cup
☞ 1/4 cup heavy cream (or soy or coconut creamer) stirred into 8 ounces chopped and melted chocolate peppermint creams (serve warm)

CHOCOLATE NIBS See COCOA NIBS/CHOCOLATE NIBS

CHOCOLATE SHELL (thin coating for cold or frozen items) – 1/2 cup
Make Your Own Melt 3 tablespoons refined coconut oil (or firm rendered leaf lard) and 3 ounces chopped dark chocolate (or 1/2 cup semisweet chocolate chips) in the microwave until smooth, stirring every 20 seconds. Let cool to room temperature, about 10 minutes. Dip frozen fruit using a toothpick or pour over ice cream. (For a thinner shell, increase the fat to 1/4 cup; for a thicker shell, increase the chocolate to up to 8 ounces.)

CHOCOLATE SYRUP – 3/4 cup (about)
- Simmer 1/2 cup water, 1/4 cup granulated sugar, 1/3 cup unsweetened cocoa powder, and a pinch of sea salt for 3 or 4 minutes. Remove from the heat and add 1/2 teaspoon vanilla; store in a lidded jar in the refrigerator. (For a sweeter syrup, increase the sugar to up to 1 cup.)

CHOCOLATE, BITTERSWEET (50 to 67% cacao) – 1 ounce
- 3 tablespoons natural unsweetened cocoa powder plus 1 tablespoon granulated sugar and 1 1/2 teaspoons shortening or vegetable oil
- 2/3 ounce unsweetened chocolate plus 2 teaspoons granulated sugar

CHOCOLATE, BITTERSWEET (50 to 67% cacao) – 4 ounces
- 4 ounces dark chocolate, such as Hershey's Special Dark
- 3 ounces semisweet chocolate plus 1 ounce unsweetened chocolate
- 3 ounces bittersweet chocolate (70 to 75% cacao) plus 2 tablespoons granulated sugar

CHOCOLATE, COUVERTURE (high-gloss coating/dipping chocolate) – 4 ounces callets or buttons
- 1 ounce finely chopped or grated dark chocolate added to 3 ounces barely melted dark chocolate and stirred until melted and smooth (use immediately)
- 1 tablespoon neutral-tasting vegetable oil added to 3 ounces barely melted dark chocolate and stirred until smooth (use immediately and consume within 3 days)

CHOCOLATE, GERMAN'S SWEET (48% cacao) – 1 ounce
- 1 ounce semisweet chocolate plus 1 1/2 teaspoons granulated sugar
- 1/2 ounce unsweetened chocolate plus 4 teaspoons granulated sugar
- 3 tablespoons natural unsweetened cocoa powder plus 4 teaspoons granulated sugar and 1 tablespoon shortening or vegetable oil

CHOCOLATE, MEXICAN (such as Ibarra or Abuelita) – 2 ounces
- 1 ounce chilled baking chocolate broken into pieces, 1 tablespoon each granulated sugar and ground almonds, and 1 teaspoon ground Ceylon/Mexican cinnamon, ground in a blender or spice/coffee grinder until fine
- 1/3 cup bittersweet chocolate chips (or 2 ounces bittersweet bar chocolate), 1 teaspoon ground Ceylon/Mexican cinnamon, and 1 or 2 drops almond extract
- 3 tablespoons natural unsweetened cocoa (for moles calling for chocolate)

CHOCOLATE, SEMISWEET (35 to 60% cacao) – 1 ounce
- 1/2 ounce unsweetened chocolate and 1 tablespoon granulated sugar
- 3/4 ounce bittersweet chocolate (70% cacao) and 1 1/2 teaspoons granulated sugar
- 1 1/2 tablespoons unsweetened cocoa powder, 3 1/2 teaspoons granulated sugar, and 1 tablespoon shortening or vegetable oil

CHOCOLATE, SWEET See CHOCOLATE, GERMAN'S SWEET

CHOCOLATE, TEMPERED See CHOCOLATE, COUVERTURE

CHOCOLATE, UNSWEETENED (99 to 100% cacao; 50 to 60% butterfat) – 1 ounce
- 3 tablespoons natural unsweetened cocoa powder plus 1 tablespoon shortening or vegetable oil
- 3 tablespoons natural unsweetened high fat (22 to 24%) cocoa powder plus 2 teaspoons shortening or butter
- 2 1/2 ounces semisweet chocolate; reduce the sugar in the recipe by 3 tablespoons and the shortening or butter by 1 1/2 tablespoons
- 3 tablespoons toasted carob powder plus 2 tablespoons water or milk; reduce the sugar in the recipe by 2 tablespoons (less flavorful)

CHOCOLATE, UNSWEETENED (99 to 100% cacao; 50 to 60% butterfat) – 4 ounces
⇨ 6 1/2 ounces bittersweet chocolate (70% cacao); reduce the butter or shortening in the recipe by 1 tablespoon and the sugar by 1/4 cup

CHOCOLATE, UNSWEETENED (99 to 100% cacao; 50 to 60% butterfat) – 8 ounces
⇨ 5 ounces natural unsweetened high fat cocoa powder plus 3 tablespoons shortening or vegetable oil
⇨ 4 1/2 ounces natural unsweetened cocoa powder plus 3 1/2 tablespoons shortening or vegetable oil

CHOKECHERRIES – 1 cup
⇨ 1 cup red currants
⇨ 1 cup small sour cherries

CIDER MOLASSES – 1 cup
⇨ 2 quarts unfiltered apple cider, gently boiled over medium heat until reduced to 1 cup, 40 to 50 minutes, stirring occasionally; store, refrigerated, for up to 1 month

CIDER, SWEET APPLE – 1 cup
⇨ 1 tablespoon boiled cider mixed with 3/4 cup water
⇨ 1 cup cold-pressed apple juice (less tangy)
⇨ 1 or 2 teaspoons cider vinegar added to 1 cup apple juice
⇨ 1 cup pear cider/perry

CINNAMON OIL – 2 drops
⇨ 1/2 teaspoon cinnamon extract
⇨ 1 1/2 to 2 teaspoons ground cassia cinnamon

CINNAMON STICK, INDONESIAN KORINTJE – 1 (3- or 4-inch) stick
⇨ 1 (5-inch) soft Ceylon cinnamon stick/canela
⇨ 2 teaspoons ground cinnamon (to replace a smashed/crushed cinnamon stick used in cooking)

- 1/4 teaspoon ground cinnamon (to replace a whole cinnamon stick removed after cooking)
- 1 tablespoon cinnamon chunks (to flavor coffee, mulled wine, or cider)

CINNAMON SUGAR – 1 cup
- 3 to 4 tablespoons ground cinnamon thoroughly mixed with 3/4 cup granulated sugar
- 2 or 3 cinnamon sticks buried in a jar containing 1 cup sugar and then left for a few weeks

CINNAMON SYRUP – 1 cup
- 4 or 5 whole cinnamon sticks added to 1 cup heated heavy syrup (*See SYRUP, SIMPLE*) and simmered 1 or 2 minutes; strain and cool before using (for more intense flavor, let the mixture sit a few hours before straining)

CINNAMON, GROUND (Ceylon, Sri Lanka, Mexican, canela) – 1 teaspoon
- 1-inch Ceylon/Sri Lanka cinnamon stick, crumbled or grated with a Microplane grater
- 2/3 teaspoon Indonesia/Korintje or China cassia cinnamon
- 1/4 to 1/2 teaspoon Vietnamese/Saigon cassia cinnamon

CINNAMON, GROUND (Indonesian, Korintje, Padang, cassia) – 1 teaspoon
- 1 1/2 teaspoons pure Ceylon/Sri Lanka cinnamon/canela
- 1/4 teaspoon cinnamon extract
- 1/2 teaspoon ground allspice plus scant 1/8 teaspoon ground nutmeg
- 1/4 teaspoon ground cardamom plus 1/8 teaspoon ground nutmeg
- 1 teaspoon apple or pumpkin pie spice

CINNAMON, GROUND (Vietnamese, Saigon cassia, Cinnamomum loureiroi) – 1 teaspoon
- 1 1/4 teaspoons Indonesian/Korintje or China/Tung Hing cassia cinnamon

⇨ 2 teaspoons pure Ceylon cinnamon/canela

CINNAMON, SOFT-QUILL *See CINNAMON, GROUND (Ceylon, Sri Lanka, Mexican, canela)*

CITRIC ACID/SOUR SALT (tart flavoring and anti-discoloration agent for fruits and vegetables) – 1 tablespoon powdered
⇨ 1 heaping tablespoon citric acid crystals (lemon salt/sour salt), finely crushed and then measured to equal 1 tablespoon (found in the canning section of supermarkets)
⇨ 1 tablespoon tartaric acid (found at wine supply stores)
⇨ 1 teaspoon ascorbic acid powder (found in drugstores)
⇨ Six (500-mg) ascorbic acid vitamin C tablets, crushed to a powder or dissolved in water
⇨ 3/4 cup bottled lemon juice, such as ReaLemon
⇨ 1 1/2 cups distilled white vinegar (5% acidity)

CITRON/YUJA (large tart citrus) – 1 fruit
⇨ 1 large lemon (juice and zest only; not the white pith)

CITRON SALT/CITRUS SALT – 1 cup
Make Your Own Thoroughly combine 1 cup coarse sea salt or flake salt and 3 tablespoons freshly grated citron zest (or lemon zest). Spread on a baking sheet and dry in a preheated 200°F oven, about 1 hour; cool completely. Store in an airtight container. Alternatively, let sit at room temperature until completely dry, 8 to 12 hours.

CITRUS OIL, PURE (lemon, lime, orange, or tangerine) – 1/2 teaspoon
⇨ 1 1/2 teaspoons pure citrus extract
⇨ 3 or 4 teaspoons finely grated citrus zest from a scrubbed fruit, preferably organic (Place the whole fruit in the freezer until partly hardened, about 30 minutes, before grating.)

CITRUS SUGAR – 1 cup

Make Your Own Process 1 cup granulated sugar and 2 to 4 tablespoons finely grated zest (lemon, lime, or tangerine) in a blender or food processor until combined, 30 to 40 seconds, or in a spice/coffee grinder in batches. Alternatively, bury thin strips of zest in the sugar and store airtight at room temperature for at least 1 week before opening.

CITRUS SYRUP – 1 cup

Make Your Own Remove 8 to 10 strips of lemon, yuzu, or lime peel (scrub the fruit first) with a vegetable peeler and scrape away any white pith. Simmer with 1 cup heavy syrup (*See SYRUP, SIMPLE*) 1 to 2 minutes; strain and cool before using.

CITRUS ZEST, DRIED See LEMON PEEL, DRIED; ORANGE PEEL, DRIED GRANULATED

CLEARJEL (modified cornstarch thickener) – 1 tablespoon

- 1 tablespoon arrowroot powder, cornstarch, potato starch, or rice starch
- 1 tablespoon quick-cooking tapioca softened in liquid/mixture for 10 to 15 minutes before cooking
- 2 tablespoons all-purpose flour, tapioca flour, or a proprietary thickener such as King Arthur Flour Pie Filling Enhancer

CLEMENTINES See MANDARIN ORANGES

CLOTTED CREAM See CREAM, CLOTTED

CLOVES, GROUND – 1 teaspoon

- 1 1/4 teaspoons whole cloves ground in a spice/coffee grinder
- 1/3 teaspoon each ground allspice, cinnamon, and nutmeg
- 1 teaspoon ground allspice

COCOA BUTTER – 1 ounce

- 4 teaspoons unsalted butter, palm oil, grapeseed oil, or other neutral-tasting oil

COCOA MIX/HOT CHOCOLATE POWDER – 1 2/3 cups

Make Your Own Whisk together 1 1/2 cups nonfat dry milk powder, 1/2 cup unsweetened cocoa powder (natural or Dutch-process), and 1/2 cup sugar. Add 1/4 cup mix to 3/4 cups hot water. Makes 10 servings. Store in an airtight container; it will keep for up to 6 months.

COCOA NIBS/CHOCOLATE NIBS (roasted shelled cocoa beans) – 4 ounces (1 cup)

⇨ 1 cup finely chopped bittersweet chocolate, preferably 70% cacao

COCOA POWDER/ DOUBLE-DUTCH DARK (ALKALIZED), UNSWEETENED (such as King Arthur) – 1 cup

⇨ 1/2 cup each Dutch-process cocoa and black cocoa

COCOA POWDER, DUTCH-PROCESS (ALKALIZED), UNSWEETENED (such as Callebaut, Droste, Pernigotti, Valrhona, or Hershey's European Style or Special Dark) – 3 tablespoons

⇨ 3 tablespoons natural unsweetened cocoa powder, preferably high fat, plus 1/8 teaspoon baking soda

⇨ 3 tablespoons natural unsweetened cocoa powder (for recipes not requiring baking powder or baking soda, such as brownies)

⇨ 1 ounce unsweetened chocolate plus 1/8 teaspoon baking soda; reduce the fat in the recipe by 1 tablespoon

COCOA POWDER, DUTCH-PROCESS (ALKALIZED), UNSWEETENED – 1 cup

⇨ 1 cup natural unsweetened cocoa powder, preferably high fat, plus 1/2 teaspoon baking soda

⇨ 1 cup all-purpose baking cocoa, such as King Arthur, or black cocoa (for more intense color)

COCOA POWDER, NATURAL (NON-ALKALIZED), UNSWEETENED (10 to 12% cocoa butter, such as Baker's, Hershey's, Ghirardelli, or Nestlé) – 3 tablespoons

⇨ 3 tablespoons European or Dutch-process cocoa powder plus 1/8 teaspoon cream of tartar (or 1/8 teaspoon lemon juice or vinegar added to the liquid in the recipe)

⇛ 3 tablespoons Dutch-process cocoa powder and omit the baking soda from the recipe (milder flavor)

⇛ 1 ounce unsweetened chocolate; reduce the fat in the recipe by 1 tablespoon

⇛ 2 ounces semisweet chocolate; reduce the fat in the recipe by 1 tablespoon and the sugar by 3 tablespoons

⇛ 4 tablespoons toasted carob powder; reduce the sugar in the recipe by 1 tablespoon and increase the fat by 1 tablespoon (less flavorful)

COCOA POWDER, NATURAL (NON-ALKALIZED), UNSWEETENED (10 to 12% cocoa butter) – 1 cup

⇛ 1 cup high fat cocoa powder (22 to 24% cocoa butter)

⇛ 1 cup European or Dutch-process cocoa powder; substitute baking powder for baking soda and double the amount (22 to 24% cocoa butter)

COCONUT BUTTER/CREAMED COCONUT – 1 cup for cooking

⇛ 1 cup vegetable shortening or unsalted butter (lacks coconut flavor)

Make Your Own Process 4 cups dried unsweetened flaked or desiccated coconut in a food processor or high-powered blender until reduced to a paste, 15 to 20 minutes, scraping down the sides of the bowl as needed. Store in a lidded jar at room temperature for up to 2 months.

COCONUT CHIPS

Make Your Own Slice fresh coconut into wafer-thin strips, sprinkle with salt (optional), spread out on baking pans, and bake at 325°F until crisp, 25 to 30 minutes, rotating the pans and flipping the chips halfway through. Cool and store in an airtight container. (Freezing the whole coconut overnight makes shelling it easier.)

COCONUT CREAM, UNSWEETENED – 1/2 cup

⇛ 1/2 cup thick liquid that rises to the top of canned or homemade coconut milk after chilling it several hours

☞ 1/2 cup light cream or whipping cream plus 1/4 teaspoon coconut extract

COCONUT MILK BEVERAGE, BOXED – 1 cup
☞ 1/4 cup canned coconut milk mixed with 3/4 cup water
☞ 1 cup hemp milk

COCONUT MILK, FRESH – 1 cup
☞ 3 tablespoons canned cream of coconut plus enough water to make 1 cup

COCONUT MILK, FULL-FAT CANNED (53 to 55% coconut extract) – 1 cup
☞ 1/4 cup (one-third of a packet) concentrated coconut cream mixed with 3/4 cup water
☞ 1/2 cup unsweetened coconut cream mixed with 1/2 cup water (whisk or stir the coconut milk before measuring)
☞ 1 cup coconut powder mixed with 1 cup water
☞ 1 cup half-and-half plus 1/2 teaspoon coconut extract (optional)
☞ 1 cup thin cauliflower puree plus 1/2 teaspoon coconut extract
Make Your Own Pour 1 1/4 cups boiling water over 1 cup packed fresh or frozen grated/shredded coconut (or unsweetened dried coconut); cool to room temperature. Process in a high-powered blender until smooth, about 2 minutes, then strain in a nutmilk bag or cheesecloth-lined sieve, pressing on the pulp to extract all the liquid. For light/lite coconut milk that resists curdling when heated, pour 1 cup water through the same puréed coconut and press again; to prevent full-fat coconut milk from curdling, add a scant 1/8 teaspoon baking soda before heating.

COCONUT MILK, LIGHT/LITE CANNED – 1 cup
☞ 1 cup of the second pressing of freshly grated coconut after making homemade coconut milk
☞ 1 cup lowfat or nonfat milk plus 1/2 teaspoon coconut extract
☞ 7/8 cup fresh coconut water plus 2 tablespoons full-fat sour cream or regular coconut milk

- ⊱ 3/4 cup canned or homemade coconut milk mixed with 1/4 cup water
- ⊱ 1/2 cup canned or homemade coconut milk mixed with 1/2 cup soymilk
- ⊱ 1/3 cup unsweetened coconut cream mixed with 2/3 cup water
- ⊱ 1 cup prepared potato milk, such as DariFree; or lactose-free milk, such as Lactaid (for coconut-free cooking; not for whipped topping)

COCONUT NECTAR/PALM SYRUP/EVAPORATED COCONUT SAP/ KITHUL TREACLE (thick, dark sweetener) – 1 cup

- ⊱ 1 cup dark agave syrup/nectar, birch syrup, brown rice syrup, maple syrup, or yacón syrup
- ⊱ 3/4 cup liquid honey plus 2 tablespoons water

COCONUT OIL, REFINED – 1 cup

- ⊱ 1 cup firm rendered leaf lard
- ⊱ 1 cup solid shortening
- ⊱ 1 cup liquid and pourable coconut oil, or neutral-flavored vegetable oil, such as canola

COCONUT PALM SUGAR, GRANULATED See PALM SUGAR, LIGHT

COCONUT SUGAR, POWDERED – 1 cup

- ⊱ 1/2 cup each confectioners' sugar and coconut milk powder, sifted together until thoroughly combined

COCONUT SYRUP, LIGHT – 1 cup See also COCONUT NECTAR

- ⊱ 1 tablespoon coconut extract added to 1 cup simple syrup (See SYRUP, SIMPLE)

COCONUT WATER/JUICE – 1 1/2 cups (contents of one young, fresh coconut)

- ⊱ 1/2 cup canned coconut milk blended with 1 cup plain water
- ⊱ 1 cup young coconut meat and 1/2 cup coconut water, pureed in a high-powered blender until smooth (add more coconut meat or water as necessary)

COCONUT WHIPPED CREAM – 1 cup
Make Your Own Beat 1 cup top layer of cream from coconut milk, 1 1/2 teaspoons sugar, 1/2 teaspoon vanilla, and a pinch of salt in a chilled bowl on low speed until small bubbles form, about 30 seconds. Increase the speed to high and beat until the mixture thickens and forms light peaks, about 2 minutes. Use immediately.

COCONUT, COLORED – 1 cup
Make Your Own Shake 1 cup flaked or shredded coconut with 3 or 4 drops food coloring, in a tightly closed jar or sealable plastic bag until the color is evenly distributed. (Alternatively, use a pinch of powdered food coloring in place of the liquid.)

COCONUT, DRY DESICCATED/MACAROON TYPE – 1 cup
- 1 1/3 cups unsweetened flaked coconut, ground in a blender or food processor until fine
- 1 1/4 cups unsweetened shredded coconut, ground in a blender or food processor until fine

COCONUT, FRESH GRATED – 1 cup
- 1 1/3 cups frozen flaked coconut (squeeze out excess water from the thawed frozen coconut and pat dry)
- 3/4 to 7/8 cup flaked or shredded unsweetened dried coconut, soaked in warm water 1 hour, using enough to barely cover the coconut; strain if necessary and pat dry (Alternatively, steam the coconut 30 minutes over simmering water.)
- 1 1/4 cups flaked or shredded unsweetened dried coconut; reduce the sugar in the recipe by 2 tablespoons

COCONUT, SWEETENED – 1 cup
- 1 cup unsweetened coconut; increase the sugar in the recipe by 1 tablespoon

COCONUT, TOASTED SHREDDED – 1 cup
Make Your Own Spread 1 cup shredded or flaked coconut (sweetened or unsweetened) in a single layer on an ungreased baking sheet

and bake at 325°F until golden, 5 to 8 minutes, stirring halfway through. Alternatively, microwave on High for 2 to 3 minutes, stirring every 30 seconds, or toast in a dry skillet over low heat, stirring frequently, 4 to 7 minutes if dry or 10 to 15 minutes if fresh. Store, tightly sealed, at room temperature for up to a month.

COCONUT, UNSWEETENED SHREDDED – 1 cup
- 1 cup sweetened coconut, rinsed and strained with water until the sugar is gone, 2 to 4 times
- 1 cup sweetened coconut; reduce the sugar in the recipe by 1 tablespoon
- 1 cup unsweetened reduced-fat coconut (40% less fat)

COFFEE-BASED CREAM LIQUEUR (such as Baileys) – 2 tablespoons for cooking
- 1 tablespoon strong coffee, 1 1/2 teaspoons each heavy cream and whiskey, and 1 scant teaspoon sugar, preferably vanilla
- 2 tablespoons *crème de noyaux* (almond-flavored), or Tiramisu liqueur (chocolate-, coffee-, and almond-flavored)
- Few drops Irish cream flavoring; increase the liquid in the recipe by 2 tablespoons

COFFEE BEANS – 1 pound
- 1 pound roasted or malted barley, carob, rice, wheat germ, or other grain coffee, such as Cafix, Guayaki, Postum, Roma, or Teeccino
- 1 pound roasted dandelion root coffee, such as Dandy Blend, or homemade (Dry large dandelion roots from old dandelion plants on a rack at room temperature for 1 to 2 weeks or in a 120°F dehydrator for 8 hours, then roast in a preheated 325°F oven until dark brown and brittle, 30 to 90 minutes. Cool, then grind.)
- 1 pound soy coffee (Soak 1 pound soybeans in water to cover for 8 to 12 hours in the refrigerator, then drain. Spread in a single layer on a baking sheet and roast in a preheated 300°F oven until dark brown, 45 to 60 minutes. Grind while hot.)

COFFEE CONCENTRATE – 1 scant cup
Make Your Own Combine 4 ounces (1 1/4 cups) regular-grind coffee with 2 cups cold water. Cover, and let sit for 12 hours before straining; store in a small bottle in the refrigerator.

COFFEE CREAMER – 1 tablespoon
⊳ 1 tablespoon instant dry milk powder
⊳ 1 tablespoon nonfat dry milk powder combined with 1 tablespoon nonfat milk (for lowfat creamer)
⊳ 1 tablespoon sweetened condensed milk (for sweetened coffee)
⊳ 1 tablespoon canned or homemade coconut milk (for a vegan alternative)

COFFEE ESSENCE – 1/3 cup
Make Your Own Bring 1/4 cup finely ground French roast or espresso roast and 1/2 cup water just to a boil, stir a few times, then cover and let steep for 3 to 4 minutes. Strain through a paper coffee filter or paper towel, then cool. Store, refrigerated, for up to 1 month.

COFFEE EXTRACT – 1 tablespoon
⊳ 1 1/2 teaspoons instant espresso powder, such as Medaglia d'Oro, or 1 3/4 espresso granules dissolved in 1 tablespoon warm water; cool before using
⊳ 2 teaspoons instant coffee granules dissolved in 1 tablespoon boiling water; cool before using
⊳ 1 tablespoon coffee-flavored syrup; reduce the sugar in the recipe by 1 or more teaspoons

COFFEE LIQUEUR/COFFEE-FLAVORED SPIRIT (such as Kahlúa, Crème de Café, Tia Maria, or Pasha) – 1 tablespoon for cooking
⊳ 1 tablespoon chocolate-, hazelnut-, or almond-flavored liqueur
⊳ 1/2 teaspoon freeze-dried instant coffee dissolved in 1 tablespoon vodka or hot water
⊳ 1/4 teaspoon chocolate extract and 1/4 to 1/2 teaspoon instant coffee dissolved in 1 tablespoon vodka or hot water
⊳ 1 tablespoon mocha-flavored espresso drink

COFFEE PASTE – 1 tablespoon
☞ 1 tablespoon instant coffee dissolved in 1 tablespoon hot water

COFFEE, CHICORY – 1 pound
☞ 1 pound dark-roasted regular coffee, such as French roast or Italian roast

Make Your Own 1 pound scrubbed and sliced chicory taproot (*Cichorium intybus*) roasted on a baking sheet in a preheated 250°F oven until fragrant, dark-brown throughout, and brittle when snapped, 2 to 4 hours. Cool and then grind. Keep tightly sealed at room temperature.

COFFEE, STRONG BREWED OR DOUBLE STRENGTH – 1 cup for flavoring
☞ The first cup from a pot of drip coffee
☞ 1 tablespoon instant espresso powder dissolved in 1 cup hot water
☞ 4 teaspoons freeze-dried instant coffee granules dissolved in 1 cup hot water

COGNAC (French brandy) – 2 tablespoons See also BRANDY
☞ 2 tablespoons Armagnac

CONDENSED MILK, DAIRY-FREE SWEETENED – 1 cup (about)
☞ 1 can full-fat coconut milk and 1/2 cup granulated sugar, simmered until the sugar is dissolved and the mixture is thick and reduced by one-quarter to one-half, about 1 hour
☞ 1 cup vegan evaporated milk and 1 1/2 cups granulated sugar, slowly heated until the sugar is dissolved and the mixture is thick *See EVAPORATED MILK, VEGAN*

CONDENSED MILK, SWEETENED – 14-ounce can
☞ 1 cup instant nonfat dry milk powder, 3/4 cups granulated sugar, 1/2 cup boiling water, and 3 tablespoons melted unsalted butter, whipped in a blender or by hand until smooth
☞ 1 cup evaporated milk and 1 1/4 cups granulated sugar, slowly heated until the sugar is dissolved

CONFECTIONERS' SUGAR See SUGAR, CONFECTIONERS'

COOKING SPRAY/NONSTICK COOKING SPRAY (oil and lecithin-based propellant used to apply a light, nonstick coating to cooking and baking pans)
- Equal parts canola, or other vegetable oil, and liquid lecithin (Combine in a food-grade pump/spray bottle; for nonstick pans or a soy-free spray, omit the lecithin and use oil only.)
- Canola oil, coconut oil, or olive oil (Spread thin with a pastry brush or paper towel, then wipe off the residue; a thin film will remain. Use 1/4 teaspoon for the equivalent of a 1- to 2-second spray, or 1 teaspoon for a 10- to 15-second spray.)

CORNFLAKE CRUMBS – 1 cup
- 4 cups cornflakes, ground in a food processor until fine, 8 to 10 seconds

CORNMEAL (for dusting pizza pans and peels) – 2 tablespoons
- 1 tablespoon coarse-ground semolina or grits
- 1 tablespoon wheat farina or dry regular Cream of Wheat
- 1 tablespoon oatmeal
- 1 tablespoon wheat bran

CORNMEAL, SELF-RISING – 1 cup
- 1 cup cornbread mix

Make Your Own Whisk together 3/4 cup fine-ground cornmeal, 1/4 cup all-purpose flour, 1/2 teaspoon baking powder, and 1/4 teaspoon each baking soda and salt.

CORNMEAL, STONE-GROUND – 1 cup See also BREADING/COATING
    MIX, GLUTEN-FREE
- 1 cup regular milled (steel-ground) cornmeal, preferably coarse-ground
- 1 cup polenta or corn grits
- 1/3 cup each almond flour, rice flour, and rice bran (for baking)

CORNSTARCH (for baking or gluten-free flour component) – 1 cup
- 7/8 cup potato starch
- 1 cup tapioca starch or arrowroot powder

CORNSTARCH (for coating/dredging or batter) – 1 cup
- 1 cup arrowroot powder
- 1 cup potato flour
- 1 cup chickpea flour
- 1 cup water chestnut flour
- 1 cup kudzu powder
- 1 cup matzo meal
- 1 cup sweet rice flour/glutinous rice flour, or brown rice flour

CORNSTARCH (for thickening) – 1 tablespoon
- 1 tablespoon waxy modified cornstarch, such as instant ClearJel (semi-translucent appearance; does not separate when frozen)
- 1 tablespoon sweet rice flour/glutinous rice flour/mochiko (opaque appearance; does not separate when frozen)
- 2 tablespoons all-purpose or quick-mixing flour (cook for 5 or more minutes after thickening to remove floury taste; opaque appearance; separates when frozen)
- 4 teaspoons arrowroot powder (clear appearance; separates when frozen; not for dairy-based sauces)
- 2 tablespoons tapioca starch, or 5 teaspoons small-pearl or quick-cooking tapioca ground in a spice/coffee grinder until powdery, about 30 seconds (clear appearance; does not separate when frozen)
- 2 teaspoons potato starch (do not let boil; semi-opaque appearance; separates when frozen)
- 1 1/2 to 2 teaspoons coconut flour (good for thickening coconut milk–based dishes)

CORN SYRUP, DARK – 1 cup
- 3/4 cup light corn syrup plus 1/4 cup unsulphured molasses
- 1 cup pure cane syrup, such as Steen's, or golden syrup, such as Lyle's (sweeter and thicker)

- 1 cup brown rice syrup/bran rice syrup
- 1 1/4 cups firmly packed brown sugar dissolved in 1/4 cup hot water (or the liquid called for in the recipe) and simmered until syrupy and reduced to 1 cup, about 5 minutes

CORN SYRUP, LIGHT-COLORED (not "lite") – 1 cup
- 1 cup liquid glucose
- 1 1/4 cups granulated sugar dissolved in 1/3 cup water (or the liquid called for in the recipe) and simmered until syrupy and reduced to 1 cup, 5 to 7 minutes

COTTAGE CHEESE – 1 cup
- 1 cup ricotta, chenna/chhena, or pot cheese
- 1 cup chopped tofu

COTTAGE CHEESE, DRY – 1 cup
- 1 cup baker's cheese, hoop cheese, or dry ricotta
- 1 cup large-curd cottage cheese, drained for 1 hour in a fine-mesh sieve set over a bowl in the refrigerator

CRAB APPLES (small tart apples high in pectin) – 1 pound
- 1 pound hawthorne fruits/thorn apples/*Crataegus monogyna* (smaller)

CRACKED WHEAT *See WHEAT, CRACKED*

CRACKER CRUMBS, FINE – 1 cup
- 1 1/4 cups unseasoned fine dry breadcrumbs *See BREADCRUMBS, DRY*

CRACKER CRUST *See CRUMB CRUST, CHOCOLATE; CRUMB CRUST, SAVORY; CRUMB CRUST, SWEET*

CRACKERS, WATER – 1 dozen
Make Your Own Mix together 2/3 cup flour, 1/4 teaspoon salt, scant 1/4 cup water, and 1 tablespoon vegetable oil and roll out as thin as

possible. Bake on a baking sheet at 350°F until light brown and crisp, about 30 minutes, flipping the crackers halfway through. Cool on a wire rack and store in an airtight container.

CRANBERRIES, DRIED UNSWEETENED – 1 cup
- 1 cup sweetened dried cranberries; reduce the sugar in the recipe by 2 tablespoons
- 1 cup raisins or sultanas/golden raisins
- 1 cup dried blueberries, bilberries, or cherries
- 1 cup dried barberries/*Berberis vulgaris*, Oregon grape berries/ *Mahonia aquifolium,* juneberries or serviceberries/*Amelanchiers* (for cooking)

CRANBERRIES, FRESH OR FROZEN – 1 cup
- 1 cup lingonberries/mountain cranberries/cowberries/*Vaccinium vitis-idaea* (smaller)
- 1 cup squashberries/*Viburnum edule* (remove large flat seeds before or after cooking)
- 1 cup sea buckthorn berries/*Hippophae rhamnoides* (deep yellow to bright orange; sweeter after freezing)
- 1 cup bilberries/blaeberries/whortleberries/*Vaccinium myrtillus* (sweeter)
- 1 cup barberries, fresh or dried (soak dried berries in water 30 minutes)
- 1 cup red currants (smaller and sweeter)
- 1 cup blueberries (smaller and sweeter)
- 1 cup red chokeberries/*Aronia arbutifolia* (more astringent; high in pectin and antioxidants; use for sorbets, jam, jelly, or juice)
- 1 cup red oval silverberries/*Elaeagnus umbellate* or *E. multiflora* (sweeter; high in vitamin C and lycopene; large seed; use raw or for fruit soup or jelly)

CRANBERRY LIQUEUR/CRANBERRY-FLAVORED SPIRIT (such as DeKuyper, Boggs, or Flag Hill) – 1 tablespoon for cooking
- 1 tablespoon cranberry syrup (sweeter)

⇛ 1/2 teaspoons cranberry extract plus 1 tablespoon water

⇛ 1 tablespoon raspberry liqueur

CREAM CHEESE (38% butterfat) – 1 cup (8 ounces)

⇛ 1 cup Neufchâtel cheese (23% butterfat; more moisture)

⇛ 1 cup reduced-fat cream cheese (16.5 to 20% butterfat; more sodium)

⇛ 1 cup fat-free cream cheese (nearly twice as much sodium; separates when heated)

⇛ 1 cup fresh goat cheese/chèvre or thick fromage blanc (softer texture)

⇛ 1 cup soy cream cheese or tofu cream cheese

⇛ 2 to 3 cups plain full-fat yogurt, Greek yogurt, quark, skyr, or labneh, drained for 12 to 24 hours in a sieve lined with dampened cheesecloth (or 2 basket-style paper coffee filters) and set over a bowl in the refrigerator (cover the sieve with a plate, cloth, or plastic wrap)

⇛ 1 1/2 cups lowfat cottage cheese, 2 tablespoons butter, and 1 tablespoon milk blended until smooth, then drained for 8 to 12 hours in a sieve lined with dampened cheesecloth and set over a bowl in the refrigerator (cover the sieve with a plate, cloth, or plastic wrap)

⇛ 2 sticks (8 ounces) vegan margarine, such as Earth Balance, plus liquid cream cheese flavoring (for cakes, cookies, fillings, or frostings)

CREAM CHEESE, CREOLE – 8 ounces (1 cup)

⇛ 1 teaspoon lemon juice stirred into 8 ounces softened cream cheese

⇛ 8 ounces fromage blanc

CREAM CHEESE, DOUBLE (60% butterfat) See PETIT SUISSE

CREAM CHEESE, WHIPPED (27.9% butterfat) – 1/2 cup

⇛ 1 (3-ounce) package room-temperature cream cheese, beaten until light and fluffy (unlike commercial whipped cream cheese, it will not separate in cooking)

CREAM, CLOTTED/DEVONSHIRE CREAM (British cream containing 55 to 75% butterfat) – 1 cup

⇨ 1/2 cup heavy cream slowly beaten into 3 ounces (1/3 cup) softened cream cheese until smooth

⇨ 1 cup mascarpone

Make Your Own Pour 4 cups heavy cream (not ultra-pasteurized) into a wide ovenproof bowl or pot and set in a preheated 175°F oven for 8 hours. Cool; cover and refrigerate for 8 to 12 hours, then remove the thick top layer of cream (use the remaining loose cream as heavy cream).

CREAM, DOUBLE/CRÈME DOUBLE (European cream containing 48% butterfat) – 1 cup

⇨ 1 1/2 cups heavy whipping cream, gently boiled in a large pan until reduced to 1 cup, about 20 minutes (Whisk the cream for a few seconds every couple of minutes, and be careful it doesn't boil over.)

⇨ 1 cup canned double cream, such as Nestlé Double Cream

⇨ 1 1/2 cups crème fraiche, drained overnight in a sieve lined with dampened cheesecloth (or 2 basket-type paper coffee filters) set over a bowl in the refrigerator (cover the sieve with a plate or plastic wrap)

CREAM, HEAVY (35 to 40% butterfat) – 1 cup

⇨ 1 cup refrigerated or shelf-stable whipping cream (30 to 35% butterfat)

⇨ 1 (8-ounce) carton unsweetened coconut cream, or 1 cup thick cream that rises to the top of canned or homemade coconut milk after chilling several hours (for cooking and whipping)

⇨ 2/3 cup undiluted icy-cold evaporated milk (for whipping)

⇨ 1 cup undiluted evaporated milk (for cooking)

⇨ 3 tablespoons powdered heavy cream mixed with 1 cup water

⇨ 2/3 cup whole milk or soy milk plus 1/3 cup melted unsalted butter, vegan butter/margarine, or coconut oil (for cooking)

⇨ 1 cup dairy-free alternative, such as Mimic Crème, So Delicious Creamer, or Silk or Mocha brand soy creamer

⇨ 1 cup brown rice cream (for cooking)

⇨ 1 cup raw cashews, soaked in water to cover for 8 to 10 hours, drained, then pulverized in a blender with 1/2 cup water

CREAM, LIGHT/SINGLE CREAM (18 to 30% butterfat) – 1 cup

⇨ 1 cup canned table cream, all-purpose light cream, or Mexican *media* cream, such as Nestlé

⇨ 1/2 cup whipping cream and 1/2 cup whole milk (18% butterfat)

⇨ 1/2 cup heavy cream and 1/2 cup half-and-half (25% butterfat)

⇨ 3 tablespoons melted unsalted butter and enough whole milk to make 1 cup (for cooking)

⇨ 1 cup canned or homemade coconut milk (dairy- and casein-free)

⇨ 1 cup coconut milk creamer (nonfat and dairy-free)

CREAM OF COCONUT (cocktail ingredient, such as Coco López) – 1 cup

⇨ 1 cup unsweetened coconut cream, whisked before measuring, plus 1/3 cup confectioners' sugar

⇨ 1 cup sweetened condensed milk plus 1/2 teaspoon coconut extract

CREAM OF COCONUT, UNSWEETENED – 1 cup

Make Your Own Heat 2 cups shredded or flaked coconut with 1 (12-ounce) can of evaporated milk until small bubbles appear around the edge, 6 to 7 minutes. Cool, then cover and refrigerate for 8 to 12 hours; strain in a cheesecloth-lined sieve, pressing firmly to extract all the liquid. Keep refrigerated; it will stay, tightly sealed, for up to 2 weeks.

CREAM OF TARTAR (potassium hydrogen tartrate/potassium bitartrate) – 1/4 teaspoon

⇨ 1/2 teaspoon distilled white vinegar (for stabilizing egg whites)

⇨ 1/4 teaspoon xanthan gum (for stabilizing egg whites)

- ⇨ 3/4 teaspoon distilled white vinegar or lemon juice (for acidifying liquids)
- ⇨ 1/8 to 1/4 teaspoon tartaric acid (for acidifying liquids)
- ⇨ Few drops distilled white vinegar (for preventing cooked sugar from crystallizing)

CREAM SHERRY See SHERRY, CREAM

CREAM, SOUR See SOUR CREAM

CREAM, WHIPPED – 1 cup (chill bowl and beaters at least 20 minutes before whipping)
- ⇨ 1/2 cup ice water, 1/2 cup instant dried milk powder, and 1 tablespoon lemon juice beaten at high speed until stiff (For nonfat dry milk powder, use 1/3 cup ice water instead of 1/2 cup; whip until slightly thickened and then add the lemon juice and continue whipping.)
- ⇨ 1 cup chilled crème fraîche whipped until fluffy; will not increase in volume (For sweetened crème, add 1 tablespoon superfine sugar, then refrigerate for at least 15 minutes before whipping; it will keep for up to 3 days.)
- ⇨ 1 (8-ounce) can thick cream, such as Nestle
- ⇨ 1/2 cup liquid nondairy whipped topping, such as MimicCreme Healthy Top, whipped for 3 to 5 minutes
- ⇨ 4 ounces frozen nondairy whipped topping, such as Cool Whip or Cool Whip Lite, thawed
- ⇨ 1/2 to 3/4 cup solid coconut fat, whipped until fluffy (Use the fat that rises to the top of canned, full-fat unsweetened coconut milk and do not overwhip; keep chilled; will melt at room temperature. For sweetened cream, add 2 to 3 teaspoons confectioners' sugar before whipping.)

CREAM, WHIPPED, LIGHT – 1 cup
- ⇨ 1/2 cup chilled heavy cream and 1/4 cup chilled plain Greek yogurt, whipped until stiff (Add sugar if desired.)

CREAM, WHIPPED, NONDAIRY See DAIRY-FREE TOPPING

CREAM, WHIPPED, STABILIZED – 1 cup cream (2 cups whipped)
- 1 tablespoon dry milk powder (or 2 tablespoons nonfat dry milk powder), sprinkled over the cream before whipping
- 1/4 cup heavy cream mixed with 1 teaspoon cornstarch and heated until thickened; cooled to room temperature; then whipped into 3/4 cup heavy cream just as it begins to thicken (For sweetened whipped cream, add 1 or 2 tablespoons confectioners' sugar when heating the cream and cornstarch.)
- 1/2 teaspoon unflavored gelatin powder softened in 1 tablespoon cold water 2 to 3 minutes, heated in the microwave 10 seconds, then cooled to room temperature; stir it into semi-whipped cream, then resume whipping
- 1 cut-up marshmallow, softened in the microwave a few seconds, then whisked a little at a time into the cold whipped cream (or use 1/4 cup marshmallow crème)
- 1/2 cup crème fraiche, folded into semi-whipped cream
- 1 or 2 tablespoons melted and cooled apple jelly used in place of sugar (the pectin acts as a stabilizer)
- 1 tablespoon, or 1 (10-gram) packet, stabilizing powder, such as Whip it or Whip Cream Aid, added before whipping; slightly decrease the amount of sugar
- 1/2 teaspoon waxy modified cornstarch, such as Instant ClearJel, mixed with the sugar before adding to the cream
- Drain the whipped cream, for at least 2 hours, in a fine-mesh sieve set over a bowl in the refrigerator and covered with plastic wrap
- Process the cream in a food processor, along with the sugar and vanilla if using. It will keep in the refrigerator for up to 2 weeks

CREAMER, NONDAIRY See COFFEE CREAMER

CRÈMA MEXICANA/MEXICAN CRÈMA – 1 cup
- 1 cup crème fraîche (richer; less salty)

☞ 1 cup *crema Salvadoreña, crema Centroamericana*, or *crema Hondureña* (darker-hued and tangier)
☞ 3/4 cup sour cream thinned with 1/4 milk or water plus salt to taste, about 1/8 teaspoon
☞ 1 cup heavy cream (for cooking)

CRÈME FRAÎCHE (French cultured cream with 48% butterfat) – 1 cup (8 ounces)

☞ 1 cup Mexican *crema/crema Mexicana* (will separate if boiled)
☞ 1 cup double cream (less tart; will not separate if boiled)
☞ 1 cup sour cream and 2 tablespoons heavy cream whisked together (will separate if boiled)
☞ 1 cup *labna* (more sour; will not separate if boiled)
☞ 1 cup mascarpone thinned with a little sour cream

Make Your Own Combine 1 tablespoon buttermilk or crème fraîche with 1 cup heavy cream, then lightly cover and leave in a warm spot until thickened, about 24 hours. Refrigerate, well covered, for up to 7 days (it will continue to thicken).

Or

Whisk together 1/2 cup heavy cream and 1/2 cup sour cream, cover lightly and leave at room temperature until thickened, 2 to 4 hours or longer. Refrigerate, well covered, for at least 4 hours before using. It will keep for up to 1 week refrigerated (it might separate if boiled).

CRÈME FRAÎCHE DIRECT-SET STARTER CULTURE – 1 packet (1/2 teaspoon)

☞ 1/3 cup buttermilk (for making crème fraîche)
☞ 1/2 teaspoon citric acid, or 1/8 to 1/4 teaspoon tartaric acid, dissolved in 1 to 2 tablespoons cool water (for making mascarpone)

CRÈME FRAÎCHE, LOW-FAT – 1 cup (8 ounces)

☞ Nonfat or 2% Greek-style yogurt, whisked until smooth
☞ 1/2 cup fat-free cream cheese (or fat-free sour cream), 1/2 cup 1% milk, and 1/4 teaspoon sugar whisked together, lightly covered, and left at room temperature until thickened, about 8 hours

Make Your Own Whisk together 1/2 cup evaporated nonfat milk, 1/2 cup plain low-fat yogurt, and 1 teaspoon lemon juice; lightly cover and leave at room temperature until thickened, about 8 hours. Will keep in the refrigerator for up to 1 week; whisk before using (might separate if boiled).

CRUMB CRUST, CHOCOLATE – 8- or 9-inch
Make Your Own Crush 9 ounces chocolate wafers (about 30) to crumbs, then process with 1/2 cup melted chocolate chips and 1 tablespoon oil or melted butter in a food processor until combined. Press against the bottom and sides of a pie pan and freeze until set, about 15 minutes.

CRUMB CRUST, SAVORY – 8- or 9-inch
Make Your Own Mix 3 tablespoons melted butter thoroughly into 1 1/3 cups savory cracker crumbs (or finely grated crusty French bread). Press against the bottom and sides of a quiche dish or pie pan and bake in a preheated 350°F oven for 10 minutes; cool to room temperature before adding a filling.

CRUMB CRUST, SWEET – 8- or 9-inch
Make Your Own Mix 3 to 4 tablespoons melted butter or canola oil thoroughly into 1 1/2 to 2 cups cookie crumbs (graham crackers, digestive biscuits, ginger or chocolate snaps, or Maria cookies). Press against bottom and sides of a greased Pyrex pie pan. Microwave on High for 2 minutes, or bake in a preheated 350°F oven for 10 to 12 minutes. Cool to room temperature before adding a filling; the crust becomes firm as it cools. (For a salty-sweet crust, substitute crushed salted pretzels. For a fat-free crust, substitute 1 egg white for the fat and coat the pan with cooking spray.)

CRUMBS See BREADCRUMBS; CRACKER CRUMBS; GRAHAM CRACKER CRUMBS; MATZO FARFEL

CURRANTS, BLACK, FRESH OR FROZEN – 1 cup *See also CURRANTS, RED*
- ⇥ 1 cup red currants (smaller; less tart; more fragile)
- ⇥ 1 cup fully ripe elderberries/*Sambucus nigra* (blue-black; sour; low in pectin)
- ⇥ 1 cup bilberries/*Vaccinium myrtillus* (purple-black; sweet and juicy)
- ⇥ 1 cup crowberries/*Empetrum nigrum* (blue-black with several seeds; freezing overnight improves flavor)
- ⇥ 1/4 to 1/3 cup thawed frozen black-currant puree

CURRANTS, DRIED (dried black Corinth or Zante grapes) – 1 cup
- ⇥ 1 cup Uvette raisins (tiny, sweet Italian raisins)
- ⇥ 1 cup black or crimson raisins, coarsely chopped or snipped (freeze the raisins to make them easier to chop)
- ⇥ 1 cup dried barberries (less sweet)
- ⇥ 1 heaping cup dried cherries, sweetened dried cranberries, dried figs, dates, or prunes, cut into tiny pieces (Coat the knife blade with a thin film of cooking spray to make the fruit easier to chop.)

CURRANTS, RED, FRESH OR FROZEN – 1 cup *See also CURRANTS, BLACK*
- ⇥ 1 cup white currants (smaller and sweeter)
- ⇥ 1 cup blueberries (purple; sweet)
- ⇥ 1 cup ripe European barberries/*Berberis vulgaris* (pink-red; tart with a smooth texture; or Japanese barberries/*Berberis thunbergii* (bright red; bitter with a mealy texture)
- ⇥ 1 cup fully ripe autumn berries/autumn-olives/*Elaeangnus umbellata* (red and juicy with soft seeds)

CUSTARD POWDER (British sweet sauce mix) – 2 tablespoons
- ⇥ 2 tablespoons dry vanilla pudding mix (not instant)
- ⇥ 2 tablespoons vegan vanilla pudding mix, such as Dr. Oetker Organics
- ⇥ 2 tablespoons cornstarch, 1/4 teaspoon vanilla powder (or extract), plus scant 1/8 teaspoon turmeric, preferably Madras (for the color only)

D

DAIRY-FREE TOPPING – 1 cup
- 1 cup soy- or rice-based topping, such as Soyatoo
- 1 cup coconut-based topping, such as CocoWhip
- 3/4 cup liquid soy-dairy creamer, such as Silk, and 2 1/2 tablespoons confectioners' sugar, beaten at high speed until soft peaks form
- 3/4 cup chilled unsweetened coconut cream (or thoroughly chilled cream from the top of no-emulsion-added canned coconut milk) plus 1 1/2 teaspoons sugar and a pinch of salt, beaten at high speed until fluffy
- 1 cup almond cream (1 1/3 cups soaked almonds blended with 1/3 cup water until creamy)
- 1 cup plain soy or coconut yogurt, sweetened with vanilla liquid stevia (thinner)

DATE HONEY/SILAN/DEVASH (Israeli sweetener) See DATE MOLASSES

DATE MOLASSES/DATE SYRUP/DIBIS TAMAR (Middle Eastern thick sweetener) – 1 cup
- 1 cup Middle Eastern grape syrup (*dibs/pekmez*) or carob syrup (*harnup pekmezi*)
- 1 cup Italian grape molasses (*vino cotto*) or fig syrup (*miele di fichi/ cotto di fichi*)
- 2/3 cup strong-flavored dark honey, such as buckwheat, chestnut, linden, or sage
- 1 cup grade A dark, robust pure maple syrup
- 1/2 cup dark molasses or treacle plus 1/2 cup light-colored corn syrup

Make Your Own Simmer 8 ounces fresh pitted Medjool dates in 2 cups water until the mixture is thick and syrupy, about 1 hour; let cool then process in a blender or food processor until smooth. Store, refrigerated, for up to 2 weeks.

DATE-PALM JAGGERY, LIQUID/JHOLA GUR (Indian sweetener) – 1/4 cup
↪ 1/4 cup coconut nectar or maple syrup
↪ 1/4 cup grated cane jaggery or other palm sugar
↪ 1/4 cup dark brown or maple sugar, moistened to a coarse paste with 1 teaspoon light molasses

DATE PASTE (thick natural sweetener) – 1 1/2 cups
Make Your Own Soak 1 pound fresh pitted Medjool dates in 1 cup warm water for 8 to 10 hours; then process to a smooth paste in a blender or food processor. Store, refrigerated, for up to 2 weeks.
Or
Simmer 1 pound chopped pitted dates with 1/2 cup water gently until the water evaporates and the dates become a soft paste. Store, refrigerated, for up to 2 weeks.

DATES, SEMI-SOFT (Deglet Noor, Thoori, Zahidi) – 1 cup
↪ 1 cup figs, prunes, or jumbo Thompson seedless raisins

DATES, SOFT (Barhi, Halawi, Hadrawi, Medjool) – 1 cup
↪ 1 cup semi-soft dates, soaked in boiling water until softened, about 60 minutes; drained; and blotted dry
↪ 3/4 cup date paste

DATE SUGAR (dehydrated ground dates) – 1 cup
↪ 1 1/3 cups light brown sugar

DESSERT SHELLS (small pastry cases for holding cold or frozen dessert items) – 1 dozen
↪ 1 dozen chocolate cups (Paint cupcake liners with melted dark chocolate, chill until firm, then gently peel the paper off.)

- 1 dozen chocolate shells (Line the inside of small scallop shells tightly with foil, then paint the foil with melted dark chocolate to form a smooth, thick coating. Chill until firm, then gently peel the foil off and repair any cracks.)
- 1 dozen wafer cups (Press freshly baked wafer cookies, such as brandy snaps, lace cookies, or tuiles, over inverted custard cups, juice glasses, or muffin cups while still warm, and then remove when cool.)
- 1 dozen gyoza cups (Brush gyoza wrappers on both sides with 1 to 2 teaspoons each water, honey, and vegetable oil. Press each wrapper into a muffin cup and bake at 375°F until golden, about 12 minutes. Cool and remove.)
- 2 dozen wonton cups (Brush wonton wrappers with melted butter and press into muffin cups (or over inverted custard cups), then bake at 375°F until golden brown, 7 to 9 minutes.)
- 1 dozen marshmallow–crisped rice cups (Mold freshly made crisped rice treat mixture over inverted muffin cups or tart shells; remove when cool.)
- 1 dozen thin, hollowed out shortcakes
- 1 dozen flat-bottomed ice cream wafer cones

DEXTROSE (finely textured glucose) – 1 tablespoon See also GLUCOSE
- 2 teaspoons granulated cane sugar

DIASTATIC MALT POWDER See MALT POWDER, DIASTATIC

DIGESTIVE BISCUITS (for crumb crust or chocolate biscuit cake) – 8 ounces
- 1 pound graham crackers (slightly sweeter)

DUTCH DARK APPLE SYRUP/APPELSTROOP – 1 cup
- 4 cups fresh apple juice, simmered until reduced to 1 cup, 45 to 60 minutes

DUTCH DARK THICK SYRUP/KEUKENSTROOP – 1 cup
☞ 1 cup molasses, treacle, coconut honey, or strong traditional honey

DUTCH THICK SWEET SYRUP/STROOP – 1 cup
☞ 1 cup golden syrup or strong honey

DYES, NATURAL FOOD See FOOD COLORING, NATURAL

E

EGG REPLACER, POWDERED – 2 teaspoons (mixed with 3 tablespoons water for baking)
- 3 tablespoons liquid egg substitute
- 1/4 cup liquid pasteurized egg
- 1 whole fresh egg
- 2 fresh egg whites

EGG SUBSTITUTE, LIQUID – 3 tablespoons
- 1 egg white, lightly beaten
- 2 teaspoons powdered egg replacer mixed with 3 tablespoons water

EGG WASH (solution brushed on pastry to seal edges, or add sheen, or help toppings adhere) – 2 tablespoons
- 2 tablespoons undiluted evaporated milk
- 2 tablespoons tapioca starch mixed with 1 tablespoon cold water
- 1 tablespoon potato starch mixed with 2 tablespoons lukewarm water
- 1 tablespoon cornstarch mixed with 2 tablespoons cold water
- 1- or 2-second spritz of egg-free finishing spray, such as Quick Shine or Bake Sheen
- 2 teaspoons ground golden flaxseed or white/Salba chia seeds soaked in 2 tablespoons water until slightly thickened, 5 to 10 minutes

EGG WHITE, LARGE FRESH – 1 (1 ounce/2 tablespoons/1 fluid ounce)
- 2 tablespoons (1 ounce) thawed frozen egg white
- 3 tablespoons pasteurized liquid egg whites, such as AllWhites or Whippin Whites; or pasteurized packaged organic, kosher egg whites, such as Eggology (ideal for uncooked or lightly cooked

preparations; takes longer to whip into foam or peaks)

☞ 1 tablespoon 100% dried/dehydrated packaged egg whites, such as Just Whites, dissolved in 2 tablespoons warm water (whips up faster than fresh whites)

☞ 1 tablespoon meringue powder dissolved in 2 tablespoons water (contains a small amount of sugar)

☞ 1 tablespoon plain agar powder whisked with 2 tablespoons water, chilled for 15 minutes, then whisked again before using

☞ 2 tablespoons aquafaba (liquid from canned chickpeas)

EGG WHITE, PASTEURIZED LIQUID – 3 tablespoons

☞ 1 fresh egg white (for cooking, baking, and Italian meringue topping)

☞

EGG YOLK, LARGE – 1 (0.6 ounce/1 1/4 tablespoons/1/2 fluid ounce)

☞ 1 1/2 tablespoons thawed frozen egg yolk

☞ 1 1/2 teaspoons powdered non-egg product, such as Ener-G Egg Replacer, plus 1 tablespoon water

☞ 2 tablespoons pasteurized liquid egg, such as Eggbeaters

☞ 1 tablespoon aquafaba (liquid from canned chickpeas)

☞ 1 tablespoon Dijon mustard or mild liquid honey (for a vinaigrette emulsion)

☞ 1/4 teaspoon xanthan gum (for a vinaigrette emulsion)

EGG, WHOLE LARGE FRESH – 1 (1.6 ounces/3 1/4 tablespoons/1 1/2 fluid ounces)

☞ 3 1/2 tablespoons thawed frozen whole egg

☞ 2 egg whites plus 1 teaspoon vegetable oil

☞ 1 egg white, 1 teaspoon vegetable oil, and 4 teaspoons water (for pancakes and moist cookies increase oil in the recipe to 1 tablespoon and omit the water)

☞ 2 large egg yolks plus 1 tablespoon cold water (omit the water for sauces, custards, or cream pie fillings)

☞ 3 tablespoons liquid egg replacement, such as Better'n Eggs or Eggbeaters

- 2 teaspoons powdered egg replacement, such as Ener-G Egg Replacer, plus 2 tablespoons water (for cookies)
- 2 1/2 tablespoons freeze-dried egg powder (powdered whole eggs) plus 2 1/2 tablespoons warm water for baking, or 4 tablespoons for scrambling (stir until smooth, or add egg powder to dry ingredients and water to other liquid called for in the recipe; use right away)
- 3 tablespoons aquafaba (viscous liquid from canned or cooked chickpeas)
- 1/4 cup (2 ounces) soft silken tofu, blotted dry and puréed until smooth (increase baking powder by 1/4 teaspoon and increase the cooking time slightly; best for brownies, coffee cakes, and quick breads)
- 2 ounces plain yogurt (whole or low-fat) mixed with 1/2 teaspoon vegetable oil (increase the cooking time slightly; best for coffee cakes, quick breads, and muffins)
- 1 tablespoon golden flaxseed meal, chia seeds, or hulled hemp seeds soaked in 3 tablespoons hot water until slightly thickened, 10 to 15 minutes, stirring occasionally (or microwaved on High until mixture bubbles and thickens slightly); cooled to room temperature (increase baking powder in the recipe by 1/8 teaspoon; best for brownies, cookies, coffee cakes, and quick breads)
- 3 tablespoons undiluted evaporated milk, cream, or soymilk creamers (for egg wash, glazing, breading)
- 2 tablespoons creamy style salad dressing, mayonnaise, or plain yogurt whisked with 1/2 tablespoon each vegetable oil and water (for breading)
- 2 tablespoons tapioca starch plus 1 tablespoon water (for sealing the edges of dough or helping toppings adhere)

EGG, WHOLE LARGE FRESH (for cakes mostly, not including chiffon, sponge, or angel food cakes)

- 2 tablespoons mayonnaise (best for chocolate cake)
- 1 teaspoon baking powder and 1 teaspoon cider or distilled vinegar (add baking powder to dry ingredients and vinegar to liquid; add at

the last minute and bake immediately after mixing; to take the place of one egg only)

EGG, WHOLE LARGE, EQUIVALENTS
⇨ 1 large = 1 jumbo, 1 extra-large, 1 medium, 2 small
⇨ 2 large = 2 jumbo, 2 extra-large, 2 medium, 3 small
⇨ 3 large = 2 jumbo, 3 extra-large, 3 medium, 4 small
⇨ 4 large = 3 jumbo, 4 extra-large, 5 medium, 5 small
⇨ 5 large = 4 jumbo, 4 extra-large, 6 medium, 7 small
⇨ 6 large = 5 jumbo, 5 extra-large, 7 medium, 8 small

EGGS, PASTEURIZED – 1 dozen:
⇨ 1 dozen whole fresh eggs submerged in hot tap water (140°F) for 3 minutes before cracking and using (if not using immediately, chill them in ice water)

ENO FRUIT SALT POWDER (Indian leavening agent) – 1 teaspoon
⇨ 1 teaspoon baking soda

ESPRESSO, BREWED – 1 (5-ounce) cup
⇨ 4 tablespoons finely ground French roast coffee added to 6 ounces boiling water, steeped 5 minutes, then strained through a coffee filter or paper towel-lined funnel (Alternatively, brew regular coffee double or triple strength.)
⇨ 2 to 4 teaspoons instant espresso granules or powder dissolved in 5 ounces boiling water

ESPRESSO EXTRACT OR POWDER – 1 teaspoon
⇨ 1 1/2 teaspoons freeze-dried instant coffee finely ground to a powder

ETROG CITRON (Israeli large pithy yellow citrus) – 1
⇨ 1 fresh Buddha's hand/fingered citron, or pomelo
⇨ 1 or 2 large, thick-skinned lemons (smaller and juicier)

EVAPORATED CANE JUICE (golden unrefined sugar crystals) See
SUGAR, TURBINADO CANE; SUGAR, GRANULATED

EVAPORATED MILK – 1 cup
- 1 cup fat-free evaporated milk (0.5% butterfat)
- 2 1/4 cups whole milk, simmered in a medium pan until reduced to 1 cup, about 20 minutes (be careful it does not boil over)
- 1/2 cup powdered whole milk blended with 2/3 cup water
- 1 cup half-and-half or light cream

EVAPORATED MILK, VEGAN – 1 cup
- 1/2 cup soymilk powder blended with enough water to make 1 cup

EXPANDEX (modified tapioca food starch) – 1 teaspoon
- 1 teaspoon xanthan gum
- 1 teaspoon guar gum

F

FARRO/EMMER WHEAT, CRACKED – 1 cup
- 1 1/4 cups whole-grain farro chopped in a blender or food processor to a cracked wheat or steel-cut oats stage, 15 to 20 seconds; sift to remove any smaller particles

FARRO/EMMER WHEAT, WHOLE-GRAIN/FARRO MEDIO (Tuscan wheat grain similar to spelt) – 1 cup
- 1 cup semi-pearled farro, pearled farro, or cracked farro
- 2 cups pre-cooked, 10-minute farro, such as Arden Farms or Trader Joe's
- 1 cup cracked wheat or bulgur (less cooking time)
- 1 cup spelt berries, hulled/pot barley, wheat berries, Kamut berries, or triticale berries (longer cooking time)

FEIJOA/PINEAPPLE GUAVA – 1 medium
- 1 medium kiwi fruit

FENNEL SEEDS, DRIED – 1 teaspoon whole seeds
- 1 scant teaspoon mature wild black fennel seeds/*Foeniculum vulgare* (more intense flavor)
- 1 1/2 teaspoons fresh green fennel seeds or 1 tablespoon minced fresh fennel leaves
- 1/2 teaspoon ground fennel seeds
- 1 scant teaspoon anise seeds
- 3/4 teaspoon caraway or dill seeds

FIGS, DRIED – 1 pound
- 1 pound pitted dried dates or prunes
- 1 pound dried apricots or mulberries

FIGS, FRESH SMYRNA/CALIMYRNA – 1 pound
- 1 pound fresh Kadota or Sierra figs
- 1 pound fresh Brown Turkey or Black Mission figs (reduce the amount of sugar called for in the recipe)
- 1 cup dried Calimyrna figs, soaked in boiling hot water until softened, about 15 minutes
- 1 pound pitted prunes plumped in cool water, if necessary (reduce the amount of sugar called for in the recipe)

FIG SYRUP/MIELE DI FICHI/COTTO DI FICHI (Italian dark thick sweetener) – 3/4 cup
- 3/4 cup grape molasses/*mosto cotto* or dark strong tasting honey
Make Your Own Stem and halve 1 pound dried figs. Simmer in 4 cups water until soft and reduced by half. Strain, then simmer the syrup until thickened and dark.

FLAXSEED MEAL/FLAXMEAL – 1 cup for baking
- 3/4 cup chia seed meal/chia powder
- 1 cup hemp powder or walnut meal (lacks gelatinous property)
- 1 cup almond meal, pecan meal, pumpkin seed meal, sesame seed meal, or sunflower seed meal (lacks omega-3s and gelatinous property)

FLAXSEEDS (brown or golden) – 1 cup
- 1 cup chia, Salba, or hemp seeds
- 1 cup sesame seeds (lacks omega-3s and gelatinous property)

FLEUR DE SEL DE GUÉRANDE See SALT, FLEUR DE SEL DE GUÉRANDE

FLOUR, ALL-PURPOSE BLEACHED OR UNBLEACHED (9.5 to 11.7% protein) – 1 cup unsifted for baking
- 1 cup plus 3 tablespoons cake flour (for cakes, biscuits, or rich short pastry; not for quick breads or cookies)
- 1 cup plus 1 tablespoon unbleached pastry flour (for cakes, biscuits, quick breads, or regular pastry)

➯ 1 cup instantized/quick-mixing flour, such as Wondra (for sponge-type cakes, flaky pastry, puff pastry, crepes, or breading)

➯ 1 cup bread flour (for strudel, phyllo, or yeast-raised breads; increase the liquid and kneading time as required)

➯ 1 cup self-rising flour (for biscuits and pancakes; omit any baking powder, baking soda, or salt in the recipe)

➯ 1 cup gluten-free all-purpose flour blend (for cakes and quick breads; will have a drier consistency; best used with buttermilk or yogurt)

➯ 1/2 cup finely ground whole-wheat flour (or whole-wheat flour ground fine in a blender, then sifted to remove any coarse particles) plus 1/2 cup cake flour (for cookies, full-bodied cakes, and quick breads; avoid overmixing)

➯ 1 cup Italian-style *Tipo 00* flour (for lighter pasta, cakes, or Italian flatbreads; more finely milled)

➯ 1 cup light spelt flour or sprouted spelt flour (if using sprouted flour, increase the baking powder in the recipe by 1/4 teaspoon, reduce the liquid in the recipe by 1 tablespoon and avoid overmixing)

➯ 1 cup whole-wheat pastry flour or soft winter whole-wheat flour with 9 to 11% protein; (for heartier, full-bodied cakes, quick breads, cookies, or pastry; increase the liquid in the recipe by 2 tablespoons)

➯ 1/2 cup whole-wheat pastry flour and 1/2 cup light buckwheat flour (for pancakes, waffles, blintzes, crepes, or pasta; increase the liquid in the recipe by 2 tablespoons and avoid overmixing)

➯ 1 cup white rice flour or superfine brown rice flour; or half rice flour and half chestnut or chickpea flour (for crepes, pancakes, or fritters; increase the liquid in the recipe by 1 to 2 tablespoons)

➯ 3/4 cup almond flour, 1/4 cup golden flaxseed meal, and 1 tablespoon coconut flour; separate the eggs, then fold the beaten whites into the batter (for muffins and cookies; for savory applications, replace the coconut flour with chickpea flour)

FLOUR, ALL-PURPOSE – 1 cup for coating dredging, dusting, and kneading

➯ 1 cup brown or white rice flour, white rye flour, or premade gluten-free flour blend (for dusting bread-kneading surfaces, bannetons, and peels; rice and rye flour absorb less moisture)

- ⊵ 1 cup grits, wheat farina, semolina, Cream of Wheat, or cornmeal (for dusting pizza-kneading surfaces and peels; absorbs less moisture and adds crunch to the dough)
- ⊵ 1 cup cornstarch, white or brown rice flour, or water chestnut flour (for dredging/coating; produces a thin crisp, coating, and fries up lighter)
- ⊵ 1 cup corn flour /finely ground yellow or white cornmeal, or rice flakes/flaked rice (for dredging/coating fish; produces a thin crunchy coating)
- ⊵ 1 cup tapioca flour (for flouring cake pans)
- ⊵ Vegetable oil (for kneading bread on a countertop or for rolling out pizza dough; doing so will prevent too much flour being absorbed)

FLOUR, ALL-PURPOSE – 1 tablespoon for thickening

- ⊵ 2 tablespoons browned all-purpose flour or rice flour (Brown the flour in a dry skillet over medium heat or on a pie pan in the oven.)
- ⊵ 1 tablespoon quick-mixing flour, such as Wondra, cake flour, pastry flour, or oat flour
- ⊵ 1 1/4 to 1 1/2 tablespoons biscuit mix or pancake mix
- ⊵ 1 tablespoon besan/chickpea flour or cashew butter (for curries)
- ⊵ 1 tablespoon finely ground brown or white rice flour, or regular rice flour ground until fine (especially for roux)
- ⊵ 1 1/2 teaspoons sweet rice flour/glutinous rice flour (does not separate when frozen)
- ⊵ 1 1/2 teaspoons cornstarch (boil no longer than 1 minute)
- ⊵ 1 1/4 teaspoons potato starch (cook until just thickened)
- ⊵ 2 teaspoons arrowroot powder (clear appearance for puddings, delicate sauces, pie filling, and glazes; stir until just thickened)
- ⊵ 1 tablespoon tapioca flour/starch, or 2 1/2 teaspoons small-pearl tapioca, ground until fine (clear appearance; does not separate when frozen)
- ⊵ 1 teaspoon instant mashed potato flakes (whisk in to avoid clumping)

FLOUR, AMARANTH See AMARANTH FLOUR

FLOUR, BREAD, UNBLEACHED/BRITISH-TYPE STRONG/GERMAN-TYPE 813/CANADIAN-TYPE ALL-PURPOSE (12 to 13.5% protein) – 1 cup unsifted

- ⇨ 1 cup high-protein all-purpose flour, such as King Arthur unbleached all-purpose flour with 11.7% protein
- ⇨ 1 cup plus 1 1/2 tablespoons national brand unbleached all-purpose flour, such as Gold Medal or Pillsbury with 10.5% protein; or 1 cup all-purpose flour plus 1 1/2 teaspoons vital wheat gluten, or 1 tablespoon wheat germ
- ⇨ 1 cup French-style flour with 11.5% protein, or European-style/ artisan flour with 11.7% protein (for French and other European breads)
- ⇨ 1 cup Indian-style finely milled soft whole-wheat flour (atta/ chapati flour) or Italian-type (*Tipo 00* flour) (for ultrathin pizza and flatbreads; reduce the liquid in the recipe by 20%)
- ⇨ 1 cup finely ground whole-wheat flour; white whole-wheat flour; or regular whole-wheat flour ground in a blender until fine (add 1 1/2 teaspoons vital wheat gluten, increase the kneading time and increase the liquid in the recipe as required)
- ⇨ 1 cup plus 2 tablespoons coarsely ground whole-wheat, wheatmeal, or graham flour (add 1 1/2 teaspoons vital wheat gluten, increase the kneading time, and increase the liquid in the recipe as required, usually about 2 tablespoons)

FLOUR, BRITISH-TYPE PLAIN UNBLEACHED See FLOUR, SOFT WINTER WHEAT

FLOUR, BRITISH-TYPE SOFT FLOUR See FLOUR, CAKE

FLOUR, BRITISH-TYPE STRONG UNBLEACHED See FLOUR, BREAD, UNBLEACHED

FLOUR, BUCKWHEAT (13 to 15% protein)
- ⇨ White, untoasted buckwheat groats (hulled seeds) or buckwheat grits, ground in a high-powered blender until powdery or in small batches in a spice/coffee grinder

⊳ Equal parts whole-wheat and all-purpose flour (contains gluten)

FLOUR, CAKE/BRITISH SOFT FLOUR/ARGENTINE HARINA 0000 (6 to 7% protein) – 1 cup sifted

Tip: Aerate the substitute flour with a whisk or sieve, lifting it above the bowl to add as much air as possible

⊳ 3/4 cup sifted bleached all-purpose flour and 2 tablespoons cornstarch or potato starch

⊳ 1 cup sifted soft Southern wheat flour with low protein content, such as White Lily all-purpose or Southern Biscuit flour with 7 to 8% protein

⊳ 1 cup unbleached (unbromated) cake flour blend, such as King Arthur with 9.4% protein (contains malted barley flour)

⊳ 3/4 cup plus 3 tablespoons pastry flour

⊳ 3/4 cup plus 2 tablespoons sifted bleached all-purpose flour, such as Pillsbury or Gold Medal

⊳ 3/4 cup potato starch and 1/4 cup matzo cake meal (for Passover)

FLOUR, CLEAR (extra fine whole-wheat flour with 11.5% protein) – 1 cup

⊳ 1 cup whole-wheat flour previously sifted through a fine-mesh sieve to remove the bran

⊳ 3/4 cup plus 2 tablespoons unbleached bread flour and 2 tablespoons whole-wheat flour

FLOUR, CORNELL (UNIVERSITY) FORMULA (enriched flour for added protein) – 1 cup

Make Your Own Whisk together 3/4 cup plus 2 tablespoons bread flour, 1 tablespoon full-fat soy flour, 1 tablespoon nonfat milk powder, and 1 teaspoon wheat germ until thoroughly combined.

FLOUR, CRACKED WHEAT – 1 cup

⊳ 1 cup cracked wheat cereal (for bread recipes when combined with other flour)

FLOUR, DURUM (13.5% to 14% protein) – 1 cup
- ☞ 1 cup finely milled semolina flour
- ☞ 1 cup wheat farina or regular Cream of Wheat, ground in a high-powered blender until extra fine or in batches in a spice/coffee grinder

FLOUR, FRENCH-TYPE 55, MEDIUM PROTEIN, HIGH-ASH BREAD FLOUR (11.5% protein) – 1 cup
- ☞ 3/4 cup unbleached all-purpose flour plus 1/3 cup unbleached bread flour

FLOUR, GERMAN-TYPE 550 UNBLEACHED See FLOUR, ALL-PURPOSE

FLOUR, GERMAN-TYPE 813 UNBLEACHED See FLOUR, BREAD

FLOUR, GERMAN-TYPE 1050 See FLOUR, HIGH-GLUTEN, UNBLEACHED

FLOUR, GLUTEN (14.5 protein; best for bread machines) – 1 cup unsifted
- ☞ 1 cup unsifted bread flour plus 2 teaspoons vital wheat gluten; decrease liquid as necessary
- ☞ 1 cup unsifted Very Strong Canadian Bread Flour/red spring wheat flour (14.8% protein; sold in Britain)

FLOUR, GLUTEN-FREE See GLUTEN-FREE GRAINS, FLOURS, and STARCHES

FLOUR, GLUTINOUS/SWEET RICE See RICE FLOUR, SWEET

FLOUR, GRAHAM/WHEATMEAL (14% protein) – 1 cup
- ☞ 3/4 cup whole-wheat flour (preferably stone-ground) plus 1/3 cup unprocessed wheat bran
- ☞ 1 cup coarsely ground whole-wheat flour (preferably stone-ground) or 1 cup plus 2 tablespoons regular whole-wheat flour
- ☞ 3/4 cup unbleached all-purpose flour, 2 tablespoons whole-wheat flour, and 2 tablespoons wheat germ

FLOUR, HIGH-EXTRACTION – 1 cup
- ⇨ 3/4 cup whole-wheat flour and 1/4 cup bread flour

FLOUR, HIGH-GLUTEN, UNBLEACHED/GERMAN-TYPE 1050 (14% protein) – 1 cup
- ⇨ 1 cup unbleached all-purpose flour plus 1 1/2 teaspoons vital wheat gluten; increase the flour in the recipe as needed
- ⇨ 1 cup unbleached bread flour; increase the flour in the recipe as needed

FLOUR, HIGH-PROTEIN, UNBLEACHED (14 1/2% protein) See FLOUR, HIGH-GLUTEN

FLOUR, IRISH WHOLEMEAL/WHOLE-WHEAT (9 to 11% protein) – 1 cup
- ⇨ 1 cup King Arthur Irish-style wholemeal flour
- ⇨ 2/3 cup whole-wheat pastry flour and 1/3 cup wheat flakes coarsely ground in a food processor

FLOUR, ITALIAN TIPO 00/GRANO TENERO (8 to 8.5% protein) – 1 cup See also FLOUR, PIZZA
- ⇨ 1 cup Argentinean soft wheat 000 flour, such as *Favorita* or *Blanca Flor*
- ⇨ 1 cup King Arthur Italian-style flour (8% protein)
- ⇨ 1/2 cup each unbleached all-purpose flour and cake flour (for pizza)
- ⇨ 2/3 cup all-purpose flour and l/3 cup fine semolina flour (for pasta)
- ⇨ 1 cup bleached all-purpose flour, such as Gold Medal (10.5% protein)

FLOUR, JAPANESE SOFT/WEAK/HAKURIKI-KO See JAPANESE SOFT/WEAK FLOUR

FLOUR, MESQUITE (11 to 17% protein) – 1 cup
- ⇨ 1 cup pure buckwheat flour
- ⇨ 1 cup coconut flour (less nutty tasting)

FLOUR, MILLET (12.8% protein) – 1 cup
- ⇨ 2/3 cup organic hulled millet, ground in a high-powered blender until powdery or in small batches in a spice/coffee grinder
- ⇨ 1 cup light-colored teff flour or quinoa flour
- ⇨ 1 cup superfine brown rice flour
- ⇨ 1 cup Kamut flour (contains gluten)

FLOUR, NUTMEAT – 1 cup
- ⇨ 3/4 cups whole nuts, ground at low speed in a blender or in small batches in a spice/coffee grinder (For baking, include a teaspoon of sugar or flour from the recipe to avoid oiliness.)

FLOUR, OAT, WHOLE-GRAIN See OAT FLOUR, WHOLE GRAIN

FLOUR, PASTA See PASTA FLOUR

FLOUR, PASTRY, UNBLEACHED (soft red winter wheat flour; 7.5 to 9.5% protein) – 1 cup See also FLOUR, WHOLE-WHEAT PASTRY
- ⇨ 2/3 cup soft white wheat berries, ground until powdery in a high-powered blender, or in small batches in a spice/coffee grinder
- ⇨ 1 cup all-purpose Southern-milled soft flour, such as While Lily; or 3/4 cup plus 3 tablespoons national brand bleached all-purpose flour, such as Pillsbury or Gold Medal (for most applications)
- ⇨ 2/3 cup bleached all-purpose flour and 1/3 cup cake flour (for most applications)
- ⇨ 3/4 cup plus 2 tablespoons quick-mixing flour, such as Wondra (for sponge-type cakes, puff pastry, flaky pastry, and crepes)
- ⇨ 1/2 cup plus 2 tablespoons cake flour and 6 tablespoons bread flour (for pastry, cookies, biscuits, pancakes, and waffles)
- ⇨ 3/4 cup plus 2 tablespoons bleached all-purpose flour and 2 tablespoons cornstarch or potato starch (for cookies, pastry, quick breads, pancakes, and waffles)

⇨ 1 cup pastry blend, such as King Arthur Perfect Pastry Blend (for pastry)

⇨ 1 cup Canadian cake and pastry flour

⇨ 1 cup Italian *Tipo 00* flour

⇨ 1 cup Argentinean or Uruguayan finely ground 000 flour

FLOUR, PATENT *See FLOUR, BREAD, UNBLEACHED*

FLOUR, PIZZA (Caputo pizza flour, Alimonti organic pasta flour; 12 to 13% protein) – 1 cup *See also FLOUR, ITALIAN TIPO 00*

⇨ 1 cup pizza flour blend, such as King Arthur

⇨ 3/4 cup plus 2 tablespoons unbleached all-purpose flour and 2 tablespoons semolina flour

FLOUR, PLAIN (British all-purpose flour with 9 to 10% protein) *See FLOUR, SOFT WINTER WHEAT*

FLOUR, POPCORN (1% protein) – 1 cup

⇨ 2 cups cold unsalted plain popcorn (preferably hot-air popped), ground in small batches in a blender or food processor until powdery

FLOUR, POTATO (15% protein) – 1/4 cup

⇨ 1/2 cup dry potato flakes/instant mashed potatoes, such as Hungry Jack

FLOUR, PUMPERNICKEL/RYE MEAL/WHOLE-RYE FLOUR (8 to 13% protein) – 1 cup

⇨ 1 cup coarsely ground stone-milled dark rye flour

⇨ 3/4 cup plus 3 tablespoons medium rye flour and 2 tablespoons wheat bran

FLOUR, QUINOA *See QUINOA FLOUR*

FLOUR, RICE, BROWN (7% protein) – 1 cup

- 3/4 cup short-grain packaged American-grown brown rice, ground until fine in a grain mill, or in small batches in a spice/coffee grinder, then sieved
- 1 cup superfine brown rice flour (less grainy)
- 1 cup stone-ground garbanzo bean flour, garbanzo–fava bean flour blend such as Authentic Foods Garfava Flour, or Indian *besan*/gram or urad dal flour
- 1 cup premade gluten-free flour blend, preferably brown rice–based

FLOUR, RICE, WHITE, SUPERFINE OR ASIAN (5 to 5.8% protein) – 1 cup

- 3/4 cup plus 2 tablespoons short- or medium-grain American-grown and packaged white rice, or dry Cream of Rice cereal, ground in small batches in a spice/coffee grinder until fine
- 1 cup oat flour (for shortbread)

FLOUR, RYE, WHITE/LIGHT (8.3% protein) – 1 cup

- 1 1/4 cups rye flakes, ground in batches in a spice/coffee grinder until powdery
- 1 cup pastry flour mixed with 1/4 teaspoon powdered rye flavoring

FLOUR, SELF-RISING SOFT FLOUR/CAKE (7 to 8% protein) – 1 cup

- 1/2 cup plus 2 tablespoons all-purpose flour, 1/3 cup cornstarch, 1 teaspoon baking powder, and 1/2 teaspoon salt, thoroughly combined with a whisk or electric mixer on low
- 1 cup cake flour plus 1 1/4 teaspoons baking powder

FLOUR, SELF-RAISING UNBLEACHED (British self-rising flour; 8 to 9% protein) – 1 cup

- 1 cup U.S. unbleached self-rising flour; reduce the salt in the recipe by 1/2 teaspoon

⇨ 1 cup pastry flour plus 1 teaspoon baking powder, thoroughly combined with a whisk or electric mixer on low

FLOUR, SELF-RISING, UNBLEACHED (U.S. self-rising flour; 8.5% to 9% protein) – 1 cup

⇨ 1 cup pastry flour, 1 1/2 teaspoons baking powder, and 1/2 teaspoon salt, thoroughly combined with a whisk or electric mixer on low

⇨ 1 cup all-purpose Southern milled flour, such as White Lily, Martha White, or Southern Biscuit; 1 teaspoon baking powder; 1/2 teaspoon salt; and 1/4 teaspoon baking soda (especially for recipes using buttermilk)

⇨ 3/4 cup plus 2 tablespoons bleached all-purpose flour, 2 tablespoons cornstarch or potato starch, 1 teaspoon baking soda, and 2 teaspoons cream of tartar (for recipes specifying buttermilk when regular milk is being substituted)

FLOUR, SEMOLINA, FINE-GRIND (13 to 16% protein) – 1 cup

⇨ 1 cup extra-fancy pasta flour or farina-grade silky fine flour

FLOUR, SOFT WINTER WHEAT ALL-PURPOSE/SOUTHERN U.S. MILLED/ UNBLEACHED BRITISH-TYPE PLAIN (7.5 to 9.5% protein) – 1 cup

⇨ 1 cup unbleached all-purpose Southern milled flour, such as White Lily or Martha White

⇨ 1 cup unbleached pastry flour (8% protein), or unbleached cake flour blend, such as King Arthur with 9.4% protein

⇨ 1 cup Italian-type 000 flour (8.5% protein)

⇨ 2/3 cup national brand bleached all-purpose flour, such as Pillsbury or Gold Medal, and 1/3 cup bleached cake flour, thoroughly combined

⇨ 3/4 cup national brand bleached all-purpose flour and 3 tablespoons cornstarch or potato starch, thoroughly combined

FLOUR, SORGHUM (11% protein) See SORGHUM FLOUR

FLOUR, SOY, FULL FAT (26 to 35% protein; 20 to 24 grams fat) – 1 cup
- ⇨ 1 cup defatted soy flour (7 grams fat)
- ⇨ 1 cup garbanzo/chickpea/*besan* flour or garbanzo-fava bean flour blend, such as Authentic Foods Garfava Flour (increase the liquid in the recipe by 2 tablespoons per cup of flour; baked goods will be slightly denser)

FLOUR, SPELT WHOLE GRAIN (13 to 15% protein) – 1 cup
- ⇨ 1 1/4 cups rolled spelt flakes, ground in batches in a spice/coffee grinder until fine, then sifted to remove any coarse bran
- ⇨ 1 cup white or light spelt flour; reduce the liquid in the recipe as required
- ⇨ 1 cup whole-wheat flour (more bitter)

FLOUR, SPROUTED WHEAT (13.5% protein) – 1 cup
- ⇨ 1 cup panocha flour/*harina para panocha*
- ⇨ 1 cup finely milled whole-wheat flour

Make Your Own Sprout 3/4 cup soft white wheat berries. Drain, then arrange the berries on dehydrator sheets and dry in a dehydrator set at 95°F to 112°F until hard, 12 to 24 hours. Grind in batches in a grain mill, high-powered blender, or spice/coffee grinder until powdery, then sift if necessary.

FLOUR, STRONG (British hard wheat flour; 11 to 12% protein) See FLOUR, BREAD

FLOUR, SUPERFINE See FLOUR, CAKE

FLOUR, TEFF (14 to 15% protein) – 1 cup
- ⇨ 1 scant cup whole-grain teff, ground until powdery in a high-powered blender, or in batches in a spice/coffee grinder
- ⇨ 1 cup finely ground millet flour (or 2/3 cup organic millet ground until powdery in a high-powered blender, or in batches in a spice/coffee grinder)

⇨ 1 cup sorghum flour or superfine brown rice flour

FLOUR, WHEATMEAL *See FLOUR, GRAHAM*

FLOUR, WHITE LILY ALL-PURPOSE – 1 cup
⇨ 1/2 cup all-purpose flour and 1/2 cup cake flour

FLOUR, WHITE WHOLE-WHEAT (13% protein) – 1 cup
⇨ 1 cup whole-wheat pastry flour
⇨ 1 cup spelt flour

FLOUR, WHOLE-WHEAT/BRITISH WHOLEMEAL FLOUR/GERMAN– TYPE 1600 FLOUR (14 to 14.4% protein) – 1 cup
⇨ 1/2 to 2/3 cup hard red winter wheat berries ground until powdery in a high-powered blender or in batches in a spice/ coffee grinder; measure after grinding and increase liquid in recipe slightly
⇨ 1 cup white whole-wheat flour (13% protein; lighter color, milder tasting; reduce the liquid in the recipe slightly)
⇨ 3/4 cup plus 2 tablespoons unbleached all-purpose flour and 2 tablespoon wheat germ
⇨ 2/3 cup unbleached all-purpose flour and 1/3 cup raw/unprocessed bran flakes (or 1/4 cup pulverized plain bran cereal; reduce the sugar in the recipe by 1 tablespoon)
⇨ 3/4 cup plus 3 tablespoons unbleached all-purpose flour, 2 tablespoons wheat bran, and 1 teaspoon wheat germ
⇨ 1 cup whole-spelt flour (lower in gluten)
⇨ 1 cup einkorn flour (lower in gluten and less dense; reduce the liquid by one-third)
⇨ 1 cup sprouted wheat flour or stone-ground whole-wheat flour (increase the liquid in the recipe as required)
⇨ 1 cup graham, Kamut, or 12-grain flour (increase the liquid in the recipe as required)

FLOUR, WHOLE-WHEAT BREAD (13 to 14% protein) – 1 cup
- 1 cup very finely ground whole-wheat flour plus 2 teaspoons vital wheat gluten
- 1 cup unbleached hard spring white flour with a high protein count, such as Wheat Montana Prairie Gold (for a sweeter, lighter, less dense loaf)
- 1 cup Hovis Granary Bread Flour or King Arthur Irish-Style Flour (coarser grind; for British wholemeal)

FLOUR, WHOLE-WHEAT CAKE (7 to 8% protein) – 1 cup
- 3/4 cup fine-grain whole-wheat flour (sifted to remove any coarse bran) plus 2 tablespoons cornstarch or potato starch
- 3/4 cup plus 3 tablespoons whole-wheat pastry flour

FLOUR, WHOLE-WHEAT PASTRY (9% protein) – 1 cup
- 1/2 to 2/3 cup soft white wheat berries, ground until powdery in a high-powered blender, or in batches in a spice/coffee grinder; increase the liquid in the recipe slightly
- 1/2 cup whole-wheat flour and 1/2 cup all-purpose flour (sift to discard any coarse bran)
- 1 cup gluten-free all-purpose flour

FLOUR, WHOLE-WHEAT SELF-RISING (9% protein) – 1 cup
- 1 cup whole-wheat flour plus 1 teaspoon baking powder

FOOD COLORING, NATURAL
- Blue: crushed and strained fresh or canned blueberries, Concord grape juice, thawed frozen grape juice concentrate, or concentrated water from boiled red cabbage
- Black: squid or cuttlefish ink, purchased or extracted from the ink sacs of fresh squid or cuttlefish
- Dark brown: caramelized sugar or baker's caramel/powdered caramel color, or strong brewed coffee, or instant or freeze-dried coffee mixed with a little hot water

- Green: spinach powder or matcha (green tea powder) dissolved in a little hot water; or fresh green vegetation (basil, coltsfoot, kale, spinach, parsley, watercress, or trimmed pandan leaves), pureed and then squeezed in cheesecloth to extract the liquid
- Orange: achiote/Bijol powder, annatto seeds soaked in a little hot water (use the water and discard the seeds), or concentrated water from boiled yellow onion skins
- Pink/red/violet: thawed frozen cranberry juice concentrate; sumac berries soaked in cold water a few hours; beet powder mixed with hot water (or sliced beets dried, then ground in a spice/coffee grinder); or juiced raw red beets especially Bull's Blood; or beets pureed, then squeezed in cheesecloth (Wear plastic gloves; 1 pound raw beets will yield 1/4 scant cup juice; the juice can be concentrated by gently boiling until reduced to 1 tablespoon.)
- Purple: fresh elderberries, cooked and then strained
- Yellow: thawed frozen orange juice concentrate, marigold flowers, or turmeric powder
- Yellow/orange: carrot juice, or half ground turmeric and half mild paprika

FRENCH FLOUR- *See FLOUR, FRENCH TYPE 55*

FRUCTOSE/LEVULOSE – 1 cup
- 1 1/2 cups superfine sugar (or 1 1/2 cups plus 1 tablespoon granulated sugar pulverized in a blender or food processor until fine-textured, 20 to 30 seconds)

FRUIT, CANDIED *See CANDIED FRUIT/GLACÉ FRUIT*

FRUIT FRESH (anti-darkening agent) – 1/4 teaspoon
- 1/4 teaspoon citric acid or 1/8 teaspoon ascorbic acid
- 1 tablespoon lemon juice

FRUIT GLAZE (apricot, cherry, raspberry, strawberry, or red currant) – 1/2 cup

Make Your Own Combine 1/2 cup (6 ounces) jelly (or jam or preserves) and 2 tablespoons water (or citrus juice or fruit-flavored liqueur) and heat over low heat, or microwave on High, until bubbling. Strain to remove seeds, if necessary, pressing hard on the solids. (For a thinner glaze add 1 or 2 more tablespoons liquid; for a thicker glaze cook, stirring frequently, until glaze is very sticky; use while warm.)

FRUIT JUICE – 1 cup for cooking
- 1 cup brewed spicy herb tea
- 1 cup canned fruit nectar; reduce the sugar in the recipe or add a few teaspoons lemon or lime juice

FRUIT SWEET/LIQUID FRUIT JUICE CONCENTRATE – 1 cup
- 12 ounces thawed frozen white grape or apple juice concentrate, gently boiled in a large pan until reduced to 1 cup, about 10 minutes (or microwaved on High in a 4-cup glass measuring cup, about 12 minutes)

FRUIT VINEGAR – 1 cup

Make Your Own Heat 1 cup vinegar (cider, wine, or unseasoned rice vinegar) and pour over 1/2 cup fresh cleaned fruit in a sterilized jar. Cool, then cover and let steep in a cool, dark place for 2 weeks. Strain and discard the fruit.

G

GARLIC BUTTER – 4 ounces (1/2 cup)

Make Your Own Stir 2 finely minced or grated garlic cloves (or 1 teaspoon or more liquid garlic seasoning or instant garlic) into 1/2 cup (1 stick) room-temperature butter. Let sit for a few minutes to develop flavor. It will keep, well sealed and refrigerated, for up to 1 week.

GELATIN, GRANULATED/POWDERED UNFLAVORED – 1 packet (1/4 ounce/1 scant tablespoon)

- 4 to 6 sheets leaf gelatin, depending upon size and grade (usually 4 sheets for silver grade)
- 4 teaspoons (.375 ounce) unflavored vegan gelatin powder (blend of vegetable gums and tapioca starch; not for highly acidic ingredients)
- 1 scant tablespoon kosher gelatin (made from fish or all-beef gelatin)
- 2 1/2 teaspoons apple pectin powder (use following the package directions; reduce sugar as necessary)
- 2 teaspoons agar powder (use 2 1/2 teaspoons for acidic ingredients, such as citrus fruit, lemon juice, vinegar, or wine)
- 2 tablespoons agar flakes, or 1 bar (increase the amount for acidic ingredients)

GELATIN SHEETS/LEAVES, SILVER GRADE – 4 sheets

- 1 package (1/4 ounce/1 scant tablespoon granulated/powdered unflavored gelatin), such as Knox, prepared according to the package directions

GIANDUJA (chocolate-hazelnut spread, such as Nutella or Noccioata) – 1 cup

- 3 ounces melted chocolate (milk or bittersweet) stirred into 1/2 cup room-temperature nut butter, preferably hazelnut

⇨ 1 cup low-carb vegan chocolate-hazelnut spread

GINGER, CRYSTALLIZED/PRESERVED – 1/3 cup
⇨ 2 tablespoons grated fresh ginger; add 3 1/2 tablespoons granulated sugar to the recipe

GINGER, DRIED
Make Your Own Cut peeled knobs of ginger into 1/8-inch slices; dry in a dehydrator at 115°F until completely dry, 4 to 8 hours, rotating the trays a few times. Let cool, and then grate.

GINGER EXTRACT – 1 cup
Make Your Own Add 1 teaspoon finely grated lemon zest and 2 tablespoons finely grated fresh ginger to 1 cup brandy or whiskey; seal tightly and leave in a cool place for 10 days, shaking the bottle daily. Strain through a cloth-lined funnel or sieve, and store tightly covered.

GINGER, FRESH MATURE TROPICAL – 1-inch peeled segment (1 tablespoon minced or coarsely grated)
⇨ 4 teaspoons fresh or frozen minced young stem ginger (no peeling required)
⇨ 4 teaspoons thawed frozen grated ginger (Flash-freeze teaspoon-size portions of grated ginger, then transfer to a small freezer bag when frozen; it will keep for up to 1 year.)
⇨ 1 tablespoon bottled ginger puree/paste
⇨ 1 1/2 teaspoons dried cracked ginger, freeze-dried minced ginger, or dried ginger slices broken into pieces (for marinades, stock, soup, and pickling)
⇨ 1/2 teaspoon ginger juice (for curries, marinades, and stir-fries)
⇨ 2 teaspoons minced or grated fresh galangal (stronger flavor; has pine notes)
⇨ 1/4 to 1/2 teaspoon powdered ginger plus few drops lemon or lime juice (for soups, curries, fruit, and baking)

➥ 1 tablespoon minced or ground fresh wild ginger rhizome/*Asarum canadense*

GINGER, GROUND DRIED/POWDERED – 1 teaspoon
➥ 1 tablespoon grated fresh ginger (freeze ginger for 30 minutes, then use a rasp-type grater)
➥ 2 tablespoons dried uncrystallized ginger, minced (or 1/4 cup crystallized ginger rinsed to remove sugar, then minced; reduce the sugar in the recipe by 2 tablespoons)
➥ 1 teaspoon ginger juice (grate fresh ginger, then squeeze to extract the juice; add to liquid ingredients)
➥ 1/4 teaspoon crumbled or ground mace and 3/4 teaspoon finely grated lemon zest

GINGER JELLY – 1/2 cup
➥ 1/2 cup apple jelly and 2 to 3 teaspoons ginger juice, gently heated together until the jelly melts; cover, and refrigerate overnight to develop the flavor (Store in the refrigerator. For jam, replace the ginger juice with 3 tablespoons minced uncrystallized ginger and add 1/2 teaspoon ground ginger.)

GINGER JUICE – 1 tablespoon (or more)
Make Your Own Peel a 1 1/2- to 2-inch piece of fresh ginger (about 1 1/2 to 2 ounces), finely grate it, and then press through a garlic press, tea strainer, fine-mesh sieve, or cheesecloth. (Freezing and thawing the ginger will produce more juice.)

GINGER JUICE – 6 tablespoons to 1 scant cup
Make Your Own Wash 1 pound unpeeled fresh ginger then chop or thinly slice (should yield 2 1/2 to 3 cups). Process in a blender or food processor for 3 to 5 minutes, then strain in a cheesecloth-lined sieve, pressing on solids to extract all the liquid. It will keep refrigerated for up to 1 week, or freeze for longer storage.

GINGER LIQUEUR/GINGER-FLAVORED SPIRIT (such as Domaine de Canton) – 1 tablespoon for cooking
⇨ 1/4 teaspoon ginger juice plus 1 tablespoon vodka or water

GINGER MARMALADE – 1/2 cup
⇨ 1/2 cup orange or lemon marmalade, 1/2 to 1 teaspoon ground ginger, and 2 to 3 teaspoons grated fresh ginger stirred together (Cover and leave at room temperature overnight to develop the flavor; then keep refrigerated.)

GINGER, POWDERED See GINGER, GROUND DRIED/POWDERED

GINGER, STEM, PRESERVED IN SYRUP – 2 tablespoons
⇨ 2 teaspoons thinly sliced soft/uncrystallized ginger; or crystallized ginger, rinsed (for ginger)
⇨ 2 tablespoons ginger syrup (for syrup) See GINGER SYRUP

GINGER SYRUP – 1 cup
⇨ 1 cup syrup from jarred preserved stem ginger (for 1 tablespoon, mix 1 teaspoon honey with 1 tablespoon ginger juice)
Make Your Own Bring to a boil 1/3 cup thinly sliced unpeeled ginger, 1/2 cup firmly packed brown sugar, and 1 cup water, then simmer until reduced and syrupy, about 10 minutes. Cool then strain. Store, refrigerated, for up to 1 month. (For more intense flavor, let the syrup sit for 45 to 60 minutes before straining.)

GLAZE See CAKE GLAZE; FRUIT GLAZE

GLUCOSE/GLUCOSE SYRUP/DEXTROGLUCOSE – 1 cup
⇨ 3/4 cup light-colored (not "lite") corn syrup brought to a full boil, cooled completely, then mixed with 1/3 cup unheated corn syrup
⇨ 1 cup light-colored (not "lite") corn syrup

GLUTEN-FREE GRAINS, FLOURS, and STARCHES

⇨ Acorn flour; almond meal; amaranth grain, flour, and flakes; arrowroot powder; brown rice flour and flakes; buckwheat flour, groats, and Cream of Buckwheat (if label reads 100% buckwheat); *canahua* grain; carob; cassava/*gari* flour; chestnut flour; chickpea/garbanzo/*besan* flour; coconut flour; corn flour; cornmeal; cornstarch; garbanzo and fava bean flour blend; glutinous rice and glutinous/sweet rice flour (despite the name, does not contain gluten); lentil flour; lupin flour; mesquite flour; hulled millet and millet flour; Montina flour (Indian ricegrass); oats and oat flour (if label reads gluten-free, such as Bob's Red Mill); potato flour and starch; quinoa flakes, flour, and grain; rice flour and rice bran/polish; sago and sago flour; sorghum flour; soy flour; tapioca and tapioca starch; teff berries and teff whole-grain flour; water chestnut flour; or yuca flour/starch

GLUTINOUS RICE FLOUR See RICE FLOUR, SWEET

GOLDEN SYRUP/LIGHT TREACLE (British pure cane sugar syrup with a butterscotch flavor) – 1 cup

⇨ 1 cup Swedish light syrup/*ljus sirap,* coconut syrup, or Steen's pure cane syrup

⇨ 3/4 cup light-colored (not "lite") corn syrup and 1/3 cup dark corn syrup, simmered, uncovered, until syrupy and reduced to 1 cup, about 5 minutes

⇨ 2/3 cup light-colored corn syrup plus 1/3 cup light unsulphured molasses or grade A golden, delicate maple syrup, heated until combined

⇨ 1/2 cup each dark corn syrup and light, mild-flavored honey, heated until combined

GOOSEBERRIES, GREEN, FRESH OR FROZEN – 1 cup

⇨ 1 cup smooth-skinned pink dessert gooseberries (reduce the sugar and cooking time)

⇨ 1 cup red or white currants (smaller; reduce the sugar and cooking time)

- 1 cup dark red Worcesterberries/*Ribes divaricatum* or purple-black Jostaberries/*Ribes nidigrolaria* (blackcurrant and gooseberry hybrids; smaller and sweeter; reduce the sugar and cooking time)
- 1 cup coarsely chopped rhubarb (less sweet; increase the sugar)

GRAHAM CRACKER CRUMBS – 1 1/4 cups packed crumbs for an 8- or 9-inch crust

- 1 package graham crackers (11 double crackers 4 7/8 x 2 3/8 inches), crushed or processed to a fine or coarse crumb
- 1 1/4 cups crushed animal crackers, arrowroot cookies, digestive biscuits, or Maria cookies
- 1 1/4 cups crushed gingersnaps, shortbread cookies/Lorna Doones, or vanilla wafers (for a crumb crust, reduce the fat and sugar in the recipe)
- 1 cup finely ground Honey Nut Chex or Cinnamon Rice Chex
- 1 1/2 cups crushed fruit-free granola (for a crumb crust, reduce the fat and sugar in the recipe)
- 1 1/4 cups crushed pretzel crumbs and scant 1/4 cup sweetened flaked coconut
- 1 1/4 cups pecan or walnut meal (for a crumb crust, use softened butter and reduce it to 1 1/2 tablespoons)

GRAPE MOLASSES/MUST SYRUP/DIBS/MOSTARDA/PEKMEZ/ PETIMÉSI (Italian, Spanish, and Middle Eastern thick syrup) – 1/4 cup

- 3/4 cup unsweetened grape juice or prune juice, gently boiled until syrupy and reduced to 1/4 cup, about 10 minutes (Stir constantly and skim the foam as necessary.)
- 1/4 cup thick fig syrup/*miele di fichi/melazzo di fichi*
- 3 tablespoons lemon juice and 4 teaspoons dark molasses (or strong-tasting honey) warmed in the microwave a few seconds, then cooled
- 3 tablespoons dark, strong-tasting/bitter honey thinned with 1 tablespoon warm water
- 1/4 cup sweet, heavy wine, such as Greek Mavrodaphne
- 2 to 3 tablespoons aged balsamic vinegar

GRAPES, RED TABLE – 1 cup
‣ 1 cup deep red to deep-purple wild fox grapes/*Vitis labrusca* or southern fox grapes/Muscardine or scuppernong/*Vitis rotundifolia* (more seeds and sour tougher skin)

GRAPPA (Italian clear distilled spirit) – 2 tablespoons
‣ 2 tablespoons Chilean or Peruvian pisco, French marc, Portuguese bagaciera, Spanish aguardiente, or very dry vermouth, such as Noilly Prat

GREEK HONEY/MELI (wildflower and herbs/Attiki, or thyme/ Hymettus) – 1 cup
‣ 1 cup Italian wildflower honey/*millefiori*
‣ 1 cup unfiltered, aromatic honey, such as pine tree or sunflower
‣ 1 cup grape must syrup/*petimezi*

GREEK-STYLE YOGURT See YOGURT, GREEK-STYLE, FULL-FAT OR 2%

GREEK SWEET WINE (Mavrodaphne, Samos, Muscat) – 1/4 cup for cooking
‣ 1/4 cup Madeira

GUAR GUM (thickening and emulsifying agent) – 1 teaspoon
‣ 1 teaspoon xanthan gum
‣ 2 teaspoons powdered unflavored gelatin or agar powder (softened in water)
‣ 1 teaspoon golden flaxmeal (ground golden flaxseed)
‣ 1 teaspoon Expandex (especially for yeast baking)
‣ 2 tablespoons potato flour
‣ 2 teaspoons psyllium powder (use 5 teaspoons for drop cookies)

GUAVA PASTE, BRAZILIAN/ATE/GOIABADA – 4 ounces
‣ 4 ounces quince paste/*membrillo*; jellied quince paste/*pâte de coing*, plumbrillo, or any tart Mexican fruit paste/*ate*

⇨ 4 ounces strawberry or raspberry paste (Cook 6 to 7 ounces strawberry or seedless raspberry jam until very thick and reduced by at least one-third, then transfer to a shallow greased dish and chill until firm.)

GUAVA PUREE – 1 cup
⇨ 1/2 to 2/3 cups guava paste and 1/2 cup water, pureed in a blender until smooth

GUM ARABIC/ACACIA GUM (natural thickening and emulsifying agent) – 1 teaspoon
⇨ 1 teaspoon xanthan gum
⇨ 1 teaspoon guar gum
⇨ 1 to 2 teaspoons instant ClearJel used following package directions

H

HALF-AND-HALF (10.5 to 12% butterfat) – 1 cup
- 3/4 cup whole milk and 1/4 cup heavy cream
- 2/3 cup nonfat or lowfat milk and 1/3 cup heavy cream
- 1/2 cup light cream and 1/2 cup whole milk
- 1 1/2 tablespoons melted unsalted butter plus enough whole milk to make 1 cup (for baking)
- 1 cup evaporated milk (for baking)
- 1 cup nondairy liquid creamer, such as Silk, So Delicious, or Organic Valley

HALLABONG JUICE (Korean citrus juice) – 1 tablespoon
- 1 1/2 teaspoons each orange and tangerine juice

HAZELNUT BUTTER See HAZELNUT PASTE

HAZELNUT MEAL/FLOUR – 1 cup
- 3/4 cup raw skinless hazelnuts ground in a food processor with 1 to 2 tablespoons flour (for nutmeal)
- 3/4 to 7/8 cup raw skinless hazelnuts ground until powdery in a high-powered blender, or in batches in a spice/coffee grinder; sift, then regrind any large particles (for flour)

HAZELNUT MILK – 4 cups
Make Your Own Soak 1 cup hazelnuts in water to cover for 8 to 10 hours. Drain, rinse, and then process with 4 cups warm water in a blender until smooth, 2 to 4 minutes. Strain through a nutmilk bag or cheesecloth-lined sieve, pressing firmly on the pulp to extract all the liquid. Store in the refrigerator, and shake before using. It will keep for up to 4 or 5 days.

HAZELNUT OIL, ROASTED (finishing oil) – 1 cup
☞ 1 cup roasted walnut oil or extra-virgin olive oil

HAZELNUT PASTE/PASTA DI NOCCIOLA – 1 cup
☞ 1 cup pistachio paste/*pasta di pistacchio*, or creamy-type almond butter

HAZELNUTS – 1 cup shelled nuts
☞ 1 cup shelled beechnuts or almonds

HEMP MILK – 4 cups
Make Your Own Soak 1 cup raw hulled hemp seeds (hemp hearts) in water to cover for 4 hours. Drain and process with 4 cups water in a blender until smooth, 2 to 4 minutes. Strain through a nutmilk bag or cheesecloth-lined sieve, pressing firmly on the pulp to extract all the liquid. Keep refrigerated and shake before using. (For hemp seeds in the shell, soak for 8 to 12 hours; for a nuttier flavor, toast the hemp seeds in a dry skillet until crisp, stirring constantly.)

HEMP SEED BUTTER – 1 cup
Make Your Own Toast 1 1/2 cups hemp seeds in a dry skillet until fragrant, 3 to 4 minutes, then process in a blender until finely ground; add 2 to 3 tablespoons grapeseed oil, and continue to process to a coarse paste. Store in a small airtight container in the refrigerator; it will keep for up to 1 month.

HEMP SEED OIL – 1 cup
☞ 1 cup walnut or flaxseed oil

HEMP SEEDS (raw or toasted) – 1/4 cup
☞ 1/4 cup sunflower seeds (raw or toasted)

HONEY–1 cup
☞ 1 cup light agave syrup/nectar
☞ 1 1/4 cups granulated sugar plus 1/4 cup liquid (for baking, use 1/4

cup more of the liquid called for in the recipe plus 1/2 teaspoon cream of tartar)

⇨ 1 1/2 cups firmly packed light or dark brown sugar plus 1/4 cup liquid

⇨ 3/4 cup unsulphured molasses or dark corn syrup plus 1/2 cup granulated sugar (for baking, increase liquid in the recipe by 2 tablespoons)

⇨ 1 cup Just-Like-Honey syrup (vegan, rice-based sweetener)

⇨ 1 cup Italian pinecone bud syrup/*mugolio* (expensive; not for cooking)

⇨ 1 cup granulated honey crystals/honey powder, dehydrated maple syrup, or molasses powder (for dry rubs and sprinkling over cereal)

HONEY, AVOCADO – 1 cup

⇨ 1 cup strongly flavored dark honey, such as buckwheat, chestnut, manuka, or pine

HONEY, BITTER/SAVORY HONEY/MIELE AMARO (Sardinian) – 1 cup

⇨ 1 cup robust or strongly flavored honey, such as avocado, buckwheat, chestnut, manuka, or pine

HONEY BUTTER – 1/2 cup

⇨ 1 or 2 tablespoons honey stirred into 4 ounces room-temperature butter (for more honey taste, beat together 1/3 cup honey and 1/2 cup butter until creamy)

HONEY, CHESTNUT (Italian) – 1 cup

⇨ 1 cup strong, earthy honey, such as Sardinian, buckwheat, pine, or eucalyptus

HONEY, KIAWE (Hawaiian) – 1 cup:

⇨ 1 cup mild-flavored honey, such as orange blossom or clover

HONEY, LAVENDER (French) – 1 cup

⇨ 1 cup wildflower, orange blossom, or any mild, fragrant honey

HONEY, LYCHEE (Asian) – 1 cup
- ⇨ 1 cup clover honey, or other mild, fragrant golden honey

HONEY, MILD – 1 cup
- ⇨ 1 cup acacia, alfalfa, blueberry, clover, kiawe, grapefruit blossom, linden blossom, or orange blossom honey
- ⇨ 1 cup Tupelo honey (sweeter)

HONEY, THYME, WILD/HYMETTUS (Greek) – 1 cup
- ⇨ 1 cup flavorful dark honey, such as berry, chestnut, or wildflower

HONEY, TIGLI (Tuscan) – 1 cup
- ⇨ 1 cup linden, lavender, or acacia honey

HUCKLEBERRIES, FRESH OR FROZEN – 1 cup
- ⇨ 1 cup blueberries (sweeter; softer seeds)
- ⇨ 1 cup bilberries/whortleberries/*Vaccinium myrtillus* (dark blue or black; smaller and tarter)
- ⇨ 1 cup salal berries/*Gaultheria shallon* (dark blue; seedy and juicy; blueberry/blackberry taste)
- ⇨ 1 cup Juneberries/serviceberries/sarvisberries/*Amelanchier alnifolia* (purple-black; some berries more tart than others; cook to soften the seeds before adding to muffin batter)
- ⇨ 1 cup black crowberries/*Empetrum nigrum* (tarter; freeze overnight to improve flavor; mix with other berries)

I

ICE CREAM CONES, MINIATURE – 1 dozen
- 1 dozen baked wafer cookies, such as brandy snaps, lace cookies, or tuiles, quickly formed into cone shapes while still hot (Insert the point of each cone into the neck of a bottle to hold its shape until it cools completely.)

INVERT SUGAR SYRUP/TREMOLINE – 1 cup
- 1 cup pure cane syrup, such as Steen's, or golden syrup, such as Lyle's
- 1 1/4 cups granulated sugar, 1/3 cup water, and 1/2 teaspoon lemon juice, simmered until syrupy and reduced to 1 cup, 7 to 8 minutes (will thicken as it cools)

ITALIAN LEAVENING (Bench Mate, Pane Angel, or Rebecchi) – 1 teaspoon
- 1/2 teaspoon each baking powder and baking soda; add 1/2 teaspoon vanilla extract to the recipe

J

JAGGERY/PALM SUGAR/GUR (Indian dark, unrefined sugar) – 1 cup grated, shaved, granulated, or jarred

- 1 cup grated or crushed Mexican unrefined sugar/*piloncillo/panela* or *panocha/panucha*
- 1 cup crushed/grated Indonesian palm sugar/*gula jawa* or Malaysian palm sugar/*gula melaka*
- 1 cup dark muscovado/Barbados sugar
- 1 cup dark brown unrefined cane sugar, such as Billington's
- 3/4 cup granulated sugar plus 5 tablespoons molasses
- 1 cup dark brown or maple sugar moistened to a coarse paste with 1 tablespoon light molasses (for jarred palm sugar)

JAPANESE SOFT/WEAK FLOUR/HAKURIK-KO – 1 cup

- 1 cup cake flour

K

KAFFIR LIME LEAF POWDER/KAFFIR POWDER – 1 teaspoon
- 4 or 5 dried kaffir lime leaves, chopped, then ground to a fine powder

KAFFIR LIME ZEST, FRESH, FROZEN, OR BRINED – 1 teaspoon finely grated
- 2 teaspoons dried zest soaked in water to rehydrate (discard soaking water)
- 1 to 2 tablespoons shredded kaffir lime leaves
- 1 1/2 teaspoons finely grated fresh citron or Persian lime zest

KAHLÚA *See COFFEE LIQUEUR*

KAYMAK/KAÏMAK/EISHTA/GAIMAR (Middle Eastern water buffalo cream) – 1/4 cup
- 1/4 cup top thick layer from creamline yogurt, such as Brown Cow
- 1/4 cup softened natural cream cheese (no gum added) lightened with a little heavy cream
- 1/4 cup clotted cream, thick crème fraîche, or mascarpone

KEUKENSTROOP *See DUTCH DARK THICK SYRUP*

KEY LIME JUICE *See LIME JUICE, KEY*

KUMQUATS, FRESH (tiny citrus fruit with sweet edible skin and tart flesh) – 2 or 3
- 2 or 3 preserved kumquats, rinsed and drained
- 2 or 3 fresh orangequats or mardarinquats (or, for a different flavor, lemonquats or limequats)

- 1 fresh calamondin/*kalamansi* (mandarin orange and kumquat hybrid; juicier)
- 2 to 3 tablespoons grated orange zest (for 2 or 3 minced kumquats in cooking)

L

LADYFINGERS/SPONGE FINGERS/SAVOIARDI (Italian) – 8 ounces

- 8 ounces pound cake, sponge cake, or génoise, cut into 3-inch by 1-inch fingers and baked at 350°F until dry and crisp, 10 to 15 minutes; cool before using (For American ladyfingers, bake cake slices until barely crisp, 7 to 10 minutes.)
- 8 ounces Champagne biscuits, or vanilla wafers

LARD, FRESH LEAF (rendered pork fat) – 1 cup

- 1 cup beef tallow (rendered beef fat)
- 3/4 cup nonhydrogenated solid vegetable shortening plus 1/4 cup chilled strained bacon drippings
- 1 cup plus 1 1/2 tablespoons supermarket lard or nonhydrogenated solid vegetable shortening
- 1 cup clarified unsalted butter
- 1 cup plus 3 tablespoons unsalted butter (for biscuits and pastry dough; reduce the liquid accordingly)
- 1 cup peanut oil plus 1 teaspoon clarified/strained bacon drippings (for frying)
- 1 cup clarified/strained bacon, poultry, or meat fat/drippings; or mild virgin olive oil (for sautéing/shallow frying, not deep fat frying)

Make Your Own Grind or finely chop 12 ounces semi-frozen unsalted pork fatback (or fat trimmed from pork shoulder without any traces of meat). Melt it in a large, heavy skillet in a preheated 200°F to 225°F oven (or with 1/4 cup water on the lowest possible stovetop setting) for 1 to 1 1/2 hours. Strain in a cheesecloth-lined sieve and cool until solid (it will be softer than leaf lard rendered from kidney fat).

LAVENDER,– 1 tablespoon dried culinary flowers

- 3 to 4 tablespoons pesticide-free fresh lavender buds (*Lavandula angustifolia* or *L. xintermedia*), stripped from stems and flower heads

↳ 1/2 teaspoon lavender extract

LAVENDER SUGAR (French) – 1 cup

Make Your Own Pulse 1 cup granulated sugar and 2 teaspoon dried lavender blossoms/culinary lavender buds in a food processor until the lavender is finely chopped; store airtight at room temperature. Alternatively, store bruised or coarsely chopped buds in a tightly sealed container with 1 cup granulated or superfine sugar until the sugar is flavored, 2 to 3 weeks, shaking the container periodically, then sift to remove the buds.

LAVENDER SYRUP – 1/2 cup

Make Your Own Add 1 tablespoon dried lavender blossoms/culinary lavender buds to 1/2 cup hot simple syrup (*See SYRUP, SIMPLE*) and cool for about 30 minutes. Strain and refrigerate; it will keep for up to 1 week.

LEKVAR See PRUNE PUREE

LEMON AGRUMATO OIL See LEMON OLIVE OIL

LEMON CURD (for cake filling) – 1 cup

↳ 1 cup lemon pudding, thinned with a little fresh lemon juice

LEMON, DAQ (small, thin-skinned Turkish lemon) – 1

↳ 1/2 Meyer lemon

LEMON EXTRACT – 1 teaspoon

↳ 1/8 teaspoon lemon oil, such as Boyajian
↳ 2 to 3 teaspoons finely grated lemon zest from a scrubbed lemon, preferably organic

Make Your Own Combine 3 tablespoons lemon zest from a well-scrubbed or organic lemon with 1/2 cup vodka and let steep in a small, dark-colored bottle for 14 or more days in a cool, dark place. Shake the bottle from time to time, then strain and store in the refrigerator. Use 1 generous teaspoon for 1 teaspoon extract.

LEMON JUICE, EUREKA/LISBON – 1 tablespoon
- 1 tablespoon Meyer lemon juice; reduce the sugar in the recipe by 1/4 teaspoon
- 2 teaspoons freshly squeezed lime juice
- 1 teaspoon lemon juice powder (for baking, increase the liquid by 1 tablespoon)
- 1/4 teaspoon citric acid powder mixed with 1 tablespoon warm water
- 1/2 teaspoon finely grated lemon zest from a scrubbed lemon, preferably organic; reduce the liquid in the recipe by 1 tablespoon
- 1 tablespoon white wine (only if lemon flavor is not needed)
- 1 1/2 teaspoons distilled white vinegar or cider vinegar (only if lemon flavor is not needed)

LEMON JUICE, MEYER – 1 tablespoon
- 2 1/2 teaspoons regular lemon juice plus 1/2 teaspoon tangerine or mandarin juice
- 1 tablespoon regular lemon juice plus a pinch of sugar

LEMON JUICE, MEYER – 1/4 cup
- 2 tablespoons each regular lemon juice and orange or tangerine juice
- 3 tablespoons regular lemon juice, 1 tablespoon orange juice, and 1/8 teaspoon sugar

LEMON JUICE POWDER – 1 tablespoon
- 2 tablespoons lemon zest
- 1 tablespoon lemon juice (reduce the liquid in the recipe by 1 scant tablespoon)

LEMON, MEYER (a cross between a lemon and a mandarin) – 1
- 1 large, thin-skinned regular Eureka lemon (more acidic)

LEMON OIL (flavoring agent) – 1/8 teaspoon
- ⇨ 1/8 teaspoon food-grade lemon essential oil
- ⇨ 1/2 teaspoon lemon extract
- ⇨ 1 1/2 teaspoons finely grated lemon zest from a scrubbed lemon, preferably organic
- ⇨ 1/4 cup coarsely grated lemon zest from a scrubbed lemon, preferably organic, squeezed in a piece of cheesecloth or a garlic press

LEMON OLIVE OIL/AGRUMATO OIL (Italian flavoring agent) – 1/2 cup
Make Your Own Combine 1/2 cup extra-virgin olive oil with 1 tablespoon lemon zest from a well-scrubbed lemon (preferably organic) and heat to 250°F. Cover and let sit for a day or two to develop the flavor, then strain. (Alternatively, use 2 teaspoons natural lemon flavor, such as Simply Organic, in place of the lemon zest.) Store, tightly covered, in the refrigerator for up to a week.

LEMON PEEL, DRIED See also LEMON ZEST
Make Your Own Finely grate the lemon zest from well-scrubbed lemons (preferably organic). Spread in a single layer and dry at room temperature for 1 to 2 days; or in a preheated 200°F oven until crisp, about 20 minutes; or in a microwave on High for 1 to 1 1/2 minutes, stirring every 30 seconds. Use it as is, or crush to a powder just before using. Store in a well-sealed container in a cool, dark place. It will keep for a few months.

LEMON POWDER
- ⇨ Dried lemon peel crushed to a powder See LEMON PEEL, DRIED

LEMON PUDDING – 1 cup (for cake or pie filling)
- ⇨ 1 cup vanilla pudding plus 1/2 teaspoon lemon extract, or to taste

LEMON, PRESERVED *See PRESERVED LEMON JUICE*

LEMON SUGAR – 1 cup
Make Your Own Peel the zest from 1 well-scrubbed lemon (preferably organic), trim any pith from the strips, then bury the strips in 1 cup granulated sugar; store airtight in a cool, dark place for 2 weeks before using.

LEMON SUGAR, SUPERFINE – 1 cup *See also VANILLA SUGAR*
Make Your Own Mix 2 tablespoons finely grated lemon zest (from a well-scrubbed lemon, preferably organic) with 1 cup granulated sugar; spread on a baking pan, and dry in a preheated 200°F oven for 20 minutes, stirring occasionally. Cool, then grind in a blender or food processor until fine, 30 to 40 seconds. Store, tightly covered, in the refrigerator. It will keep for a few months.

LEMON ZEST – 1 teaspoon
- 1 teaspoon grated Buddha's hand citron (more aromatic)
- 1/2 (scant) teaspoon lemon extract
- 1/3 teaspoon dried minced lemon peel, softened for 15 minutes in 1 teaspoon water (or other liquid from the recipe)
- 1/4 (generous) teaspoon lemon juice powder (powdered lemon peel)
- 1 1/2 teaspoons frozen lemon peel (Freeze the peel in strips, then finely mince before using; for a non-organic lemon, dunk it into boiling water and firmly wipe off the wax before freezing.)
- 1/16 to 1/8 teaspoon lemon oil, such as Boyajian (double the amount for a cooked dish)
- 2 teaspoons grated or minced candied lemon peel (Rinse to remove sugar before grating or reduce sugar in the recipe by 1/2 teaspoon; for easier grating or mincing, pulse with the flour or sugar called for in the recipe.)
- 1 teaspoon finely grated lime zest

LEMON ZEST, MEYER – *1 tablespoon*
⇨ 2 teaspoons regular lemon zest and 1 teaspoon tangerine or orange zest

LIME, AUSTRALIAN FINGER/DOOJA LIME, PULP/JUICE VESICLES – *1 tablespoon*
⇨ 1 1/2 teaspoons each lemon juice and lime juice
⇨ 1 tablespoon Meyer lemon juice

LIME, BEARSS SEEDLESS – *1*
⇨ 1 Meyer lemon (sweeter)
⇨ 2 Persian limes (more acidic)

LIME, BITTER/LIMA/CITRUS LIMETTA (Yucatecan seasoning) – *1*
⇨ 1/2 Seville orange
⇨ 1 Persian lime plus a little grapefruit zest

LIME CITRUS OIL/PURE LIME OIL – *1/8 teaspoon*
⇨ 1/8 teaspoon food-grade lime essential oil
⇨ 1/2 teaspoon lime extract
⇨ 1 teaspoon finely grated lime zest

LIME JUICE, KEY – *1/2 cup*
⇨ 1/2 cup Persian lime juice plus 1 teaspoon finely grated lime zest
⇨ 1/4 cup Persian lime juice and 1/4 cup lemon juice
⇨ 1/2 cup bottled Key lime juice, such as Floribbean, Nellie and Joe's, or Rose's

LIME JUICE POWDER – *1*
⇨ 2 tablespoons lemon zest
⇨ 1 tablespoon lemon juice (reduce the liquid in the recipe by 1 scant tablespoon)

LIME, PERSIAN – 1
- 2 Key limes
- 1 Eureka/Lisbon lemon, or 1/2 Meyer lemon

LIME, RANGPUR, JUICE – 1 tablespoon
- 2 teaspoons Key or Persian lime juice and 1 teaspoon tangerine juice

LIME, RANGPUR, ZEST – 1 teaspoon
- 1 teaspoon Key lime, tangerine, or tangelo zest

LIME, SWEET/LIMO/NARAN-KAI/SOM KLEANG (mild-tasting citrus fruit) – 1
- 1 Meyer lemon

LIME, THAI
- Key lime (for zest)
- Key lime juice plus a dash of Meyer lemon juice (for juice)

LIME ZEST – 1 teaspoon
- 1 teaspoon limequat, lemon, or orange zest
- 1/3 teaspoon dried lime peel, softened in 2 teaspoons water for 15 minutes
- 1/2 teaspoon lime extract
- 1/8 teaspoon lime citrus oil

LINGONBERRIES, FRESH OR FROZEN (Scandinavian tart berries) – 1 cup
- 1 cup fresh or frozen cranberries, halved
- 1 cup highbush cranberries/*Viburnum trilobum*, large flat seeds removed before cooking
- 1 cup red or black currants

LIQUID FRUIT JUICE CONCENTRATE – 1 cup *See also FRUIT SWEET*
- 1 cup white grape juice concentrate or apple juice concentrate

LJUS SIRAP (Swedish light syrup) *See GOLDEN SYRUP*

LOQUATS, FRESH (small sweet-sour yellow fruits) – 1 pound
- 1 (15-ounce) can loquats, drained
- 1 pound fresh acerola or apricots

LÚCUMA/LÚCMO (Peruvian yellow-fleshed, starchy fruit) - 1
- White sapote or sapodilla (juicier texture)
- Frozen lúcuma puree (per recipe directions)
- Lúcuma powder/*Pouteria lúcuma* (for baking; use following the package directions, usually 2 parts powder to 1 part liquid)

LÚCUMA PULP, FRESH OR FROZEN (Peruvian fruit puree) – 1/2 cup
- 3/4 cup lucuma powder mixed with 3/4 cup cool water and left to thicken for 2 to 3 hours

LUMPIA WRAPPERS (Filipino fresh pastry wrappers) – 8 wrappers
- 8 spring roll wrappers
- 8 Shanghai-style egg roll wrappers
- 8 ounces rice paper/wafer paper or phyllo pastry cut to size (thinner, more delicate)

Make Your Own Blend or process 2/3 cup cornstarch, 1 egg, 1/2 cup plus 2 tablespoons water, and a pinch of salt until smooth; let sit for 15 minutes. Working with 1 1/2 tablespoons batter at a time, cook in a preheated, lightly oiled nonstick skillet about 1 1/2 minutes, spreading out the batter with a spoon to about 6 inches in diameter. Place cooked lumpia on a plate and keep covered with a damp towel while you make the rest. They will keep in the refrigerator for a day or two or frozen for a few months.

LYCHEE/LITCHI PUREE – 1/4 cup
- 8 canned litchis pulsed in a blender until smooth

LYCHEES/LITCHIS, FRESH – 1 bunch (about 20), peeled and seeded
- 2 ounces dried lychees softened in warm water
- 1 (20-ounce) can lychees/litchis, rambutans, or longans, drained
- 20 fresh or frozen pulasans, rambutans, or longans, peeled and seeded
- 20 large fresh grapes, such as Red Globe, Tokay, or Muscat, seeded and peeled

LYE MICROBEADS/PELLETS, FOOD-GRADE/SODIUM HYDROXIDE (alkali for pretzel wash) – 1 ounce (2 tablespoons)
- 2 tablespoons sodium carbonate (Make the sodium carbonate by drying 1 1/3 cups baking soda/sodium bicarbonate for 2 hours on a foil-lined baking sheet in a preheated 250°F oven.)
- 1/4 cup baking soda/sodium bicarbonate

LYLE'S SYRUP See GOLDEN SYRUP/LIGHT TREACLE

M

MACADAMIA NUTS – 1 pound
☞ 1 pound Brazil nuts, hazelnuts, beechnuts, cashews, or almonds

MACE – 1 mace blade (1 teaspoon crumbled/flakes)
☞ 1/2 teaspoon ground mace
☞ 1 scant teaspoon freshly grated nutmeg, or 1/2 teaspoon fine-ground nutmeg
☞ 1/2 teaspoon ground allspice

MADEIRA (Portuguese fortified wine) – 2 tablespoons
☞ 1 tablespoon Banyuls, semi-dry Marsala, port, dry sherry, or dry vermouth

MAHLAB/MAHLEB/MAHLEPI (Turkish, Middle Eastern, and Greek aromatic flavoring) – 1 teaspoon powdered or crushed
☞ 1 drop each almond extract and cherry extract
☞ 1 teaspoon ground cardamom

MAIDA/NAAN FLOUR (Indian all-purpose soft white flour) – 1 cup
☞ 2/3 cup unbleached all-purpose flour and 1/3 cup pastry flour
☞ 1 cup pastry flour

MALAI (Indian clotted cream) See CREAM, CLOTTED

MALTED MILK POWDER – 1 tablespoon
☞ 1 tablespoon non-diastatic malt powder

MALTED WHEAT FLAKES (yeast bread flavoring) – 1 tablespoon
☞ 1 tablespoon Maltex wheat cereal

MALTOSE/MALT SUGAR – 1 cup
- 3/4 cup rice bran syrup, corn syrup, golden syrup, or clear honey (increase the liquid in the recipe by 1/4 cup if necessary)

MALT POWDER, DIASTATIC (amylase enzyme dough improver) – 1 tablespoon
- 1 tablespoon sprouted wheat flour/wheat malt (sprouted wheat berries dried on a tray in a food dehydrator set at 120°F until brittle, then ground; use 1/4 teaspoon per large loaf)
- 1/4 cup sprouted wheat berries, pureed in a blender with part of the liquid called for in the recipe (use 1/4 cup per large loaf)

MALT POWDER, NON-DIASTATIC (flavoring agent and sweetener) – 1 tablespoon
- 1 tablespoon packed light brown sugar (for pretzel, bagel, pancake, or waffle batter)
- 1 tablespoon barley malt syrup/plain malt syrup or honey (for boiling water bath for bagels)
- 1 tablespoon granulated sugar, honey, or agave syrup/nectar (for yeast or flatbread dough)

MALT SUGAR See MALTOSE/MALT SUGAR

MALT SYRUP, BARLEY, NON-DIASTATIC See BARLEY MALT SYRUP, PLAIN

MANDARIN ORANGES, CANNED NO SUGAR ADDED – 8 ounces
- 8 to 10 ounces fresh Satsumas, small Pixies, clementines, or Kishu mandarins, sectioned, seeded if necessary, and microwaved on High until softened, 20 to 30 seconds

MANGO PUREE, FROZEN – 1 cup
- 1 cup canned Alphonso mango pulp (or Kesar variety for Indian dishes)
- 2 fresh ripe Alphonso or Ataulfo/honey mangos, peeled and pureed

MAPLE SUGAR CRYSTALS *See SUGAR, MAPLE*

MAPLE SYRUP – 1 cup
- 1 cup gluten-free, sugar-free maple syrup
- 1 cup agave syrup/nectar, birch syrup, brown rice syrup, or Swedish light syrup/*ljus sirap*
- 1 1/4 cups barley malt syrup (reduce the liquid in the recipe by 1/4 cup)
- 3/4 cup plus 2 tablespoons honey thinned with 2 tablespoons apple juice
- 1/2 cup finely grated maple sugar (increase the liquid in the recipe by 1/4 cup)
- 1 cup homemade maple brown sugar syrup (Simmer 2 cups dark brown sugar and 1 cup water until syrupy, then cool. Add 1 teaspoon maple extract and leave for 24 hours to develop the flavor. Store, refrigerated, for up to 6 months.

MARASCHINO LIQUEUR/MARASCHINO-FLAVORED SPIRIT (such as Luxardo or Maraska) – 2 tablespoons
- 2 tablespoons cherry liqueur or bottled maraschino cherry juice

MARSALA, COOKING (Sicilian fortified wine) – 2 tablespoons
- 1 tablespoon each sweet vermouth and dry sherry
- 2 tablespoons Madeira or dry sherry, such as Dry Sack
- 2 tablespoons white wine (or white grape juice) and 1/2 teaspoon brandy

MARSALA, SWEET COOKING (Sicilian fortified wine) – 2 tablespoons
- 1 tablespoon dry Marsala sweetened with a little sugar

MARSHMALLOW CRÈME – 1 (7-ounce) jar
- 1 (16-ounce) package marshmallows melted with 2 1/2 tablespoons light-colored corn syrup until smooth (Melt the marshmallows in the microwave on High, about 1 1/2 minutes, stirring every 45 seconds; or in a double boiler over simmering water. For 1 cup of crème, use

16 large marshmallows and 2 teaspoons light corn syrup.)
↳ 7 ounces Ricemellow (brown rice vegan crème alternative)

MARSHMALLOWS, MINIATURE – 1 cup (1 1/2 ounces)
↳ 8 regular-size marshmallows, cut into pieces with kitchen shears (dust the shears with cornstarch or flour)

MARZIPAN – 10 ounces (1 1/4 cups)
↳ 1 cup (9 to 10 ounces) almond paste, 1/2 cup powdered sugar, and 1 tablespoon light-colored corn syrup (not Lite), kneaded together until combined

MASCARPONE – 1 cup
↳ 3/4 cup natural cream cheese (no gum added), 1/4 cup heavy cream, and 1 1/2 tablespoons sour cream, blended together until smooth
↳ 1/2 cup softened natural cream cheese and 1/2 cup sour cream, blended until smooth
↳ 1/2 cup ricotta and 1/2 cup heavy (or whipping) cream, beaten until very smooth

Make Your Own Heat 1 1/2 cups light cream to 185°F; stir in 2 teaspoons fresh lemon juice and then let it sit off the heat for 20 minutes. Line a sieve with dampened cheesecloth and set it over a bowl; transfer the mixture to the sieve, place in the refrigerator, and let drain for 12 to 24 hours.

MATCHA/MACCHA (Japanese culinary-grade green tea powder)
↳ Japanese new crop green tea/Sencha, ground, pressed through a fine-mesh sieve, then spread on parchment paper to dry, about 1 hour (less colorful)
↳ Green food coloring powder (for baking; use following package directions; less flavorful)

MATZO (Jewish unleavened bread) – 8 ounces
↳ 2 cups all-purpose flour and 1/2 cup water mixed until smooth; rolled thin and immediately baked at 500°F for 10 minutes
↳ 8 ounces crisp lavash

MATZO CAKE MEAL – 1 cup
- 1 cup finely ground matzo meal (or 4 ounces unsalted matzo broken up and pulverized to a fine powder)
- 1 1/4 cups sifted cake flour (sifted before measuring)

MATZO CAKE MEAL, GLUTEN-FREE – 1 cup
- 1 cup potato starch

MATZO FARFEL (crumbled matzo) – 1 cup
- 1 1/2 matzo sheets, crushed to the consistency of fine breadcrumbs

MATZO MEAL, FINE GRIND – 1 cup
- 4 ounces (3 pieces) unsalted matzo or 4 1/2 matzo crackers, finely ground in a blender or food processor
- 2 cups matzo farfel ground fine
- 1 cup finely ground water cracker crumbs

MEDLAR/AZGIL (small brown fruit) – 1 soft bletted medlar
- 1 unripe green medlar, frozen until hard, then left at room temperature until bletted (freezing and thawing hastens bletting)
- 1/4 cup apple butter plus a very tiny pinch of ground cinnamon

MEMBRILLO/COTOGNATA See QUINCE PASTE

MERINGUE POWDER – 1 tablespoon
- 1 tablespoon dried/powdered egg white
- 1 large fresh egg white or 2 to 3 tablespoons thawed frozen egg white

MILK, LOW-FAT/1% (102 calories; 8.2 to 10 g protein; 2.4 to 5 g fat; 3 g saturated fat; 14 g carbs; 13 g sugars; 31 to 35% DV calcium) – 8 ounces (1 cup)
- 1 cup nonfat milk plus 1 to 2 teaspoons unsalted butter or unsalted stick margarine

- 1/2 cup each nonfat milk and whole milk
- 1 cup seven-grain milk (140 calories; 2 to 3 g protein; 2 to 2.5 g fat; 0 g saturated fat; 27 to 28 g carbs; 16 g sugars; 35% DV calcium)
- 1 cup almond milk (30 to 60 calories; 1 g protein; 2 to 3 g fat; 0g saturated fat; <1 to 8 g carbs; 0 to 7 g sugars; 20% to 45% DV calcium)
- 1 cup camel's milk (110 calories; 5 g protein; 4.5 g fat; 3 g saturated fat; 15 mg cholesterol; 30% DV calcium)
- 1 cup cashew milk (25 calories; <1 g protein; 2 g fat; 0 g saturated fat; 1 g carbs; 0 g sugars; 45% DV calcium)
- 1 cup coconut milk beverage (45 to 80 calories; 0 to 1 g protein; 4.5 to 5 g fat; 0 g saturated fat; 1 g carbs; 1 g sugar; 10 to 45% DV calcium)
- 1 cup flax milk (50 to 60 calories; 2 to 5 g protein; 2.5 g fat; 0 g saturated fat; 2 g carbs; 0 g sugars; 30% DV calcium)
- 1 cup hazelnut milk (110 calories; 2 g protein; 3.5 g fat; 0 g saturated fat; 18 to 19 g carbs; 14 g sugars; 30% DV calcium)
- 1 cup hemp milk (70 to 140 calories; 2 to 3 g protein; 0.5 to 6 g fat; 0 to 0.5 g saturated fat; 1 to 9 g carbs; 6 g sugars; 30 to 50% DV calcium)
- 1 cup oat milk (130 calories; 4 g protein; 0 to 2.5 g fat; 0 g saturated fat; 24 g carbs; 19 g sugars; 35% DV calcium)
- 1 cup potato milk (70 calories; 0 g protein; 0g fat; 0 g saturated fat; 20 g carbs; 2 g sugars; 30% DV calcium)
- 1 cup rice milk (90 to 130 calories; 1 g protein; 2 to 2.5 g fat; 0 g saturated fat; 23 to 27 g carbs; 10 g sugars; 30% DV calcium)
- 1 cup soymilk (80 to 110 calories; 4 to 7 g protein; 1.5 to 4.5g fat; 0.5 g saturated fat; 3 g carbs; 1 g sugars; 20 to 45% DV calcium)
- 1 cup sunflower milk (70 to 80 calories; 2 g protein; 3.5 to 4 g total fat; 0.5 g saturated fat; 4 to 10 g carbs; 6 g sugars; 8% DV calcium)
- 1 cup water (for cookies, muffins, pancakes, waffles)

MILK, NON-FAT/SKIM (<0.5% butterfat; 90 calories) – 1 cup
- 1/3 cup instant nonfat dried milk powder and 3/4 cup water
- 1/4 cup regular nonfat dried milk powder (or soymilk powder) and 1 cup water

- ⇨ 1/2 cup fat-free evaporated milk and 1/2 cup water
- ⇨ 1 cup fat-free evaporated milk (use undiluted for low fat but full-bodied sauces)
- ⇨ 1 cup potato milk
- ⇨ 1 cup seltzer or sparkling water (for extra-light pancakes and batter)

MILK, NUT See ALMOND MILK; CASHEW MILK; COCONUT MILK; HAZELNUT MILK; WALNUT MILK

MILK, SOUR/CLABBERED – 1 cup for baking
- ⇨ 1 cup buttermilk
- ⇨ 1 cup milk and 3/4 teaspoon baking soda
- ⇨ 1 cup milk and 1 tablespoon distilled white vinegar

MILK, WHOLE (3.5% butterfat) – 1 cup
- ⇨ 1/4 cup dried whole milk powder and 7/8 cup water
- ⇨ 1/3 cup instant nonfat dried milk powder, 3/4 cup water, and 2 1/2 teaspoons melted unsalted butter or stick margarine
- ⇨ 3/4 cup plus 3 tablespoons nonfat milk and 2 1/2 teaspoons melted unsalted butter
- ⇨ 1/2 cup plus 2 tablespoons nonfat milk and 6 tablespoons half-and-half
- ⇨ 3/4 cup plus 2 tablespoons nonfat milk and 2 tablespoons heavy cream
- ⇨ 1 cup low-fat/1% milk and 2 teaspoons melted unsalted butter
- ⇨ 2/3 cup low-fat/1% milk and 1/3 cup half-and-half
- ⇨ 3/4 cup reduced fat/2% milk and 1/4 cup half-and-half
- ⇨ 1 cup reduced fat/2% milk and 1 1/2 teaspoons melted unsalted butter
- ⇨ 1/2 cup each full-fat evaporated milk and water
- ⇨ 1/2 cup each thick cashew cream and water
- ⇨ 1 cup full-fat unsweetened soy milk or reconstituted soy milk powder (avoid using with acidic ingredients such as lemon juice, chocolate, or wine, or letting it boil; doing so will cause it to curdle)

☞ 1 cup buttermilk (for baking, add 1/2 teaspoon baking soda and reduce any baking powder in the recipe by 2 teaspoons)

☞ 1 cup sparkling or seltzer water; or 1 cup plain water plus 1 egg yolk (for pancakes, waffles, fritters, or batter mix; makes them extra-light

☞ 1 cup silken tofu puréed with 1 or 2 tablespoons water until completely smooth (for salad dressings, dips, cream soups)

MIXED SPICE, SWEET (British spice blend) – 4 teaspoons

☞ 1 teaspoon each ground allspice, cloves, and coriander plus 1/2 teaspoon each grated nutmeg and ground Ceylon cinnamon

☞ 4 teaspoons pumpkin pie spice

MIZUAME *See STARCH SYRUP*

MOLASSES, DARK/REGULAR UNSULPHERED – 1

☞ 1 cup cane syrup, dark honey, dark corn syrup, dark treacle, palm syrup/kithul treacle, or very dark, strong maple syrup

MOLASSES, LIGHT/MILD UNSULPHERED – 1 cup

☞ 1 cup *yacón* syrup, sorghum syrup, or Swedish dark syrup/*mörk sirap*

☞ 1/2 cup dark molasses and 1/2 cup light-colored corn syrup

☞ 3/4 cup dark brown sugar dissolved in 1/4 cup hot water (or other liquid in the recipe)

MOLASSES, MIDDLE EASTERN *See DATE MOLASSES; GRAPE MOLASSES; POMEGRANATE MOLASSES*

MORA BERRY/RUBUS GLAUCUS (South American fruit) *See BLACKBERRIES*

MOSTO COTTO/SABA/SAPA *See GRAPE MOLASSES*

MULBERRIES, WHITE, DRIED – 1 cup
- 1 cup red or black mulberries (larger and tarter)
- 1 cup golden raisins/sultanas or chopped dried figs

MULBERRIES, PERSIAN BLACK, FRESH – 1 cup
- 1 cup fresh, fully ripe Chinese white mulberries (milder; sometimes seedless)
- 1 cup fresh, fully ripe white mulberries from the weeping mulberry plant (bland; best for drying)
- 1 cup fresh, fully ripe (purple) red mulberries
- 1 cup fresh blackberries, boysenberries, loganberries, or olallieberries

MUSCATEL SWEET WHITE WINE VINEGAR – 1 tablespoon
- 1 tablespoon sherry vinegar, champagne vinegar, or seasoned rice vinegar

N

NAARTJIE (South African tangerine) – 1 *See also MANDARIN ORANGES, CANNED*
- 1 Clementine, satsuma mandarin, or tangelo

NAARTJIE ZEST *See TANGERINE ZEST*

NAN/NAAN FLOUR *See MAIDA/NAAN FLOUR*

NARANJILLA/LULO JUICE, FROZEN (Ecuadorian fruit juice) – 1 (14-ounce) package
- Pulp from 2 pounds thawed frozen naranjillas (about 8 large fruits), blended with 1 cup water and strained
- 14 ounces passion fruit juice

NARANJA AGRIA *See ORANGE, SOUR/BITTER/SEVILLE/NARANJA AGRIA*

NARANJILLA/LULO PUREE, FROZEN (Ecuadorian fruit puree) – 1 (7-ounce) package
- Pulp from 6 thawed frozen naranjillas, lightly mashed
- 1 cup frozen passion fruit puree

NIGELLA SEEDS/KALONJI/KALIJEERA/CHARNUSHKA (Indian and Middle Eastern seasoning) – 1 teaspoon
- 1 teaspoon ajwain/ajowan seeds, black cumin seeds, black sesame seeds, caraway seeds, or cracked black pepper (for garnish, not taste)

NUTELLA *See GIANDUJA*

NUT-FLAVORED LIQUEUR (such as Frangelico, Nocciole, Noisette) – 1 tablespoon for cooking
- 1/4 teaspoon almond, hazelnut, or walnut extract, plus 1 tablespoon water

NUT FLOUR See FLOUR, NUTMEAT

NUTMEG, EAST INDIAN – 1 teaspoon fine ground
- 2 teaspoons freshly grated East Indian nutmeg
- 1 1/3 teaspoons freshly grated Grenadian West Indian nutmeg
- 2/3 teaspoon fine ground Grenadian West Indian nutmeg
- 3/4 teaspoon crumbled mace blade or 1/2 teaspoon ground mace
- 1 teaspoon ground allspice or cinnamon
- 1 teaspoon apple pie spice or pumpkin pie spice

NUTMEG, GRENADIAN WEST INDIAN – 1 teaspoon fine ground
- 2 teaspoons freshly grated Grenadian nutmeg
- 1 tablespoon freshly grated East Indian nutmeg
- 1 1/3 teaspoons fine ground East Indian nutmeg

NUT MILK See ALMOND MILK; CASHEW MILK; COCONUT MILK; HAZELNUT MILK; WALNUT MILK

NUTRITIONAL YEAST See YEAST, NUTRITIONAL

NUTS, CHOPPED – 1 cup for baking
- 1 cup toasted rolled oats (Toast old-fashioned oats on a baking sheet in a preheated 400°F oven until golden, 15 to 20 minutes, stirring halfway through; or in a large skillet over medium heat for 4 to 5 minutes, stirring frequently; or in a microwave on High for 3 to 5 minutes, stirring every minute. Cool before using.)
- 1 cup chopped pretzels
- 1 cup coarsely crushed thick unflavored potato chips
- 1 cup crisped rice cereal, crushed cornflakes, or whole grain wheat and barley cereal, such as Grape-Nuts

- 1 cup toasted pumpkin or sunflower seed kernels (Toast raw kernels in a dry skillet over medium heat, stirring frequently, until golden and fragrant, about 5 minutes; cool before using.)
- 1 cup coarsely ground hot-leached acorns
- Browned butter/*beurre noisette* (for the flavor only; use in place of the butter specified the in the recipe)

NUTS, UNSALTED – 1 cup

1 cup salted nuts blanched in boiling water for 1 or 2 minutes (or rinsed in a colander under cool water), then dried on a baking sheet in a preheated 300°F oven for 4 or 5 minutes; or in a dry skillet over low heat, shaking the pan constantly; or on a paper or cloth towel at room temperature, 1 or 2 hours

O

OAT BRAN – 1 cup
- 1 cup rice bran
- 1 1/2 cups wheat bran
- 1 scant cup toasted wheat germ
- 1 cup plain instant oatmeal
-

OAT BRAN FLOUR (16% protein) – 1 cup
- 1 cup oat bran, ground until fine in a blender or food processor, or in batches in a spice/coffee grinder

OAT FLOUR, WHOLE-GRAIN (17% protein) – 1 cup
- 1 1/4 cups whole oat groats, ground in a high-powered blender until powdery, or in small batches in a spice/coffee grinder

OAT MILK – 1 quart
Make Your Own Soak 1 cup oat groats in water to cover 8 to 10 hours. Drain, then blend with 2 cups fresh water until smooth, 2 to 3 minutes; let steep 30 to 45 minutes. Strain through a cheesecloth-lined sieve, pressing firmly on the pulp to extract all the liquid. Add 2 cups more water and refrigerate. Shake before using; it will keep in the refrigerator for up to 3 days. (For 1 pint use 1 cup old-fashioned rolled oats and 1 1/2 cups water and blend until smooth; it will keep in the refrigerated for up to 3 days.)

OATS, OLD-FASHIONED ROLLED – 1 cup
- 1 cup rolled barley flakes, quinoa flakes, buckwheat flakes, rye flakes, Kamut flakes, spelt flakes, triticale flakes, or whole-wheat flakes (for cooked cereal and baking)
- 2/3 cup all-purpose flour (for baking)

OATS, QUICK-COOKING – 1 cup
- ↦ 1 cup plus 2 tablespoons old-fashioned or thick-cut rolled oats, pulsed briefly in a food processor

OIL, MILD/NEUTRAL TASTING – 1 cup
- ↦ 1 cup canola or safflower oil

OIL, NUT (almond, hazelnut, macadamia, pecan, pine, pistachio, walnut) – 1 cup
- ↦ 1 cup poppy seed oil or squash seed oil
- ↦ 1 cup mild-tasting extra-virgin olive oil

OIL OF BITTER ALMONDS – 1 drop
- ↦ 1/2 teaspoon almond extract

OIL OF PEPPERMINT – 1 drop
- ↦ 1/8 to 1/4 teaspoon mint extract
- ↦ 1 tablespoon chopped fresh peppermint
- ↦ 1 teaspoon dried cut-leaf peppermint or leaves from a peppermint tea bag

OIL, VEGETABLE – 1 cup for baking
- ↦ 1 1/4 cups nonhydrogenated solid vegetable shortening
- ↦ 1 cup mayonnaise (not reduced-fat or fat-free; best for chocolate cake)
- ↦ 1/2 cup thick unsweetened applesauce, drained for 15 minutes, and 1/2 cup well-shaken buttermilk (for recipes where oil is the only liquid)

ONION JUICE
- ↦ Fresh onion squeezed through a garlic press, or grated on large holes of a box grater then pressed through a fine-mesh sieve

ONION POWDER – 1 teaspoon
- ↦ 2 1/2 tablespoons jarred minced onion
- ↦ 1/2 cup chopped fresh onion

- 1 tablespoon dried minced onion, onion flakes, or instant minced onion
- 1 teaspoon onion salt; reduce the salt in the recipe by 1 teaspoon

ONION SALT – 1 tablespoon
- 1 teaspoon onion powder mixed with 2 teaspoons kosher or coarse sea salt

ONIONS, FRIED, CANNED (for casserole topping) – 1 cup
- 1 cup Southeast Asian packaged fried shallots
- 1 cup crushed onion-flavored soy crisps

ORANGE BITTERS (such as Fee Brothers, Pomeranzen, Regans', Angostura Orange) – 1 dash
- 1/16 teaspoon orange extract

ORANGE, BLOOD (thin-skinned orange with deep red interior) – 1
- 1 small Ruby Red pink grapefruit (tarter)
- 1 Cara Cara orange, or another naval-type orange (a little sweeter)

ORANGE, BLOOD, JUICE – 1 cup
- 1 cup Florida orange juice plus 1 tablespoon grenadine
- 3/4 cup plus 2 tablespoons Florida orange juice and 2 tablespoons unsweetened pomegranate juice

ORANGE BLOSSOM WATER See ORANGE FLOWER WATER

ORANGE, CARA CARA (low-acidity, sweet navel orange with deep-pink flesh)
- Fully ripe naval orange; or sweet blood orange, preferably Tarocco

ORANGE CITRUS OIL/PURE ORANGE OIL – 1/8 teaspoon
- 1/2 teaspoon orange extract
- 1 or 2 teaspoons finely grated orange zest

ORANGE EXTRACT – 1 teaspoon
- ⇨ 1 teaspoon dried granulated orange peel or orange juice powder
- ⇨ 1 tablespoon finely grated orange zest from a well-scrubbed orange, preferably organic
- ⇨ 2 teaspoons grated candied orange peel (Rinse to remove the sugar before grating or reduce the sugar in the recipe; for easier grating, pulse with the flour called for in the recipe.)
- ⇨ 1/4 cup orange juice; reduce the liquid in the recipe by 1/4 cup

ORANGE FLOWER WATER/ORANGE BLOSSOM WATER – 1 tablespoon
- ⇨ 1/2 teaspoon orange extract
- ⇨ 1/16 to 1/8 teaspoon orange citrus oil, such as Boyajian (double the amount for a cooked dish)
- ⇨ 2 teaspoons finely grated orange zest
- ⇨ 1/3 teaspoon Sicilian flower essence/*Fiori di Sicilia* (has vanilla and orange aroma)

Make Your Own Steep 2 teaspoons crushed or minced dried orange peel (preferably sour) for 2 days in 1 cup sweet, non-sparkling white wine. Strain through a fine-mesh sieve; discard the peel. Use 1 tablespoon for each tablespoon in the recipe. Store in a sterilized jar in the refrigerator up to 7 days. Makes 1 cup.

ORANGE JUICE CONCENTRATE – 2 tablespoons
Make Your Own: Gently boil 1 cup fresh orange juice until reduced to 2 tablespoons, 10 to 12 minutes; or microwave it on High in a 4-cup glass measuring cup coated with cooking spray until reduced to 2 tablespoons.

ORANGE JUICE, FRESH – 1 cup
- ⇨ 1/4 cup frozen orange juice concentrate mixed with 3/4 cup water
- ⇨ 2 cups brewed orange herbal tea; reduce the liquid in the recipe by 1 cup

ORANGE JUICE POWDER – 1 tablespoon
- ⇨ 2 tablespoons orange zest

⇨ 1/2 teaspoon orange extract

ORANGE LIQUEUR/ORANGE-FLAVORED SPIRIT (such as Bauchant, Citrónge, Cointreau, Curaçao, Gran Torres, Grand Marnier, Leopold Bros., Triple Sec) – 1 tablespoon for cooking

⇨ 1/2 teaspoon orange extract and 2 1/2 teaspoons water
⇨ 1 1/2 teaspoons frozen orange juice concentrate and 1 1/2 teaspoons water
⇨ 1 tablespoon fresh orange juice and 1/2 teaspoon finely grated orange zest (or 1/4 teaspoon orange extract)
⇨ 1 teaspoon finely grated orange zest

ORANGE PEEL, DRIED GRANULATED – 1 tablespoon

⇨ Strips of orange peel (removed with a paring knife or vegetable peeler and any white pith scraped away) dried at room temperature for 3 to 7 days, or in the microwave on High for 2 to 3 minutes; crushed or ground as needed
⇨ 1 tablespoon finely grated fresh orange zest
⇨ 2 teaspoons grated candied orange peel; reduce sugar in the recipe by 1/2 teaspoon
⇨ 1/2 teaspoon orange extract

ORANGE, SOUR/BITTER/SEVILLE/NARANJA AGRIA (high-acid orange) – 1

⇨ 1 calamondin/kalamansi, or 3 kumquats

ORANGE, SOUR/BITTER/SEVILLE/NARAJIA AGRIA, JUICE – 1 tablespoon

⇨ Juice of 3 large kumquats
⇨ 1 teaspoon each lemon juice, grapefruit juice, and sweet orange juice
⇨ 1 1/2 teaspoons each lime or lemon juice and sweet orange juice
⇨ 2 teaspoons sweet orange juice and 1 teaspoon distilled white vinegar (for savory dishes only)

ORANGE, SOUR/BITTER, JUICE – 1/2 cup
- 1/4 cup lime juice and 2 tablespoons each orange and grapefruit juice
- 5 tablespoons lemon or lime juice and 3 tablespoons orange juice
- 1/2 cup verjuice

ORANGE, SOUR/BITTER, ZEST – 1 tablespoon
- 2 teaspoons grated orange zest, and 1 teaspoon grated lemon zest
- 1 tablespoon grated lime zest

ORANGE ZEST – 1 tablespoon
- 1 teaspoon dried minced orange peel, softened for 15 minutes in 1 tablespoon water
- 1 tablespoon tangerine or kumquat zest
- 1 1/2 teaspoons orange extract
- 2 tablespoons fresh orange juice (reduce the liquid in the recipe by 2 tablespoons)
- 1/2 teaspoon orange citrus oil, such as Boyajian (double the amount for a cooked dish)
- 1 tablespoon grated or minced candied lemon peel (Rinse to remove the sugar before grating or reduce the sugar in the recipe by 1/2 teaspoon; for easier grating or mincing, pulse with the flour or sugar called for in the recipe.)

OUARKA See BRIK PASTRY

P

PALM SUGAR, LIGHT/COCONUT PALM SUGAR (Southeast Asian unrefined sugar) –1 (1-inch) piece chopped or shaved See also JAGGERY
- 2 tablespoons coconut sugar crystals or Sucanat
- 1 tablespoon each maple sugar and light brown sugar
- 2 tablespoons firmly packed light brown sugar
- 4 teaspoons granulated sugar

PALM SUGAR SYRUP, HEAVY – 1 cup
- 2 cups light palm sugar, melted over very low heat until liquefied (add a little maple syrup if desired)
- 1 cup each shaved palm sugar and water, simmered until thick and syrupy and reduced to 1 cup
- 1 cup golden syrup, such as Lyle's

PALM SUGAR SYRUP, LIGHT – 1 cup
- 1 cup each shaved (or jarred) palm sugar and water heated until sugar is dissolved
- 1 cup simple/stock syrup

PALM SYRUP See COCONUT NECTAR

PANCAKE MIX See BAKING MIX/ALL-PURPOSE

PANEER/PANIR (Indian fresh curd cheese) – 4
- 4 ounces pressed farmer cheese or queso fresco
- **4 ounces** drained extra-firm tofu
- 4 ounces halloumi cheese (saltier; reduce the salt in the recipe by 1/2 teaspoon)

PANELA (Latin American loaf sugar) *See PILONCILLO*

PARMESAN CHEESE – 1 ounce
- ⇨ 1 ounce Grana Padano, aged Asiago, or Pecorino Romano (sharper-tasting)

PARMESAN CHEESE, VEGAN – 1 cup
- ⇨ 1 cup nutritional yeast powder or flakes (has a cheesy taste)
- ⇨ 5 ounces hazelnuts, 1 chopped garlic clove, plus a pinch of sea salt pulsed in a food processor until finely chopped (has a savory taste; store, tightly sealed, in the refrigerator)

PASSION FRUIT – 1 fruit (1 tablespoon pulp with seeds)
- ⇨ 1/2 large yellow passion fruit (transparent flesh; sweeter)
- ⇨ 1 tablespoon mango or guava pulp plus a few drops of Key lime juice
- ⇨ 1 1/2 teaspoons frozen unsweetened passion fruit concentrate or frozen tropical fruit puree (for strained pulp)
- ⇨ 1 ripe yellow or orange maypop/passionflower fruit (*Passiflora incarnata* and *P. caerulea*)
- ⇨ 1 or 2 tablespoons passion fruit liqueur (for flavoring only)

PASSION FRUIT JUICE – 1 cup
- ⇨ 6 large yellow passion fruits (or 12 purple), pulp removed and pureed in a blender 1 minute, then strained
- ⇨ 3/4 cup plus 2 tablespoons canned passion fruit nectar and 1 or 2 tablespoons lemon or lime juice
- ⇨ 1/2 cup each pineapple juice and lime juice, preferably Key lime
- ⇨ 1 1/3 cups frozen *naranjilla* juice, thawed and strained

PASSION FRUIT PULP – 1 (generous) cup
- ⇨ 6 large yellow, or 12 small purple, passion fruits, halved and pulp removed
- ⇨ 2 cups frozen passion fruit puree, such as Goya

PASTA FLOUR (very fine and silky hard durum wheat flour) – 1 cup

- 1/2 cup each golden semolina flour and durum wheat flour (best for ravioli)
- 1/3 cup each semolina, golden durum, and unbleached all-purpose or whole-wheat flour
- 1 cup unbleached all-purpose flour with 10% protein, or equal parts cake and all-purpose flour to approximate 10% (best for delicate stuffed pasta)

PASTRY CASES *See DESSERT SHELLS*

PASTRY CREAM MIX – 4 ounces

- 4 ounces vanilla pudding mix, custard powder, or vegan pudding mix, such as Dr. Oetker Organics, prepared following the package directions

PEACHES – 1 pound

- 1 pound nectarines (firmer texture)

PEANUT BUTTER – 1 cup

- 1 cup sunflower butter/sunbutter/sunflower seed spread
- 1 cup almond butter, cashew butter, hemp butter, or toasted sesame tahini
- 1 cup soy nut butter or golden peabutter (legume flavor)
- 2 cups dehydrated peanut butter powder mixed with 1 cup water (less calories and fat)

Make Your Own Toast 2 cups skinless peanuts on a baking sheet in a preheated 350°F oven until fragrant, 7 to 10 minutes, stirring halfway through. Transfer to a food processor while warm and process until reduced to a paste, about 15 minutes, scraping down the sides of the bowl as needed. (For chunky butter, stir in 1/4 cup chopped peanuts.) Store it in a sterilized jar in the refrigerator; it will keep for up to 3 months.

PEANUT FLOUR (28% fat) – 1 cup
Make Your Own Grind 3/4 cup plus 2 tablespoons raw skinless peanuts in a high-powered blender until powdery, or in batches in a spice/coffee grinder. Sift, then regrind any large pieces.

PEANUT OIL, ROASTED – 2 tablespoons
⇨ 2 tablespoons virgin peanut oil/arachis oil (has a roasted flavor)
⇨ 1 tablespoon toasted sesame oil/Chinese sesame oil (has a stronger flavor)
⇨ Cold-pressed peanut oil (has a milder flavor)

PEANUTS – 1 cup
⇨ 1 cup wild jungle peanuts (heirloom variety from the Amazon; does not contain aflatoxin found in American peanuts)
⇨ 1 cup roasted pumpkin seeds (pepitas) or sunflower seeds

PEANUTS, DRY-ROASTED – 1 cup
Make Your Own Roast 1 cup raw peanuts on a baking sheet in a preheated 325°F oven until fragrant, 5 to 6 minutes; then rub them in a cotton kitchen towel to remove the skins.

PEARS – 1 pound
⇨ 1 pound Asian pears (crisper; slightly longer cooking time)
⇨ 1 pound apples

PECAN BUTTER – 1 cup
Make Your Own Process 2 cups raw or toasted pecans in a food processor until reduced to a paste, 10 to 15 minutes, scraping down the sides of the bowl as needed. Store, refrigerated, in a sterilized jar for up to 1 month.

PECANS – 1 cup shelled
⇨ 1 cup shelled walnuts

PEKMEZ/PETIMEZI (thick Turkish sweetener) See GRAPE MOLASSES

PEPPERMINT, FRESH – 1/4 cup chopped
- 1 tablespoon dried peppermint, or leaves from 2 to 3 peppermint tea bags

PERSIMMON, DRIED/HOSHIGAKI – 8 ounces
- 8 ounces unsulphured dried apricots

PERSIMMON, FUYU, FRESH – 1 pound
- 1 pound Israeli sharon fruit/kaki persimmon

PERSIMMON, HACHIYA, FRESH – 1 pound
- 5 ounces Japanese dried persimmon/*hoshigaki*, softened in boiling water for 30 to 45 minutes, or in apple juice 8 to 12 hours
- 1 pound ripe plums, mamey sapote, cherimoya, or mango

PERSIMMON PUREE – 1 cup for baking
- 1 cup thick applesauce, canned pumpkin, or thawed frozen mango puree

PETIT SUISSE (French double-crème cheese) – 1 ounce
- 1 ounce Caprini, Fin de Siècle, Gratte-Paille, Le Coutances, Père Michel, Supreme, or natural cream cheese

PHYLLO/FILO DOUGH (paper-thin sheets of pastry dough) – 1 pound
- 1 pound frozen whole-wheat phyllo dough (slightly thicker; easier to handle and using clarified butter ensures crispiness, as it does for all phyllo dough)
- 1 pound frozen Armenian or Turkish *yufka* dough (slightly thicker; comes in 16-inch rounds)
- 1 pound country-style phyllo dough/*horiatiko* (thicker and crunchier; easier to work with; use fewer sheets)
- 1 pound frozen preshredded Greek phyllo dough/*kataifi/kadayfi* (does not roll but is easier to work with for a top and bottom crust; toss with melted butter rather than brushing it on)
- 1 pound frozen puff pastry, regular/vegan, or all-butter (thicker)

- 1 pound (8- or 10-inch) lumpia wrappers
- 1 pound (8 by 8-inch) rice-flour spring roll wrappers (for gluten-free alternative; slightly thicker)

PHYLLO/FILO DOUGH, COUNTRY-STYLE/HORIATIKA (thick sheets of pastry dough) – 1 pound
- 1 pound regular phyllo dough (brush unsalted clarified butter between each double layer; and to prevent the edges drying out, brush from outside to center)

PILONCILLO/PANELA/PANOCHA (Mexican and South American unrefined cane sugar) – 1 (8-ounce) cone or 8 (1-ounce) cones See also JAGGERY
- 1 1/4 cups Indian palm sugar/jaggery/gur
- 1 cup dark brown sugar and 2 tablespoons unsulphured molasses
- 3/4 cup granulated sugar and 5 tablespoons molasses

PIMENTO BERRIES, DRIED See ALLSPICE, JAMAICAN

PINE NUTS/PIGNOLI/PINYON/PIÑON – 1 cup shelled
- 1 cup sunflower seed kernels, pumpkin seed kernels/pepitas, hempseeds, or slivered blanched almonds

PISTACHIO CREAM/CREMA DI PISTACCHIO (Italian sweetened, enriched pistachio paste) – 1 cup
- 1 cup chocolate-hazelnut spread, such as Nutella or Rawtella, or other sweetened spread (different flavor)

PISTACHIO FLOUR – 1 cup
- 1 cup almond or chestnut flour

Make Your Own Grind 1 1/2 cups chilled unsalted peeled pistachios in a blender or food processor until powdery, or in small batches in a spice/coffee grinder. Sift and regrind any large pieces.

PISTACHIO OIL – 1 cup
▹ 1 cup almond oil or extra light olive oil

PISTACHIO PASTE/PASTA DI PISTACCHIO (Italian nut paste) – 1 cup
▹ 1 cup hazelnut paste/*pasta di nocciole*
▹ 1 cup smooth-style almond butter; or creamy peanut butter
Make Your Own Process 1 1/4 cups raw shelled pistachios and 1/4 cup neutral-tasting vegetable oil in a high-powered blender until smooth, scraping down the sides of the bowl as needed. It will keep in a sterilized jar in the refrigerator for up to 1 month.

PIZZA CRUST (for baking on a baking/pizza stone or inverted baking sheet at 450 to 500°F)
▹ 1 1/2 cups packaged biscuit mix and 1/3 cup boiling water, stirred briskly until the dough holds together, then kneaded or processed until smooth and no longer sticky, 1 to 2 minutes (roll out and bake for 5 minutes before adding the toppings)
▹ Refrigerated French bread dough; refrigerated yeast rolls, such as crescent; or biscuit dough (for a thin, crispy Roman-type crust; roll and stretch the cold dough as thinly as possible and bake immediately)
▹ Country-style filo/*horiatiko* or refrigerated piecrust (for St. Louis or delicate-type pizza; partly bake before adding the toppings)

PIZZA CRUST, PREPARED (for baking on a baking/pizza stone at 450°F; or for baking/cooking in a preheated baking sheet or skillet until browned on the bottom then broiling until the top is golden)
▹ Large whole-wheat pocketless pita bread/*pide*, or large pocket pitas, separated at the seams
▹ Middle Eastern whole-grain flatbread, such as soft lavash, cut to size
▹ Indian flatbread, such as chapati or naan
▹ Ciabatta or focaccia halved horizontally

- Thin roll halves, such as Sandwich Thins; English muffin halves; or thin bagel halves (for individual pizzas)
- 1 (11- to 13-inch) flour tortilla
-

PIZZA FLOUR *See FLOUR, PIZZA*

PIZZA SAUCE – *1 cup*

Make Your Own Combine 1 (15-ounce) can crushed tomatoes with 1 1/2 to 2 teaspoons pizza seasoning, or 1 teaspoon Italian seasoning plus 1/8 teaspoon garlic powder. (For a thicker sauce, puree the mixture until almost smooth, then simmer, uncovered, until thickened, about 30 minutes.)

Or

Drain half of 1 (28-ounce) can whole peeled tomatoes (preferably San Marzano), then press through a food mill, and combine with 2 to 3 teaspoons olive oil, 1/4 teaspoon each salt and crumbled dried oregano, and 1 minced garlic clove (optional).

PIZZA SEASONING – *1 tablespoon*

- 1 teaspoon Italian seasoning
- 1 teaspoon each dried thyme and granulated garlic, and 1/2 teaspoon each ground fennel and dried oregano

PLUMS – *1 pound*

- 1 pound plumcots or Pluots (green-yellow or black fruit; a cross between plum and apricot)
- 1 pound plum cherry hybrid, such as Pixie Sweet Cherrium, Cherub, or Verry Cherry
- 1 pound wild plums/*Prunus americana* (red or yellow small tart fruits for jam), or wild sloes of the blackthorn bush/*Prunus spinosa* (small purple sour fruits for jam)

POLENTA MEAL (*Italian stone-ground yellow cornmeal*) – *1 cup*

- 1 cup dry corn kernels (or buckwheat groats), coarsely ground in a grain mill or in batches in a spice/coffee grinder (Dry-roasting the buckwheat groats enhances their aroma and taste; soaking them 8 to 12 hours before cooking makes the polenta creamier and more digestible.)

⊫ 1 cup yellow corn grits (coarse-grind degerminated cornmeal) or medium-grind cornmeal

⊫ 1 cup quick-cooking polenta (Use 3 1/2 cups water and cook for 8 to 15 minutes, stirring frequently.)

⊫ 1 cup instant (precooked) polenta (Use 3 cups water and cook for 2 to 3 minutes.)

⊫ 1 cup fine-grind yellow or white cornmeal for creamier polenta/ *polentina* (Use 4 cups water and cook for 10 to 15 minutes.)

⊫ 1 cup whole-grain teff (Use 3 cups water and cook for 20 minutes.) or whole-grain amaranth (Use 2 cups water and cook for 15 to 20 minutes.) (Both grains can be chilled, baked, or pan-fried like polenta; they will have slightly stickier consistency.)

⊫ 1 cup granulated buckwheat or Cream of Buckwheat (Cook following the package directions; makes a polenta-like side dish.)

POMEGRANATE CONCENTRATE/ROB-E ANAR (Middle Eastern souring agent) – 1/4 cup

⊫ 3 tablespoons pomegranate molasses

Make Your Own Boil 2 cups fresh or bottled pure unsweetened pomegranate juice gently over medium heat in a wide, uncovered pan, stirring occasionally, until thickened and reduced to 1/4 cup, 20 to 30 minutes. Use immediately, or store in a small sterilized jar in the refrigerator; it will keep for a couple of weeks.

POMEGRANATE JUICE – 1 cup

⊫ 2 cups pomegranate seeds, pureed in a blender, then strained in a cheesecloth-lined fine-mesh sieve, pressing to release the juice

⊫ 3 tablespoons pomegranate concentrate combined with enough water to make 8 ounces

⊫ 3 tablespoons freeze-dried pomegranate powder combined with 8 ounces water

⊫ 1 cup cranberry juice or tart 100% cherry juice

POMEGRANATE JUICE, SOUR (Middle Eastern souring agent) – 1/3 cup
- 1/3 cup pure unsweetened pomegranate juice and 1 teaspoon lemon or lime juice
- 1 tablespoon pomegranate concentrate added to 4 1/2 tablespoons water
- 1/3 cup pure 100% unsweetened cranberry or sour/tart cherry juice

POMEGRANATE MOLASSES/DIBIS ROUMAN/DIBS RUBBA (Middle Eastern seasoning and souring agent) – 1/4 cup
- 2 cups fresh or bottled pure pomegranate juice, 2 tablespoons granulated sugar, and 1 tablespoon lemon juice, gently simmered until syrupy and reduced to 1/4 cup, about 30 minutes
- 3 1/2 tablespoons pomegranate concentrate plus 1 teaspoon fresh lemon juice
- 1/4 cup cherry syrup (for brining)
- 3 tablespoons lemon juice and 1 generous tablespoon unsulphured molasses (or strong flavored honey), warmed in the microwave a few seconds, then cooled
- 1 to 2 tablespoons aged balsamic vinegar

POMEGRANATE SEEDS/ARILS, FRESH – 1 tablespoon
- 1 tablespoon fresh papaya seeds (for salad; silvery-black and peppery tasting)
- 1 tablespoon snipped dried barberries or cranberries (for salad or garnish)
- 1 tablespoon pomegranate molasses, applied in tiny drops (for garnish)

POMEGRANATE SEEDS, DRIED SOUR/ANARDANA (Indian and Middle Eastern souring agent) – 1 tablespoon
- 1 tablespoon pomegranate molasses, lemon juice, or lime juice (for souring agent)
- 1 tablespoon snipped dried barberries or cranberries (for garnish)

POMEGRANATE SYRUP See POMEGRANATE MOLASSES

POPPY SEEDS, BLUE/BLACK – 1 cup

- 1 cup black amaranth grain, softened in hot water for 8 to 12 hours (for muffins, cakes, and pastries)
- 1 cup packaged ground black poppy seeds or canned poppy seed paste (for pastry filling)
- 1 cup nigella seeds; sesame seeds, preferably black; hulled hemp seeds; chia seeds; dark flaxseeds; Salba seeds; or lamb's quarter seeds (as topping for baked goods)

POPPY SEEDS, GROUND – 1 cup

- 1 1/4 cups dark/blue/black poppy seeds, toasted in a dry skillet over medium-high heat, stirring constantly until fragrant, 2 to 3 minutes. Cooled, then ground in a spice/coffee grinder until fine

PORCINI MUSHROOM/KING BOLETE/PENNY BUN, FRESH – 1 pound

- 1 pound fresh portobello mushrooms, gills removed
- 3 ounces dried porcini/*cèpes* or dried Polish mushrooms, soaked in warm water until softened, 30 to 40 minutes
- 3 ounces dried shiitake mushrooms (for more meaty, umami flavor) soaked in warm water until softened, 30 to 40 minutes
- 1 (10-ounce) can whole or quartered *cèpes*

PORCINI POWDER – 1/3 cup

Make Your Own Break up 1/2 ounce (3 or 4) smooth or cleaned dried porcini mushrooms and grind to a fine powder in a coffee/spice grinder. Sift out large pieces, then regrind and sift again. Store in an airtight container in a cool, dark place; it will keep for up to 3 months.

PORCINI SALT – 1/2 cup

Make Your Own Thoroughly combine 1 tablespoon porcini powder and 1/2 cup kosher salt. Store in an airtight container in a cool, dark place; it will keep for up to 2 months.

PORT, RUBY OR TAWNY (sweet fortified wine) – 2 tablespoons

- 2 tablespoons Banyuls, Madeira, Moscatel, or sweet vermouth

PORTOBELLO MUSHROOMS, FRESH – 1 pound
- 1 pound large fresh cremini, porcini, or matsutake mushrooms
- 3 ounces dried porcini mushrooms, soaked in warm water until softened, 30 to 40 minutes
- 1 (10-ounce) can whole or sliced mushrooms

POTASSIUM BICARBONATE/BICARBONATE OF POTASH (leavening agent) – 0.1 ounce (1 teaspoon)
- 1 teaspoon baking soda (sodium bicarbonate)

POTATO MILK – 4 cups
- Scant 2/3 cup potato milk powder, such as Darifree, blended with 1 cup hot or cold water, then added to 1 quart additional cold water and blended until smooth

Make Your Own Boil 1 cup chopped potatoes in 3 cups mildly salted water until soft. Cool, then add 1/4 cup soaked sliced almonds and enough cold water to equal 4 cups; blend until smooth, about 5 minutes, then strain in a fine-mesh sieve. Store, refrigerated, for up to 3 days.

POTATO STARCH (for thickening) – 2 teaspoons See also FLOUR, POTATO
- 1 tablespoon cornstarch or glutinous sweet rice flour
- 4 teaspoons arrowroot powder
- 2 tablespoons tapioca starch, or 5 teaspoons quick-cooking or small-pearl tapioca, ground until powdery
- 2 tablespoons all-purpose or quick-mixing flour (cook at least 5 more minutes after thickened)

POWDERED SUGAR See SUGAR, CONFECTIONERS'

PRESERVED LEMON JUICE (Moroccan seasoning) – 1/4 cup
- 1/4 cup fresh lemon juice mixed with 1 1/2 teaspoons kosher salt

PROVOLONE (Italian stretched-curd cheese) – 1 ounce
☞ 1 ounce young *caciocavallo*, scamorza, domestic fontina, mozzarella, or asadero/*queso Oaxaca*

PROVOLONE PICANTE (Italian well-aged grating cheese) – 1 ounce
☞ 1 ounce aged Asiago, Parmesan, Pecorino Romano, Sbrinz, or domestic Romano

PRUNE PLUMS, ITALIAN (small, purple oval plums) – 1 pound
☞ 1 pound Damson or Mirabelle plums
☞ 1 pound wild purple beach plums/*Prunus maritime* (smaller; more tart)

PRUNE PUREE/PRUNE BUTTER (butter alternative for low-fat baking) – 3/4 cup
☞ 3/4 cup baby food prunes

Make Your Own Process 6 ounces pitted prunes (1 cup packed) with 1/2 cup boiling water to a smooth paste in a blender or food processor. Store in the refrigerator for up to 3 months.

PSYLLIUM HUSK FIBER (bulking agent used in gluten-free recipes) – 1 tablespoon
☞ 2 1/2 teaspoons ground flaxseed or chia seeds

PUDDING MIX, INSTANT – 1 package using 2 cups milk
☞ 1/4 cup instant dry milk powder, 1/3 cup each instant Clearjel and powdered sugar, plus 1/2 teaspoon fine sea salt (For vanilla add 1 teaspoon vanilla powder; for cocoa add 1/4 cup cocoa powder.)

PUFF PASTRY DOUGH, SHORTENING- OR BUTTER-BASED – 1 pound
☞ 1 pound commercial phyllo/filo dough, or slightly thicker country-style filo/*horiatiko*, brushed with butter or oil
☞ 1 pound commercial *yufka* dough (thicker than regular phyllo and crunchier)

PUMMELO/POMELO/SHADDOCK (large yellow-green thick-skinned citrus) – 1
- 1 large Oroblanco citrus (hybrid of pummelo and grapefruit; juicier)
- 2 or 3 mondelos/mandalos (sweeter; more seeds)
- 2 medium pink grapefruits

PUMPKIN, FRESH – 1 cup chopped fresh
- 1 cup chopped fresh orange-fleshed winter squash (Ambercup, buttercup, butternut, calabaza, Dickinson, Jarrahdale, Hubbard, Queensland blue, or sweet dumpling)
- 1 cup chopped fresh sweet potato such as Beauregard, Garnet, or Jewel (takes longer to cook)

PUMPKIN PIE SPICE – 1 teaspoon
- 1/2 teaspoon ground cinnamon, 1/4 teaspoon ground ginger, 1/8 teaspoon ground nutmeg, and 1/8 teaspoon ground allspice (or cloves)

PUMPKIN PUREE, CANNED – 1 (29-ounce) can
- 4-pounds fresh Sugar or pie pumpkin, baked, scooped out, seeded, pureed, and then drained in a fine-mesh sieve for at least an hour
- 2 pounds sweet potatoes such as Garnet or Jewel, baked, peeled, and mashed
- 1 (29-ounce) can yams, drained, mashed, and strained

PUMPKIN SEED MEAL/FLOUR – 1 cup
- 1 1/4 cups pumpkin seeds, ground until powdery in a high-powered blender, or in batches in a spice/coffee grinder

PUMPKIN SEED OIL – 1 cup
- 1 cup extra-virgin olive oil, preferably deeply colored and flavorful

PUMPKIN SEEDS/PEPITAS – 1 cup
- 1 cup butternut or acorn squash seeds
- 1 cup winter melon seeds

- 1 cup Lady Godiva, Triple Treat, or Hungarian Mammoth squash seeds (hull-less green seeds, three times the size of regular hulled pumpkin seeds)
- 1 cup sunflower seeds

Q

QUINCE/CYDONIA OBLONGA (high-pectin, hard yellow fruit) – 1 pound

- ☞ 1 pound Japanese flowering quince/*Chaenomels speciosa* (smaller and more sour)
- ☞ 1 pound crab apples or unsprayed hawthorne fruits/thorn apples/ *Crataegus* species (smaller)
- ☞ 1 pound tart apples, such as Granny Smith (less sour; reduce the cooking time)

QUINCE PASTE/MEMBRILLO/COTOGNATA/PÂTE DE COINGS (Latin American cheese accompaniment) – 1 ounce

- ☞ 1 ounce guava paste, such as Goya, homemade plum paste/ *plumbrillo*, or any tart Mexican fruit paste/*ate*

QUINOA FLOUR – 1 cup

- ☞ 3/4 cup prewashed whole light quinoa, such as Bob's Red Mill triple-washed, or 1 cup quinoa flakes, ground in batches in a spice/coffee grinder until the consistency of fine-ground cornmeal
- ☞ 7/8 cup brown rice flour

QUINOA MILK, UNSWEETENED – 1 quart

- ☞ 1 cup cooked white quinoa plus 3 cups filtered water, blended until smooth, then strained in a nutbag or fine-mesh sieve. Keep refrigerated and shake before using. It will keep for up to 3 days.

R

RAGI/FINGER MILLET (Sri Lankan flatbread flour) – 1 cup
- 1 cup unbleached whole-wheat flour

RAISINS, HIMALAYAN HUNZA – 1 pound
- 1 pound seedless golden raisins or dried red barberries

RAISINS, SEEDED (Muscatel) – 1 pound
- 1 pound dark seedless raisins (preferably extra-large) and 1 cup sugar, steeped in 2 cups hot water for 1 hour (drain and pat dry, if necessary)

RAISINS, SEEDLESS (Thompson dark or golden) – 1 cup
- 1 cup organic sun-dried Black Monukka or Italian Zibibbo raisins (for dark; larger and sweeter)
- 1 cup Himalayan Hunza or Sicilian Sultanina raisins (for golden; larger and moister)
- 1 cup Italian Uvette raisins or dried currants (smaller and sweeter)
- 1 cup dried unsweetened cranberries or barberries (less sweet)
- 1 cup cut-up dates, figs, or prunes

RAMBUTAN/HAIRY LYCHEE/MAMON (Southeast Asian small, white-fleshed fruit)
- Fresh, canned, or frozen *pulasans*, longans, or lychees

RAPADURA (Brazilian evaporated cane sugar) – 1 cup
- 1 cup Sucanat, organic cane sugar, pre-grated *panela*, or finely grated or shaved *piloncillo/panela*

RASPBERRIES, RED – 1 cup
- ⇨ 1 cup black raspberries (drier and seedier)
- ⇨ 1 cup golden raspberries (sweeter)
- ⇨ 1 cup small strawberries, such as Alpine/*fraises des bois,* Earliglow, or wild strawberries (sweeter and firmer)
- ⇨ 1 cup loganberries or moras/*Rubus glaucus* (medium red; less sweet; cross between blackberry and raspberry)
- ⇨ 1 cup wineberries/*Rubus phoenicolasius* (golden orange or scarlet; larger)
- ⇨ 1 cup salmonberries/*Rubus spectabilis* (orange or crimson; soft with delicate flavor)
- ⇨ 1 cup wild thimbleberries/*Rubus parviflorus* (pale or bright red; larger)
- ⇨ 1 cup cloudberries/*Rubus chamaemorus* (amber; raspberry-size; tart and juicy)

RASPBERRY LIQUEUR/RASPBERRY-FLAVORED SPIRIT (such as Chambord or DeKuyper) – 1 tablespoon for cooking
- ⇨ 1 tablespoon raspberry brandy/framboise, cranberry liqueur, or raspberry balsamic vinegar
- ⇨ 1/2 teaspoon raspberry extract plus 2 1/2 teaspoons water

RASPBERRY VINEGAR – 1 cup
- ⇨ 1 cup red wine vinegar plus a little raspberry liqueur, such as Chambord
- ⇨ 1 cup cranberry vinegar or other red fruity vinegar

Make Your Own Lightly mash 1 pint/12 ounces fresh ripe raspberries, combine with 1 cup red wine vinegar, cover, and let sit at room temperature for 1 week. Strain in a cloth-lined sieve, then bottle and refrigerate for up to 6 months.

RED FOOD COLORING – 1 bottle (1 fluid ounce/2 tablespoons) *See also FOOD COLORING, NATURAL*
- ⇨ 1/3 teaspoon gel food coloring dissolved in 2 tablespoons water

RHUBARB, FRESH OR FROZEN – 1 pound
- 1 pound gooseberries
- 1 pound young Japanese knotweed stems/*Polygonum cuspidatum*

RICE FLOUR See FLOUR, RICE, BROWN; FLOUR, RICE, WHITE

RICE FLOUR, SWEET/GLUTINOUS RICE FLOUR/SWEET RICE POWDER (thickening agent such as Erawan or Mochiko) – 1 tablespoon
- 2 tablespoons tapioca starch; or 5 teaspoons pearl or quick-cooking tapioca, ground in a spice/coffee grinder until powdery, about 30 seconds
- 1 tablespoon cornstarch (separates when frozen)
- 2 1/4 teaspoons potato starch (separates when frozen)
- 4 teaspoons arrowroot powder (separates when frozen)
- 3 tablespoons kudzu powder (separates when frozen)
- 2 tablespoons all-purpose or quick mixing flour (cook at least 5 more minutes after thickened; separates when frozen)

RICE MEAL (Indian) – 1 cup
- 3/4 cup plus 2 tablespoons white or brown rice, ground until fine in a blender, or in small batches in a spice/coffee grinder

RICE POWDER, ROASTED/KHAO KHUA (Southeast Asian thickener) – 1/2 cup
- 1/2 cup uncooked sticky rice (or long-grain rice) toasted in a dry skillet over medium heat, stirring frequently, until golden, 8 to 10 minutes; cooled, then ground in small batches in a spice/coffee grinder until sandy-textured. Store, tightly covered, in the refrigerator (for best flavor store toasted rice and grind just before using). For Chinese brown rice powder/*chau mi fen,* use brown rice
- 1/2 cup toasted chickpea/garbanzo flour

RICE, PUFFED BASMATI/KURMURA (Indian) – 1 cup
- 1 cup puffed rice cereal, puffed wheat, or air-puffed millet or sorghum

RICE SYRUP *See BROWN RICE SYRUP*

ROCK SUGAR *See SUGAR, BROWN ROCK; SUGAR, YELLOW/CLEAR ROCK*

ROSE EXTRACT/ESSENCE (food flavoring agent) – 1 teaspoon
⇨ 1 1/2 tablespoons rose water (reduce the liquid in the recipe by 1 tablespoon)

ROSE GERANIUM SYRUP – 1 cup
Make Your Own Add 2 or 3 unsprayed rose geranium sprigs (including leaves) to 1 cup hot simple syrup (*See SYRUP, SIMPLE*). Cool, then remove the sprigs and store, tightly covered, in the refrigerator; it will keep up to 7 days.

ROSE HIP SYRUP – 1 cup
Make Your Own Halve, seed, and rinse 8 ounces fresh unsprayed rose hips. Simmer, uncovered, with 1 cup water until softened, 20 to 30 minutes. Strain, discard the hips and then boil the liquid with 1 cup sugar until clear, about 2 minutes. Cool and store, refrigerated, in a sterilized jar for up to 6 weeks. (Wear plastic gloves when handling the rose hips, and remove the seeds with a small demitasse spoon.)

ROSE WATER (food flavoring agent) – 1 tablespoon
⇨ 1/2 teaspoon food-grade pure rose extract/essence (reduce the liquid in the recipe by 1 tablespoon)
Make Your Own Simmer 3/4 cup purified water and 1/2 cup trimmed, fresh, pesticide-free rose petals, covered, for 30 minutes. Cool, strain, then add 1 or 2 teaspoons vodka. Store in a sterilized bottle in the refrigerator. Makes 1/3 cup; use 1 tablespoon for each tablespoon in the recipe. Use within 7 days.

RUM – 2 tablespoons for cooking
- ⮞ 1/2 teaspoon imitation rum extract plus 1 1/2 tablespoons vodka or water
- ⮞ 2 tablespoons bourbon or brandy
- ⮞ 1/8 to 1/4 teaspoon butter-rum flavor/extract (if the recipe contains butter)

RUM EXTRACT – 1 teaspoon
- ⮞ 2 tablespoons rum; omit 2 tablespoons liquid from the recipe

S

SABA/SAPA/MOSTO COTTO (Italian grape must syrup) *See GRAPE MOLASSES*

SACHA INCHI NUTS, ROASTED (large Peruvian oil-rich nuts) – 1 ounce
- 1 ounce macadamia nuts

SACHA INCHI OIL (Peruvian oil high in omega-3 fatty acids) – 1 tablespoon
- 1 tablespoon hemp or flaxseed oil

SAFFLOWER/SAFFRON THISTLE/FALSE SAFFRON/TURKISH SAFFRON/ MEXICAN SAFFRON (coloring agent) – 1 teaspoon dried compressed petals
- 1 teaspoon pesticide-free dried marigold petals, preferably pot marigold/*Calendula officinalis*, steeped in a little warm water for about 5 minutes (use the liquid for color and discard the petals)
- 1/2 teaspoon ground annatto seeds
- 1 teaspoon whole annatto seeds, steeped in a little hot water for about 5 minutes (use the liquid for color and discard the seeds)
- 1/4 teaspoon sweet California or Hungarian paprika plus 1/2 teaspoon ground turmeric, preferably Madras

SAFFRON/COUPÉ/SARGO – 1/2 teaspoon (10 to 15 threads/pinch)
- 1/8 teaspoon ground/powdered saffron
- 2 or 3 drops of saffron extract
- 1 1/2 teaspoons safflower stigmas/Mexican saffron/*azafrán*, soaked in 1 tablespoon warm water for 20 minutes, then added to the dish along with the water (for color)
- 1 teaspoon pesticide-free dried marigold petals, preferably pot

marigold/*Calendula officinalis*, steeped in 1 or 2 tablespoon warm water for 5 minutes (use the liquid for color and discard the petals)
- 1/2 teaspoon ground annatto seeds (for color)
- 1 teaspoon whole annatto seeds, steeped in a little hot liquid (use the liquid for color and discard the seeds)
- 1/4 to 1/2 teaspoon powdered Madras turmeric, or just enough for color

SAGO STARCH – 1 tablespoon
- 1 tablespoon tapioca starch, or 2 1/2 teaspoons quick-cooking tapioca, ground until powdery
- 2 teaspoons arrowroot powder
- 1 1/2 teaspoons cornstarch or sweet rice flour/glutinous rice flour/mochiko
- 2 tablespoons all-purpose flour or quick-mixing flour, such as Wondra (cook 5 minutes after thickening)

SAHLAB/SALEP POWDER (Greek and Turkish ground orchid root thickener) – 1 tablespoon pulverized
- 2 teaspoons cornstarch (lacks flavor; for flavor add 1/2 teaspoon rose water, orange blossom water, or one or two drops of elderflower cordial)

SALT, FLEUR DE SEL DE GUÉRANDE (fine-grained finishing salt from Brittany) – 1 teaspoon
- 1 teaspoon French *fleur de sel de Camargue* (from the Mediterranean coast) or *fleur de sel ile de Ré* (from the Atlantic coast)
- 1 1/2 teaspoons crystalline-flake sea salt, such as Maldon, Cornish, or Halen Môn (finishing salt)
- 1 teaspoon coarse-grain moist French sea salt/*sel gris Marin/sel gris de Guérande,* moist Baja sea salt, Korean sea salt, or Maine sea salt
- 3/4 teaspoon finely ground refined sea salt such as Baja, Atlantic, or Mediterranean

SALT, HIMALAYAN PINK (rose-colored, mineral-rich salt) – 1 tablespoon
- 1 tablespoon Bolivian Rose, Hawaiian Haleakala Ruby, Hawaiian Red Alaea Volcanic, Australian Murray River (peach or rose-color), or Peruvian Pink salt (pinkish-beige color)

SALT, KOSHER/KOSHERING SALT (additive-free salt with irregular coarse grains) – 1 teaspoon Diamond Crystal or 3/4 teaspoon Morton
- 1/2 teaspoon non-iodized table salt
- 1 teaspoon coarse or extra-coarse sea salt (non-iodized and additive-free)
- 3/4 teaspoon pickling, canning, or cheese salt (non-iodized and additive-free)

SALT, LAVENDER (French seasoning) – 1 tablespoon
- 1 teaspoon French dried lavender blossoms and 1 tablespoon coarse sea salt, pulverized until fine, then left several days to develop flavor

SALT, PINK, NATURAL See SALT, HIMALAYAN PINK

SALT, SEA, FINE-GRAIN – 1 teaspoon
- 1 teaspoon table salt
- 1 1/2 teaspoons coarse-grain sea salt, pulsed in a spice/coffee mill until fine, then measured (Clean the mill immediately after use to prevent corrosion.)
- 1 1/2 teaspoons Morton kosher salt or Morton coarse sea salt
- 2 teaspoons Diamond Crystal kosher salt, Morton extra-coarse sea salt, or coarse gray sea salt

SALT, SOUR See CITRIC ACID/SOUR SALT

SARDINIAN BITTER HONEY See HONEY, BITTER

SELF-RISING CORNMEAL See CORNMEAL, SELF-RISING

SELF-RISING FLOUR See FLOUR, SELF-RISING

SELF-RISING WHOLE-WHEAT FLOUR *See FLOUR, WHOLE-WHEAT SELF-RISING*

SEMOLINA/FARINA/SEMOLA (coarsely ground durum wheat) – 1 cup *See also FLOUR, SEMOLINA, FINE-GRIND*
- 1 cup dry whole-wheat farina or dry regular Cream of Wheat

SESAME BUTTER/SESAME PASTE - 1/4 cup
- 1/4 cup smooth unsweetened peanut butter plus few drops of light sesame seed oil

SESAME SEED FLOUR – 1 cup
- 1 1/4 cups hulled/white sesame seeds, ground in batches in a spice/coffee grinder until fine
- 1 cup pumpkin seed flour/meal, sunflower seed meal, or hempseed meal

SESAME SEEDS, HULLED WHITE/MUKI GOMA (Japanese condiment) – 1 ounce
- 1 ounce white poppy seeds, sunflower seed kernels, golden flaxseeds, hulled hemp seeds, Salba seeds, or finely chopped blanched almonds

SEVILLE ORANGE *See ORANGE, SOUR/BITTER/SEVILLE*

SHERRY, CREAM (sweet, dark fortified wine) – 2 tablespoons for cooking
- 2 tablespoons dry sherry plus 1/2 teaspoon dark brown sugar
- 2 tablespoons Madeira
- 2 tablespoons apple juice plus a few drops mild vinegar

SHERRY, DRY (fortified wine) – 2 tablespoons for cooking (not cooking sherry, which has salt added)
- 2 tablespoons dry vermouth or saké
- 2 1/2 tablespoons white wine (regular or nonalcoholic) plus few grains light brown sugar

SHORTENING, VEGETABLE (100% fat) – 1 cup

- 1 cup nonhydrogenated palm fruit oil shortening
- 1 cup chilled refined coconut oil or coconut butter
- 1 cup plus 2 tablespoons unsalted butter or unsalted stick margarine (if there is liquid in the recipe, reduce the liquid by 2 ounces/4 tablespoons; if the butter is salted, reduce the salt in the recipe by 1/2 teaspoon)
- 3/4 cup plus 2 tablespoons rendered leaf lard (for biscuits and pastry crusts)
- 7/8 cup strained bacon, poultry, or meat fat/drippings (for biscuits, cornmeal, savory crusts, and frying; not for deep-fat frying)
- 3/4 cup vegetable oil (for cookies, quick breads, and pastry; for flaky pastry, mix the oil with 1 1/2 cups flour taken from the recipe; freeze until solid, 1 or 2 hours, then grate or process into the rest of the flour mixture)

SICILIAN CITRUS FLAVORING/FIORI DI SICILIA – 1 teaspoon

- 1/8 teaspoon orange citrus oil, such as Boyajian, plus 1/2 teaspoon vanilla extract

SIMPLE SYRUP See SYRUP, SIMPLE

SKYR (Icelandic thick yogurt) – 1 cup

- 1 cup full-fat plain Greek-style yogurt, *fromage blanc*, quark, or *gvina levana* (Israeli soft white cheese)

SMETANA/SMATANA/SMITANE (Eastern European fermented cream) – 1 cup

- 1/2 cup heavy cream and 1/2 cup sour cream, whisked together, lightly covered, and left at room temperature for 2 to 4 hours. It will keep, tightly covered, in the refrigerated for up to 1 week.
- 1/2 cup each sour cream and crème fraîche (less fat)
- 1 cup Mexican sour cream/*crema Mexicana agria* (less fat)

SORGHUM FLOUR – 1 cup

- ☞ 1 cup light-colored teff flour
- ☞ 1 cup superfine brown rice flour
- ☞ 1 cup quinoa flour
- ☞ 1 cup whole-wheat pastry flour (contains gluten)

SORGHUM SYRUP/SORGHUM MOLASSES/SWEET SORGHUM (Southern U.S. sweetener with a malty flavor) – 1 tablespoon

- ☞ 1 tablespoon cane syrup, golden syrup, dark honey, light unsulphured molasses, or maple syrup
- ☞ 4 teaspoons dark corn syrup

SOUR CREAM (18% butterfat) – 1 cup

- ☞ 1 cup crème fraîche, Mexican *crema,* or Venezuelan *nata* (higher fat; less sour)
- ☞ 1 cup *smetana/smitane* or quark (thinner consistency; lower-fat)
- ☞ 1 cup plain full-fat Greek-style yogurt (thicker consistency; more calories)
- ☞ 1 tablespoon lemon juice (or distilled white vinegar) stirred into 1 cup heavy cream (or evaporated milk); left at room temperature until slightly thickened, 30 to 40 minutes; and refrigerated for 4 hours before using
- ☞ 3/4 cup natural cream cheese, 1/4 cup milk or water, and a dash of lemon juice blended until smooth and creamy
- ☞ 1/2 cup each plain yogurt and creamed cottage cheese, blended until smooth and creamy
- ☞ 1 cup (8 ounces) firm or extra-firm silken tofu, 1 to 4 tablespoons canola or olive oil, 2 tablespoons lemon juice, and 1 teaspoon salt, processed in a blender until smooth and creamy
- ☞ 1 cup soaked cashews, 1/2 cup water, 2 (or more) tablespoons lemon juice, and 1/4 to 1/2 teaspoon sea salt, processed in a high-powered blender until smooth and creamy
- ☞ 1 cup small-curd or creamed cottage cheese, 1/4 cup plain yogurt or buttermilk, and 1 or 2 teaspoons lemon juice (optional), processed until smooth, then drained 2 or 3 hours in a sieve lined with

dampened cheesecloth (Alternatively, use 2 tablespoons milk and 1 teaspoon lemon juice in place of the yogurt or buttermilk.)

SOUR CREAM – 1 cup for baking
- 3/4 cup whole milk and 1/3 cup butter, heated until the butter melts, then mixed with 1 tablespoon lemon juice or distilled white vinegar and left at room temperature until slightly thickened, about 30 minutes
- 1 cup soy sour cream, coconut yogurt, or thick canned coconut milk (dairy- and lactose-free)
- Sour cream powder rehydrated with water following the package directions

SOUR CREAM, FAT-FREE OR LOW-FAT – 1 cup
- 1 tablespoon lemon juice or distilled white vinegar, stirred into 1 cup fat-free evaporated milk and left at room temperature until slightly thickened, about 30 minutes (chill for 4 hours before using)
- 1 cup plain nonfat or low-fat quark (richer texture)

SOUR CREAM, MEXICAN See CRÈMA MEXICANA

SOURDOUGH STARTER (tangy leavener for bread and pastries) – 1 cup (8 to 9 ounces)
- 1 teaspoon dry active yeast sprinkled over 1/2 cup lukewarm water and left to dissolve, 3 to 5 minutes, before stirring in 1/2 cup all-purpose or whole-grain flour (Cover loosely with plastic wrap and leave at room temperature until thick and bubbly, 2 to 3 days.)
- 1/8 teaspoon dry powdered/dehydrated sourdough starter (per loaf in the recipe)
- 2 to 3 teaspoons instant sourdough flavoring (per cup of flour in the recipe; not for leavening or better keeping qualities)
- 1/4 teaspoon citric acid (per each loaf in the recipe; for sour flavor only, not for leavening or better keeping qualities)
- 1 cup overnight poolish (for a little sourdough flavor only)

☞ Strained dill pickle brine in place of half the water (for tangy sourdough flavor in rye bread)

☞ Yeasted whole-wheat, no-knead-type dough fermented at room temperature for up to 18 hours (for slightly tangy sourdough flavor only)

☞ Yeasted white bread dough stored for several days in the refrigerator after the first rise and before the second rise (for sourdough flavor only)

SOY BUTTER – 2 cups

Make Your Own Combine 3/4 cup powdered soy milk, 3/4 cup water, 1 teaspoon salt in a double boiler and cook for 25 minutes; gradually whisk in 1 cup canola oil and beat until thick. Store, refrigerated, in a tightly sealed container. It will keep for up to 1 month.

SOY MILK – 2 cups

☞ 1/2 cup soy powder (powdered soy milk) and 1 3/4 cups water, blended until smooth

☞ 8 ounces soft silken tofu and 1 cup cold water blended until smooth (For thinner soy milk, increase the amount of water; for sweeter soy milk, add 2 teaspoons rice syrup or light agave syrup.)

☞ 2/3 cup soy flour and 2 cups water, whisked together; simmered for 30 minutes, stirring occasionally; strained through a fine-mesh sieve; and flavored with sweetener or vanilla, if desired

SOY NUT BUTTER – 8 ounces

Make Your Own Process 8 ounces plain or roasted cooked soybeans, 1/4 teaspoon salt (optional), and 1 to 2 tablespoons vegetable oil in a high-power blender or food processor until reduced to a paste, scraping down the sides of the bowl as needed. It will keep in a sterilized jar in the refrigerator for up to 1 month.

SPELT FLOUR See FLOUR, SPELT

SPLENDA (sucralose and maltodextrin sweetener) – 1 cup
- 1 cup granulated sugar (has more browning properties)
- 1 cup stevia and maltodextrin sweetener, such as Stevia Extract in the Raw
- 1 1/3 cups erythritol/fermented cane sugar, such as Z-sweet or Organic Zero

SPRINKLES, INDIVIDUAL COLORED – 1 ounce
- 1 ounce white sprinkles shaken with a pinch of powdered food coloring in a tightly closed jar or sealable plastic bag

SPRUCE TIP SYRUP (Norwegian honey-like sweetener) – 1/2 cup (about)
- 1 cup young, tender, unsprayed spruce sprigs/tips/*Picea* species, about 2 inches long (or balsam, Douglas fir, pine, or other fir sprigs), boiled in a simple syrup (1 cup each water and granulated sugar) until thick and syrupy (strain through a fine-mesh sieve and discard the spruce)

STAR ANISE (Chinese seasoning) – 1 whole star (8 points)
- 3/4 teaspoon crushed or broken star anise pieces
- 1/2 teaspoon ground star anise
- 3/4 teaspoon anise seeds (crushed with the side of a knife)
- 1/2 teaspoon ground anise or fennel
- 1/2 teaspoon Chinese five-spice powder (for savory dishes)

STAR ANISE, GROUND – 1 teaspoon
- 2 whole star anise, crushed; or 1 1/2 teaspoons broken pieces
- 1 1/2 teaspoons anise or fennel seeds, ground in a pepper mill or spice/coffee grinder
- 1 teaspoon ground anise
- 1 teaspoon Chinese five-spice powder (for savory dishes)

STARCH SYRUP/MIZUAME (Japanese natural sweetener) – 1 cup
- 1 cup light-colored (not "lite") corn syrup

☞ 1 cup mild, light-colored honey
☞ 1 cup golden syrup (adds color)

STEVIA LEAF EXTRACT (liquid herbal sweetener) – 8 ounces (1 cup)
Make Your Own Add 3/4 cup lightly crushed dried stevia leaves/ *Stevia rebaudiana* to 1 1/2 cups 180° F water; cover and steep for 40 minutes. Strain and transfer to a dark-colored bottle; it will keep in the refrigerator for up to 2 weeks. (One teaspoon equals 1 tablespoon granulated sugar.)

STRAWBERRIES – 1 cup
☞ 1 cup raspberries
☞ 1 cup tayberries (a cross between blackberry and red raspberry; bright deep purple)
☞ 1 cup loganberries (a cross between blackberry and raspberry; reddish purple)
☞ 1 cup berrylike fruits of strawberry spinach/*Chenopodium capitatum* (for cooking and jellies; bright red)
☞ 1 cup strawberry guava (smaller and sweeter version of guava; reddish purple)

STRAWBERRY DUST
☞ Freeze-dried strawberries, pulverized in a spice/coffee grinder

STRAWBERRY SUGAR
☞ Equal parts freeze-dried strawberries and granulated sugar, pulverized in a food processor or spice/coffee grinder

STROOP *See DUTCH THICK SWEET SYRUP/STROOP*

STRUDEL DOUGH – 1 pound
☞ 1 pound fresh or frozen regular or whole-wheat phyllo/filo dough (thaw overnight if frozen)

- ☞ 1 pound frozen Armenian or Turkish *yufka* dough (little thicker; comes in round sheets)
- ☞ 1 pound frozen all-butter, ready-to-bake puff pastry (less crisp)

SUCANAT (dried sugarcane juice) *See SUGAR, GRANULATED*

SUCRALOSE *See SPLENDA*

SUET, BEEF – 4 ounces grated (1/2 cup)
- ☞ 1/2 cup shredded vegetarian suet, such as Atora light
- ☞ 1/2 cup coarsely grated frozen or chilled leaf lard
- ☞ 1/2 cup coarsely grated frozen or chilled shortening
- ☞ 1/2 cup plus 1 tablespoon finely chopped frozen unsalted butter (if there is liquid in the recipe, reduce the liquid by 2 tablespoons)

SUET, VEGETARIAN – 1/2 cup
- ☞ 1/2 cup coarsely grated frozen or chilled nonhydrogenated solid vegetable shortening

SUGAR, BAKER'S *See SUGAR, SUPERFINE; SUGAR, GOLDEN BAKER'S*

SUGAR, BARBADOS *See SUGAR, MUSCOVADO*

SUGAR, BROWN *See SUGAR, DARK BROWN; SUGAR, LIGHT BROWN/ GOLDEN*

SUGAR, BROWN ROCK/SLAB (Chinese large-crystal sugar) – 1 (5 x 1-inch slab) (3 1/4 ounces coarsely grated or finely chopped)
- ☞ 1/2 cup firmly packed dark brown sugar plus 1 teaspoon unsulphured molasses

SUGARCANE, FRESH – 1 (12-inch-long) cane
- ☞ 1 (20-ounce) can sugarcane sticks in syrup

SUGAR, CASTOR/CASTER *See SUGAR, SUPERFINE*

SUGAR, COCONUT PALM See JAGGERY/PALM SUGAR/GUR

SUGAR, COLORED/DECORATING – 1 cup
- 1 cup sanding or coarse sugar sprinkled with 6 to 8 drops liquid food coloring (or 1 or 2 drops gel), shaken in a tightly closed jar or kneaded in a sealable plastic bag, then spread on a parchment-lined baking sheet and dried at room temperature, 2 to 3 hours

SUGAR, CONFECTIONERS'/POWDERED/ICING – 1 cup
- 2/3 cup granulated sugar plus 1/2 teaspoon cornstarch or potato starch (optional), pulverized in a blender or food processor until powdery, 2 to 3 minutes (Let the sugar settle before removing the cover, then strain, if necessary, to remove any large particles. For glazing sugar, omit the starch.)
- 1 cup non-melting confectioners'-type sugar, such as King Arthur topping sugar
- 1 cup xylitol, such as Ideal confectioners' sugar

SUGAR, CORN – 3/4 cup
- 2/3 cup granulated sugar
- 3/4 cup malt powder
- 1 1/4 cup dry malt extract

SUGAR, CRYSTALLIZED/CRYSTAL/SPARKLING/DECORATING – 1 cup
- 1 cup Swedish pearl sugar
- 1 heaping cup white rock sugar or sugar pearls, chopped into small pieces
- 1 cup maple sugar/crystals (darker)
- 1 cup turbinado or Demerara sugar (darker smaller crystals)

SUGAR, DARK BROWN – 1 cup
- 1 1/4 cups light muscovado/Barbados sugar
- 1 cup chopped or shaved palm sugar/jaggery, *panela, panocha*, or *piloncillo* (for baking, melt with liquid ingredient)

- ☞ 1 cup light brown sugar plus 1 tablespoon unsulphured molasses (pulse in a food processor, or add the molasses to the wet ingredients)
- ☞ 1 cup granulated sugar mixed with 2 tablespoons unsulphured molasses (pulse in a food processor, or add the molasses to the wet ingredients)

SUGAR, DECORATING See SUGAR, COLORED; SUGAR, CRYSTALLIZED

SUGAR, DEMERARA (coarse-grained, pale brown, dry semi-refined sugar) – 1 cup
- ☞ 1 cup turbinado/semi-refined sugar, such as Sugar in the Raw
- ☞ 1 cup pregrated Brazilian semi-refined sugar/*rapadura*
- ☞ 1 cup pregrated Columbian semi-refined sugar/*panela*

SUGAR, FLAVORED See CINNAMON SUGAR; CITRUS SUGAR; LAVENDER SUGAR; LEMON SUGAR; STRAWBERRY SUGAR; VANILLA SUGAR

SUGAR, FRUCTOSE See FRUCTOSE

SUGAR, GLAZING See SUGAR, CONFECTIONERS'

SUGAR, GOLDEN BAKER'S (British fine-grained unrefined sugar) – 1 cup
- ☞ 1 cup plus 1 tablespoon Demerara or turbinado sugar, pulverized in a blender or food processor until fine-textured, about 20 seconds
- ☞ 1 cup superfine sugar (lacks color and caramel taste)

SUGAR, GRANULATED/WHITE SUGAR (medium-crystal cane or beet sugar) – 1 cup
- ☞ 1 cup granulated sugarcane juice, such as Sucanat (more granular texture)
- ☞ 1 cup semi-refined granulated castor sugar or superfine/castor sugar (for cakes, custards, and meringues)
- ☞ 1 cup firmly packed light or dark brown sugar (For baking with dark brown sugar, add 1/4 teaspoon baking soda, and reduce the oven temperature by 25°F to avoid over-browning.)

- 1 3/4 cups unsifted confectioners' sugar (will make cookies less crisp)
- 3/4 cup mild-flavored honey (Reduce the oven temperature by 25°F, reduce the liquid in the recipe by 1/4 cup or add 3 extra tablespoons flour, and, unless buttermilk, yogurt, or sour cream is called for in the recipe, add 1/4 teaspoon baking soda.)
- 1 cup sucralose and maltodextrin, such as Splenda Granulated or Essential Everyday No Calorie Sweetener
- 1 cup chicory root dietary fiber/inulin and erythritol, such as All Natural SomerSweet
- 1/2 cup sucralose and sugar, such as Splenda Sugar Blend for Baking; or 1/2 cup stevia leaf extract and sugar, such as Truvia Baking Blend
- 1 cup xylitol sweetener, such as Ideal Granular Blend or XyloSweet (not for yeast bread or hard candies)
- 1 3/4 cups chicory root dietary fiber/inulin, such as Just Like Sugar Baking Sweetener
- 1 1/3 cups erythritol and stevia, such as Z-sweet, Organic Zero, or Emerald Forest
- 1/3 cup homemade stevia leaf extract (for fruit desserts and drinks)
- 2/3 cup granulated fructose (not for baked goods except in pies)
- 2/3 cup light agave syrup/nectar or coconut nectar (for fruit desserts and drinks; reduce the other liquids in the recipe by 1/4 cup)
- Agave nectar: Substitute it for no more than half of the granulated sugar in a recipe. For every cup of sugar, use only 2/3 cup agave nectar, and reduce the other liquids in the recipe by 1/4 cup.
- 8 ounces rock sugar (for glazes and drinks; dissolves rapidly and evenly)

SUGAR, LIGHT BROWN/GOLDEN – 1 cup
- 1/2 cup dark brown sugar mixed with 1/2 cup granulated sugar
- 1 cup granulated sugar mixed with 1 tablespoon unsulphured molasses (combine in a food processor or electric mixer, or add the molasses to the wet ingredients)
- 1 cup light muscovado/Barbados sugar, rapadura, or coconut crystals (air-dried coconut sap)

- 1/2 cup brown sucralose, such as Splenda Brown Sugar Blend
- 1 cup white sucralose, such as Splenda or Essential Everyday No Calorie Sweetener, plus 1/4 cup maple syrup (reduce the liquid in the recipe by 2 tablespoons)
- 2/3 cup dark agave syrup/nectar (reduce the liquid in the recipe by 1/4 cup, or add 1/3 cup extra flour; reduce the oven temperature by 25°F and increase the baking time by a few minutes)

SUGAR, LUMP – 6 ounces (1 cup)
- 3/4 cup granulated sugar

SUGAR, MALT See MALTOSE

SUGAR, MAPLE (dried crystallized maple syrup) – 1 cup
- 2/3 cup Grade A dark, robust maple syrup (reduce the liquid in the recipe by 2 tablespoons or add 2 tablespoons extra flour)
- 1 cup light or dark muscovado/Barbados sugar
- 1 cup (or more) birch sugar (less sweet)
- 1 cup granulated sugar plus 2 teaspoons maple extract, or 2 tablespoons maple syrup

Make Your Own Boil 1 1/2 cups Grade A dark, robust maple syrup to the soft ball stage (240°F), then stir until thick and creamy. Pour into a greased baking dish, let sit until firm, then break up for coarse crystals or pulverize for medium-fine crystals.

SUGAR, MUSCOVADO/BARBADOS, LIGHT OR DARK (moist, fine-textured unrefined sugar) – 1 cup
- 1 cup dark brown sugar
- 1 cup finely grated *piloncillo/panela* or panocha/*panucha* (Mexican unrefined sugar)

SUGAR, PALM See JAGGERY

SUGAR, RAW/UNREFINED See JAGGERY; PILONCILLO; SUGAR, MUSCOVADO; SUGAR, TURBINADO CANE

SUGAR, ROCK *See SUGAR, BROWN ROCK; SUGAR, YELLOW/CLEAR ROCK*

SUGAR, SANDING/PEARL (extra-large-crystal cane or beet sugar) – 1 ounce
- ⇥ 1 ounce Asian rock sugar, coarsely grated or finely chopped
- ⇥ 1 ounce sugar pearls or sugar cubes, coarsely crushed
- ⇥ 1 tablespoon Turbinado/semi-refined sugar

SUGAR, SUPERFINE/ULTRA FINE/BAKER'S/CASTOR/CASTER (fine-crystal cane or beet sugar) – 1 cup
- ⇥ 1 cup golden castor sugar/golden baker's sugar
- ⇥ 1 cup plus 2 teaspoons granulated sugar, pulverized in a blender or food processor until finely textured, 20 to 30 seconds (let the sugar dust settle before opening lid)
- ⇥ 1 cup granulated sugar (takes longer to dissolve)

SUGAR SYRUP *See SYRUP, SIMPLE*

SUGAR, TURBINADO CANE (coarse-grained light-brown unrefined sugar) – 1 cup
- ⇥ 1 cup unrefined sugar, such as Sugar in the Raw; or Demerara sugar, such as Florida Crystals
- ⇥ 1 packed cup light brown sugar (if sprinkled, press through a sieve)

SUGAR, YELLOW/CLEAR ROCK (large-crystal Asian sugar) – 1-inch crystal piece (scant 1/2-ounce) coarsely grated or finely chopped: *See also SUGAR, BROWN ROCK*
- ⇥ 1 tablespoon granulated or turbinado sugar

SUNFLOWER MILK – 1 quart
Make Your Own Soak 1 cup raw unsalted sunflower seeds in water to cover for 4 to 8 hours; drain, rinse, then blend with 4 cups water until smooth, about 3 minutes. Strain in a nutmilk bag or fine-mesh sieve,

pressing firmly on the pulp to extract all the liquid. Keep refrigerated and shake before using. It will keep for up to 3 days.

SUNFLOWER OIL – 1 cup
 ☞ 1 cup light peanut oil

SUNFLOWER SEED BUTTER – 1 cup
 ☞ Golden peabutter (made from brown peas)

Make Your Own Toast 1 1/2 cups sunflower seed kernels in a dry skillet until fragrant, 3 to 4 minutes. Process with 1/4 teaspoon salt (optional) in a blender or food processor until finely ground, then add 2 to 4 tablespoons grapeseed oil, and process to a coarse paste, scraping down the bowl as needed. Store, refrigerated, in a small sterilized jar. It will keep up to 1 month.

Or

Toast 2 cups sunflower seed kernels on a baking sheet in a preheated 350°F oven until golden, 15 to 20 minutes; cool a few minutes then process in a food-processor until reduced to a paste, about 25 minutes, scraping down the sides every 2 to 3 minutes. Add 1/4 teaspoon salt if desired and process a few minutes longer.

SUNFLOWER SEED KERNELS – 1 cup
 ☞ 1 cup hulled hemp or pumpkin seeds
 ☞ 1 cup pine nuts or slivered almonds
 ☞ 1 cup chia or Salba seeds

SUNFLOWER SEED MILK See SUNFLOWER MILK

SUPERFINE SUGAR See SUGAR, SUPERFINE

SÜZME (Turkish extra-thick yogurt for dips and desserts)– 1 cup

Make Your Own Line a sieve with a double layer of dampened cheesecloth (or 2 basket-type paper coffee filters) and set it over a bowl. Put 2 cups plain full-fat yogurt (without pectin or additives) in the sieve and drain for 8 hours in the refrigerator.

SWEDISH DARK SYRUP/MÖRK SIRUP – 1 cup
☞ 1 cup light molasses or treacle

SWEDISH LIGHT SYRUP/LJUS SIRAP – 1 cup:
☞ 1 cup golden syrup, such as Lyle's
☞ 1 cup light corn syrup

SWEETENED CONDENSED MILK See CONDENSED MILK, SWEETENED

SWEET RICE FLOUR See RICE FLOUR, SWEET

SYRUP, FLAVORED – 1 cup See also ALMOND SYRUP; CINNAMON SYRUP; CITRUS SYRUP; COCONUT SYRUP; ROSE GERANIUM SYRUP
☞ 1 cup heavy simple syrup (See SYRUP, SIMPLE) flavored with 1/2 to 1 teaspoon extract (such as vanilla, almond, butterscotch, walnut, coffee, or eggnog in season)
☞ 1 cup sugar-free, calorie-free flavored syrup, such as Torani
☞ 1 cup syrup from canned fruit packed in heavy syrup

SYRUP, REFINER'S/INVERT – 1 cup
☞ 1 cup golden syrup, such as Lyle's
☞ 1 cup light or dark corn syrup

SYRUP, SIMPLE/STOCK SYRUP, REGULAR – 1 cup
☞ 1/2 cup each honey and boiling water, stirred until combined, then cooled
☞ 1/2 cup each light agave syrup/nectar and hot water, stirred until combined, then cooled
☞ 1 cup each superfine sugar and water, shaken in an airtight container until the sugar dissolves

Make Your Own Bring 1 cup granulated sugar and 1 cup water to a gentle simmer over medium heat, then simmer, stirring, until the sugar dissolves, 1 to 2 minutes. Cool and store, refrigerated, for up to 6 months. (For light syrup, reduce the sugar to 1/2 cup; for heavy syrup increase the sugar to 1 1/2 cups.)

SYRUP, SIMPLE/STOCK SYRUP, RICH/DOUBLE STRENGTH – 1 tablespoon

⇨ 1 tablespoon light agave syrup/nectar

Make Your Own Gently simmer 2 cups sugar, 1 tablespoon corn syrup or glucose, and 1 cup water until the sugar dissolves, 2 to 3 minutes. Or omit the corn syrup or glucose and gently simmer, covered, for 10 minutes. Cool and measure out 1 tablespoon. The syrup will keep in the refrigerator for up to 6 months.

T

TANGERINE ZEST – 1 teaspoon
- 2 tablespoons tangerine juice; reduce the liquid in the recipe by 2 tablespoons
- 1/2 teaspoon tangerine or orange extract
- 1 teaspoon grated orange zest
- 1/8 teaspoon tangerine citrus oil, such as Boyajian

TAPIOCA STARCH – 1 tablespoon for thickening
- 2 1/2 teaspoons quick-cooking tapioca ground in a spice/coffee grinder until powdery
- 1 1/2 teaspoons cornstarch or sweet rice flour/glutinous rice flour
- 1 1/4 teaspoons potato starch
- 2 teaspoons arrowroot powder
- 1 tablespoon all-purpose flour (cook for at least 5 minutes after thickening)

TAPIOCA, GRANULAR/QUICK-COOKING – 1 tablespoon for thickening
- 2 tablespoons small pearl tapioca, soaked in 1/4 cup milk or water until the liquid is completely absorbed, about 12 hours
- 1 1/2 tablespoons tapioca starch
- 1 1/2 tablespoons sago starch
- 1 1/2 teaspoons sweet rice flour/glutinous rice flour
- 2 teaspoon arrowroot powder (separates when frozen)

TEFF FLOUR See FLOUR, TEFF

TEMPURA FLOUR/TEMPURA KO (Japanese) – 1 cup
- 3/4 cup plus 2 tablespoons cake flour and 2 tablespoons cornstarch or potato starch

TIPO 00 FLOUR *See FLOUR, ITALIAN TIPO 00*

TREACLE, DARK (British dark thick syrup) – 1 tablespoon
  ☞ 1 tablespoon blackstrap molasses *See also MOLASSES*

TRIMOLINE/NULOMOLINE (inverted sugar) – 1 cup
  ☞ 1 cup liquid glucose

U

UGLI/UNIQ FRUIT (thick-skinned orange colored citrus) – 1
- 1 pink grapefruit or pomelo (less sweet and juicy)

V

VANILLA BEAN PASTE – 1 teaspoon
- 1 teaspoon vanilla powder
- 4 drops concentrated vanilla essence

VANILLA BEAN, BOURBON/MADAGASCAR OR MEXICAN – 3- to 4-inch section
- 1/4 to 1/2 teaspoon ground whole vanilla bean
- 1 teaspoon pure vanilla extract, vanillin/vanilla powder, vanilla bean paste, vanilla bean crush, vanilla flavoring, or imitation vanilla
- 1 tablespoon vanilla sugar (reduce the sugar in the recipe by 1 tablespoon)
- 4 drops concentrated vanilla essence (add after removing from the heat)

VANILLA BEAN, TAHITIAN – 1 whole bean including scraped seeds
- 2 Bourbon-Madagascar or Mexican vanilla beans
- 1 teaspoon ground whole vanilla beans
- 1 tablespoon vanilla bean paste, pure vanilla extract, vanillin/vanilla powder, or vanilla flavoring (add toward the end of cooking, or after removing from the heat)

VANILLA EXTRACT – 1 teaspoon
- 1 teaspoon vanilla bean paste or vanilla flavoring
- 1/4 to 1/2 teaspoon ground whole vanilla beans
- 1/2 teaspoon double strength vanilla extract
- 1 (2- to 3-inch) piece Bourbon-Madagascar vanilla bean, or 1(1- to 2-inch piece) Tahitian vanilla bean, split and seeds scraped out (add early in the recipe; for puddings, custards, sauces, or ice cream)
- 4 drops concentrated vanilla essence
- 1 teaspoon imitation clear vanilla or vanillin/white vanilla powder (for no color)

- 1 teaspoon alcohol-free vanilla extract, such as Trader Joe's
- 1 tablespoon vanilla sugar (Reduce the sugar in the recipe by 1 tablespoon. Alternatively, grind a piece of vanilla bean with a little sugar, then add it to the granulated sugar before weighing or measuring.)

VANILLA EXTRACT – 8 ounces
Make Your Own Split 1 Bourbon-Madagascar, or cheaper grade B/ extract, vanilla bean lengthwise. Scrape out the seeds and thinly slice the bean. Add the bean and seeds to 1 cup brandy, aged rum, or vodka in a dark-colored 8-ounce bottle; seal tightly and store in a cool, dark place for at least 3 months, shaking the bottle from time to time. (The higher the alcohol proof the better; for wheat-free extract, choose brandy or rum.)

VANILLA EXTRACT, DOUBLE-STRENGTH – 4 ounces
- 1 split and sectioned vanilla bean, gently inserted into a 4-ounce bottle of vanilla extract and left to steep at least 7 days

VANILLA POWDER See VANILLA BEAN PASTE

VANILLA SUGAR – 1 cup
Make Your Own Pulse 1 cup granulated or powdered sugar and 1 teaspoon vanilla powder (or half a vanilla bean cut in half) in a blender or food processor until thoroughly combined and well distributed.
Or
Split 1 vanilla bean lengthwise, then place in a jar with 1 cup granulated or powdered sugar and let sit for 1 to 2 weeks. Replenish the sugar as needed until the bean loses its flavoring capability.

VERJUICE/VERJUS/AGRESTO/HOSRUM/KORUK/ABGHOOREH (unripe grape juice) – 2 tablespoons
- 1/4 to 1/3 cup hard, sour green grapes, pureed and strained to measure 2 tablespoons
- 1 tablespoon each white grape juice and cider vinegar

- ⇨ 1 tablespoon each white wine and unseasoned rice vinegar
- ⇨ 1 1/2 tablespoons white wine and 1/2 tablespoon distilled white vinegar or lemon juice
- ⇨ 1 1/2 teaspoons dried sour grape powder and 2 tablespoons water

VIETNAMESE YOGURT/SUA CHUA/DA UA – 1 cup
- ⇨ 1 (3.5-ounce) can sweetened condensed milk stirred into 3/4 cup plain Greek-style yogurt until thoroughly incorporated. Will keep, tightly covered, in the refrigerator for up to 2 weeks.

VIOLETS, CANDIED/VIOLETTES DE TOULOUSE (French) – 4 ounces
Make Your Own Beat 1 pasteurized egg white with 1 tablespoon water; brush onto 3 ounces pesticide-free, edible violets; then dredge them in superfine sugar. Place on a rack or parchment-lined baking sheet and dry in a cool place for 24 hours. (To keep the best shape, dry the violets upside down suspended by their stems.) Store the candied violets in an airtight container at room temperature. Use within 2 months.

VITAL WHEAT GLUTEN (high protein flour used to increase gluten content in bread recipes) – 1 tablespoon
- ⇨ 1 tablespoon whole-grain bread improver blend, such as King Arthur (omit ascorbic acid if called for in the recipe)
- ⇨ 2 tablespoons high-gluten flour (reduce the flour in the recipe by 1 tablespoon if necessary)

W

WALNUT FLOUR – 1 cup
Make Your Own Grind 1 3/4 to 2 cups shelled walnut halves in a food processor until powdery, or in batches in a spice/coffee grinder.

WALNUT LIQUEUR/WALNUT-FLAVORED SPIRIT (such as Flaschengeist, Lantenhammer, Nocino, or Nux Alpina) – 1 tablespoon for cooking
☞ 1/4 teaspoon walnut extract and 1 tablespoon water

WALNUT MILK – 4 cups (about)
☞ 4 cups almond milk or hazelnut milk,
Make Your Own Soak 1 to 1 1/2 cups raw walnut halves in water to cover for 4 to 8 hours; drain, rinse, and then process with 4 cups warm water in a blender or food processor until smooth, 2 to 3 minutes. Strain through a nutmilk bag or cheesecloth-lined sieve, pressing firmly on the pulp to extract the liquid. Keep refrigerated and shake before using; it will keep for up to 5 days.

WALNUT OIL – 1/2 cup
☞ 1/2 cup hazelnut, macadamia nut, or extra-virgin olive oil
Make Your Own Toast 1/2 cup shelled walnuts. Process with 1/2 cup neutral-tasting vegetable oil in a blender or food processor until smooth. Strain and refrigerate for 2 or 3 days to develop the flavor; use immediately or store, tightly covered, in the refrigerator for up to 3 months.

WALNUTS, ENGLISH – 1 cup
☞ 1 cup butternuts/*Juglans cinerea* or pecans
☞ 1 cup hickory nuts (harder shells)
☞ 1 cup black walnuts (firmer; harder shells; more bitter)

WARKA/WARKHA/WARQA/OUARKA See BRIK PASTRY

WATER CHESTNUT POWDER (Asian thickening agent) – 1 tablespoon
- 1 tablespoon lotus root starch or cornstarch

WHEAT BRAN, UNPROCESSED/MILLERS BRAN
- Whole-wheat flour, sifted through a fine-mesh sieve to extract the bran; use the flour in making country French bread
- Oat bran or rice bran (measure by weight, not volume)

WHEAT, CRACKED – 1 cup
- 1 generous cup hard red wheat berries, chopped to the cracked-wheat stage in a blender, 15 to 20 seconds, or in small batches in a spice/coffee grinder (sift to remove any smaller particles)
- 1 cup cracked rye (rye chops), coarse-ground bulgur (grind #3), or whole-wheat Israeli couscous
- 1 cup buckwheat groats or kasha (for a gluten-free alternative)

WHEAT GLUTEN See VITAL WHEAT GLUTEN

WHEAT MALT SYRUP (non-diastatic liquid malt) – 1 tablespoon
- 1 tablespoon barley malt syrup
- 1 1/2 teaspoons granulated sugar, or 1 tablespoon light brown sugar

WHEY (the watery part of milk left over from cheese making) – 2 tablespoons
- 2 tablespoons plain yogurt, kefir, or buttermilk (for adding to soaking water for grains)
- 2 tablespoon lemon juice (for adding to soaking water for legumes)
- 1 to 2 teaspoons additional salt (for starter culture for lacto-fermented vegetables)

WHIPPED TOPPING See CREAM, WHIPPED; DAIRY-FREE TOPPING

WHISKEY SAUCE – 1 1/2 cups
- 1/4 cup whiskey, thoroughly stirred into a 14-ounce can warmed sweetened condensed milk (low-fat or regular)

WHITE WINE VINEGAR – 1 tablespoon
- 1 tablespoon champagne vinegar or unseasoned rice wine vinegar

WHOLE-GRAIN BREAD IMPROVER – 1 tablespoon
- 1 tablespoon vital wheat gluten plus scant 1/8 teaspoon ascorbic acid

WINE – 1 cup for sweet dishes
- 1 cup grape juice made from varietal wine grapes, such as Merlot or Cabernet
- 3/4 cup unsweetened apple juice or cran-apple juice and 1 tablespoon lemon juice or mild vinegar
- 1 cup nonalcoholic fruity wine
- 3/4 cup water and 3 tablespoons lemon juice

WINE, RED – 1 cup for cooking
- 1 cup red vermouth plus a few drops of red wine vinegar or lemon juice
- 1/2 cup each balsamic vinegar and water
- 1 cup soaking liquid from sun-dried tomatoes or dried mushrooms plus 1 teaspoon cider vinegar (Strain the mushroom liquid through dampened cheesecloth or a paper coffee filter to remove any grit.)
- 1/2 to 3/4 cup unsweetened red grape juice (not Concord), cranberry juice, or pomegranate juice plus 1 tablespoon white vinegar and enough water to measure 1 cup
- 1 cup beef or vegetable broth, plus 1 teaspoon red wine vinegar stirred in just before serving; reduce the salt in the recipe accordingly
- Red wine powder (used dry in cooking or spice rubs)

WINE, SPARKLING - 1 cup for cooking
- 1 cup sparkling white grape juice or sparkling apple cider

WINE, WHITE – 1 cup for cooking

- ⇨ 3/4 cup dry white vermouth (opened vermouth will last for 3 months in the refrigerator)
- ⇨ 1 cup white low-alcohol wine, or de-alcoholized wine (0.3 to 0.5%)
- ⇨ 1 cup pear or apple cider (or unsweetened apple juice plus a few drops of cider vinegar)
- ⇨ 1 cup chicken or vegetable broth (or the juice from canned mushrooms), plus 1 teaspoon white wine vinegar or lemon juice, stirred in just before serving (reduce the salt in the recipe accordingly)
- ⇨ 1 cup ginger ale, white grape juice, or white cranberry juice drink

X

XANTHAN GUM (thickening, emulsifying, and stabilizing agent) – 1 teaspoon (4 g)
- 1 teaspoon guar gum (3 teaspoons for drop cookies)
- 2 teaspoon unflavored gelatin powder, pectin, or agar powder
- 2 teaspoon psyllium powder (5 teaspoons for drop cookies)
- 2 tablespoons potato flour

XOCOLATA A LA PEDRA (Catalonian chocolate) See CHOCOLATE, MEXICAN

XTABENTUN (Yucatan anise-flavored spirit) – 2 tablespoons
- 2 tablespoons Absente, anisette, Galliano, Herbsaint, ouzo, Pernod, or other anise-flavored liqueur

XYLITOL (low-calorie natural sweetener) – 1 tablespoon
- 1 tablespoon sucralose, such as Splenda
- 1 tablespoon Sucanat, granulated sugar, or raw/unrefined sugar (more calories)
- 1 to 4 drops liquid stevia (or to desired sweetness)

Y

YACÓN SLICES, DRIED (South American tuber) – 1 cup
➼ 1 cup dried apple slices

YACÓN SYRUP (South American thick brown sweetener) – 1 cup
➼ 1 cup date syrup, palm honey/syrup, blackstrap molasses; amber agave syrup/nectar, coconut nectar, or Swedish dark syrup/*mörk sirap*

YEAST, ACTIVE DRY – 1 teaspoon
➼ 3/4 teaspoon instant yeast (add dry to ingredients; let the dough rise only once and reduce the rising time by 40 to 50%)
➼ 2 teaspoons compressed fresh yeast (crumble dry into ingredients)
➼ 1/2 teaspoon each baking soda and lemon juice stirred together (add to wet and dry ingredients at the end; use for no-rise pizza dough)

YEAST, ACTIVE DRY – 1 packet (1/4 ounce/2 1/4 teaspoons)
➼ 1 (1/4-ounce) packet instant yeast (add to dry ingredients and reduce the rising time by 40 to 50%; not for refrigerated dough)
➼ 1 (0.6-ounce) cake (1 tablespoon plus 1 teaspoon) compressed fresh yeast (crumble into dry ingredients)
➼ 1/2 teaspoon instant yeast (add to dry ingredients; knead the dough half as long, then let rise 2 to 3 times longer than normal, deflating and turning it over every 1 1/2 to 2 hours)

YEAST, COMPRESSED FRESH/BAKER'S YEAST – 1 (0.6-ounce) cake
➼ 1 (1/4-ounce) packet instant yeast (add to dry ingredients; let the dough rise only once and reduce the rising time by 40 to 50%)
➼ 1 (1/4-ounce) packet active dry yeast (dissolve the yeast in 1/4 cup

110°F water following the package directions)
- 2 cups fermented yeast starter/sponge/sourdough starter (use at room temperature and reduce the liquid in the recipe by 1 cup)
- 1/2 teaspoon active dry yeast (let the dough rise in the refrigerator for 12 to 24 hours, then bring to room temperature and let finish rising before shaping and proofing)

YEAST COMPRESSED, FRESH/BAKER'S YEAST – 2 ounces
- 3 small (0.6-ounce) cakes fresh compressed yeast
- 1 ounce (3 tablespoons) active dry yeast or 4 (1/4-ounce) packages (dissolve the yeast in 1 cup 110°F water following the package directions)

YEAST, INSTANT/RAPID RISE/FAST RISING/BREAD MACHINE YEAST – 1 teaspoon
- 1 1/4 teaspoons active dry yeast (dissolve the yeast in 1/4 cup 110°F water; let the dough rise twice, and increase the rising time)
- 2 teaspoons compressed fresh yeast (crumble into dry ingredients; let the dough rise twice and increase the rising time)
- 1/2 teaspoon active dry yeast plus 1 1/2 cups pre-ferment starter or sponge (increase the salt in the recipe by 1/4 teaspoon and decrease the water accordingly, by about 1 tablespoon)
- 1/2 teaspoon active dry yeast (let the dough rise in the refrigerator for 12 to 24 hours, then bring to room temperature and, if necessary, let finish rising before shaping and proofing)
- 1/2 teaspoon each baking soda and lemon juice stirred together, then added to the batter at the end (for no-rise pizza dough)

YEAST, NUTRITIONAL (dietary supplement and vegan cheese flavoring condiment) – 1 tablespoon powdered
- 2 tablespoons nutritional yeast flakes (smoother texture)
- 2 to 3 teaspoons brewer's yeast or debittered brewer's yeast (more bitter)
- 2 to 3 teaspoons yeast extract paste, such as Marmite or Vegemite (saltier and stronger)

☞ 1 tablespoon finely grated, very sharp Parmesan or Romano cheese (for the cheese flavoring only)

YEAST STARTER, WILD (starter for rye bread)
☞ 1 cup strained brine from a jar of dill pickles or cornichons at room temperature

YOGURT, FULL-FAT/WHOLE (3.5 to 5% fat content) – 1 cup
☞ 2/3 cup 2% Greek-style yogurt and 1/3 cup milk
☞ 2/3 cup full-fat Greek-style yogurt and 1/3 cup water
☞ 1 cup nonfat yogurt (lower in calories; higher in sugar and protein)
☞ 1 cup nondairy yogurt, such as almond, coconut, rice, or soy (lower in protein; higher in sugar)
☞ 1/2 cup each full-fat Greek-style yogurt and plain nonfat yogurt
☞ 1 cup low-fat yogurt plus 1 tablespoon heavy cream
☞ 1 cup goat's milk yogurt (tarter tasting; does not curdle when heated)
☞ 1 cup sheep's milk yogurt (creamy consistency; higher in calcium and protein)
☞ 1 cup Bulgarian buttermilk (tarter tasting; thinner consistency)
☞ 1 cup sour cream, crème fraîche, or Mexican *crèma agria* (for cooking or as a condiment)
☞ 1 cup fruit puree or thick unsweetened applesauce (for cooking)
☞ Nonfat yogurt powder (for dressings, sauces, and casseroles)

YOGURT, GREEK-STYLE, FULL-FAT OR 2% – 1 cup
☞ 1 1/2 to 2 cups plain yogurt (full-fat or low-fat, without pectin or additives) drained for several hours in the refrigerator, in a sieve lined with a double layer of dampened cheesecloth (or a basket-type paper coffee filter)
☞ 1 cup Icelandic-style skyr yogurt
☞ 1 cup *labna* (richer)
☞ 1 cup reduced-fat sour cream (for cooking)

YOGURT STARTER/CULTURE – 1 teaspoon Bulgarian 411 powdered culture; or 1 (5-gram) package freeze-dried starter

- 2 tablespoons very fresh room-temperature plain yogurt (full-fat, low-fat, nonfat, or Greek-style) with live active cultures and without additives
- 3 crushed acidophilus tablets (this makes 1 quart when combined with 4 cups pasteurized whole milk, heated and cooled to 115°F, then incubated undisturbed at 100°F to 110°F for 8 to 12 hours)

YUZU ZEST – 1 teaspoon

- 1/3 teaspoon dried yuzu peel, softened in 2 teaspoons warm water for 15 minutes, then finely chopped
- 3/4 to 1 teaspoon yuzu powder
- 1 to 2 teaspoons lemon zest or fully ripened Key lime zest

Z

ZERESHK *See BARBERRIES, DRIED*

ZEST, CITRUS *See LEMON ZEST; LEMON ZEST, MEYER; LIME ZEST; LIME, RANGPUR, ZEST; ORANGE, SOUR/BITTER ZEST; ORANGE ZEST; TANGERINE ZEST; YUZU ZEST*

FOOD EQUIVALENTS AND YIELDS

Ingredient	Weight	Amount
A		
Agave syrup, light or dark	1 ounce	1 tablespoon plus 1 teaspoon
	11 1/2 ounces	1 cup; 8 fluid ounces
Almond paste	9 1/8 ounces	1 cup
Almonds, blanched slivered	4 ounces	1 scant cup
Almonds, chopped	4 1/2 ounces	1 cup
Almonds, ground fine/meal	4 ounces	1 cup
Almonds, shelled	1 ounce	20 to 24 whole raw nutmeats; 1/4 cup finely chopped or ground
	1 pound	3 cups whole; 3 1/2 cups coarsely chopped; 4 cups slivered or finely chopped; 4 1/2 cups sliced; 4 cups ground
Almonds, sliced	3 1/2 ounces	1 cup
Almonds, unshelled	1 pound	1 to 1 1/2 cups shelled; 5 to 7 ounces
Amaretti cookies	3 ounces	20 (about)
Anise seeds, whole	1 ounce	1/4 cup; 2 2/3 tablespoons ground seed
Apple pie filling	20-ounce can	2 1/2 cups; enough for 1 (9-inch) pie
Applesauce, sweetened	9 ounces	1 cup
Applesauce, unsweetened	8 3/4 ounces	1 cup
Apples, dried	1 pound	4 1/2 cups; 8 cups cooked
Apples, fresh	1 pound	2 large; 3 medium; 4 to 5 small; 2 1/2 to 3 cups pared, cored, sliced/chopped; 2 cups grated; 1 1/4 to 1 1/2 cups sauce
Apricots, canned	15-ounce can	16 unpeeled halves; 1 3/4 cups drained
Apricots, dried California	1 pound	75 to 95 large halves; 120 to 130 medium halves; 2 2/3 to 3 cups; 5 1/2 to 6 cups cooked

Apricots, dried, diced	5 3/4 ounces	1 cup (1/8- to 1/4-inch dice)
Apricots, dried Turkish/ Mediterranean	1 pound	50 to 72 whole; 2 3/4 to 4 cups
Apricots, fresh	1 pound	5 to 6 large; 8 to 14 medium; 4 cups pitted and halved; 2 1/2 cups pitted and sliced; 2 cups cooked and drained
Arrowroot powder	1 ounce	1/4 cup scooped and leveled
	4 1/2 ounces	1 cup spooned and leveled

B

Baking mix, gluten-free	1 pound	2 2/3 cups
Baking powder	1 ounce	2 2/3 tablespoons
Baking soda	1 ounce	2 1/2 tablespoons
Banana powder, freeze-dried	4 ounces	1 cup
Bananas, dried	1 pound	4 1/2 cups dried slices
Bananas, fresh	1 medium	1 cup sliced; 1/2 cup mashed
	1 pound	2 large; 3 to 4 medium; 5 to 6 baby; 2 to 2 1/2 cups sliced; 1 1/2 to 2 cups mashed; 1 to 1 1/4 cups mashed overripe
Bananas, fresh mashed	8 ounces	1 cup (about 2 medium)
Barberries, dried	1 ounce	1/2 cup
Barley powder, roasted	4 ounces	1 cup
Blackberries, fresh	6 ounces	1 1/2 to 1 2/3 cups
Blackberries, frozen	1 pound	3 to 3 1/2 cups
Blueberries, canned	15-ounce can	1 1/2 cups drained
Blueberries, dried	1 pound	2 1/2 cups
Blueberries, fresh	12 ounces	1 pint; 2 to 2 1/4 cups
Blueberries, frozen	1 pound	3 to 3 1/2 cups
Boysenberries, fresh or frozen	4 1/2 ounces	1 cup
	1 pound	3 1/2 cups
Brazil nuts, shelled	1 ounce	6 large or 8 medium whole nutmeats
	5 ounces	35 to 40 whole nutmeats; 1 cup
	1 pound	3 1/4 cups whole nutmeats; 2 1/2 cups chopped
Brazil nuts, unshelled	1 pound	45 to 57 nuts; 1 1/2 cups shelled; 8 ounces
Breadcrumbs, dried	3 1/2 ounces	1 cup; 3 to 4 bread slices dried and crushed

Breadcrumbs, fresh	2 1/4 ounces	1 cup; 2 bread slices crumbled or ground
Breadcrumbs, panko-style	2 ounces	1 cup
Bread, traditional white and whole-wheat	1 ounce	1 slice; 1/2 cup soft crumbs piled lightly; 3 tablespoons to 1/4 cup fine dry crumbs
	16-ounce loaf	15 to 18 medium-thick slices; 24 to 28 thin slices; 8 to 11 cups cut or torn into 1/2- or 1-inch pieces, loosely packed; 8 to 9 cups soft crumbs
Butter	1 ounce	2 tablespoons (1/4 stick/1/8 cup)
	1 1/2 ounces	3 tablespoons
	2 ounces	4 tablespoons (1/2 stick/1/4 cup)
	3 ounces	6 tablespoons (3/4 stick)
	4 ounces	8 tablespoons (1 stick/1/2 cup/1/4 pound
	6 ounces	12 tablespoons (1 1/2 sticks/3/4 cup
	8 ounces	16 tablespoons (2 sticks/1 cup
	1 pound	2 cups (4 sticks
Butter, clarified	6 7/8 ounces	1 cup
Buttermilk	8 1/2 ounces	1 cup; 8 fluid ounces
Buttermilk powder	4 1/4 ounces	1 cup
Butter size of an egg	2 ounces	4 tablespoons (1/2 stick/1/4 cup)
Butter size of a walnut	1 ounce	2 tablespoons
Butter, whipped	1-pound tub	3 cups

C

Cake crumbs	3 ounces	1 cup
Cake meal, matzo	4 1/2 ounces	1 cup
Cake meal, gluten-free	4 1/4 ounces	1 cup
Candied cherries	6 ounces	1 cup
Candied fruit, chopped	1 pound	3 cups loosely packed; 2 cups firmly packed
Candied peel	6 ounces	1 cup
Caramel, block	10 ounces	1 cup cut into 1/2-inch pieces
Caramel syrup/paste	11.5 ounces	1 cup
Carob flour	3 2/3 ounces	1 cup
Cashews, shelled	1 ounce	14 large; 18 medium; 26 small
	1 pound	3 1/3 to 3 1/2 cups whole
Cheese, aged/hard/grating	1 ounce	1/4 cup ground in a food processor; 1/3 to 1/2 cup grated on a box grater;

		3/4 to 1 cup shaved on a rasp grater
	1 pound	4 cups ground in a food processor;
		5 1/3 to 8 cups grated on a box grater;
		16 cups shaved on a rasp grater
Cheese, American processed	1 pound	16 (1-ounce) slices; 4 cups cubed
Cheese, cottage	1-pound tub	2 cups
Cheese, farmer-type	7 1/2 ounces	1 cup packed
Cheese, firm/medium hard	1 ounce	1/4 cups shredded, lightly packed;
		1/3 cup coarsely grated, lightly packed
	4 ounces	1 cup shredded, lightly packed;
		1 cup cubed
	1 pound	4 cups shredded, lightly packed;
		2 2/3 to 3 3/4 cups cubed;
		12 to 16 (1/4-inch) slices;
		2 cups melted
Cheese, goat, aged	3 ounces	2/3 cup grated
Cheese, goat, fresh mild	3 ounces	1/2 to 2/3 cup crumbled (chill in freezer 20 minutes to make it easier to crumble)
Cheese powder, Cheddar	4 ounces	1 cup firmly packed
Cheese, queso fresco	3 ounces	1/2 cup crumbled
Cheese, ricotta, whole-milk	15 ounces	1 3/4 to 2 cups
Cheese, shredded	8-ounce bag	2 cups
Cherimoya	1 pound	2 small; 2 cups peeled and cubed; 1 1/2 cups mashed
Cherries, canned sour	16-ounce can	1 1/2 cups drained
Cherries, dried Bing	8 ounces	2 cups
Cherries, dried Montmorency	8 ounces	1 1/2 to 1 2/3 cups
Cherries, fresh sour	1 pound	3 cups; 2 cups pitted
Cherries, fresh sweet pitted	1 pound	55 to 65; 2 3/4 to 3 1/4 cups; 1 1/2 cups juiced
Cherries, fresh sweet unpitted	1 pound	75 (about); 3 1/2 to 4 cups; 3 1/4 cups stemmed, not pitted; 2 1/3 to 3 cups pitted 1 1/2 cups juice
Cherries, glacéed/candied	6 ounces	1 cup loosely packed
Cherries, jarred Morello/sour	24.7-ounce jar	2 cups cherries; 1 cup juice
Cherries, maraschino	10-ounce jar	25 to 33 cherries in syrup 1 cup drained and chopped
Cherry pie filling	20-ounce can	2 1/3 cups; enough for 1 (9-inch) pie

Chestnut puree	8 ounces	1 cup
Chestnuts, dried	1 ounce	7 to 8 chestnuts
	6 to 7 ounces	1 cup; 1 pound rehydrated
Chestnuts, fresh	1 pound	20 to 24 large; 2 1/4 to 2 1/2 cups peeled and diced; 2 scant cups pureed
Chestnuts, peeled roasted	1 ounce	3 peeled nutmeats
	14-ounce bag	42 to 48; 2 1/2 cups vacuum-packed
Chia seeds	5 3/4 ounces	1 cup
Chocolate, bittersweet or unsweetened	1 ounce	1 envelope liquid chocolate; 1 square; 3 to 4 tablespoons finely chopped or grated 2 tablespoons melted
Chocolate chips, bittersweet	5 ounces	1 cup
Chocolate chips, semisweet	1 ounce	2 heaping tablespoons
	6 ounces	1 cup; 3/4 cup finely chopped; 2/3 cup melted
Chocolate, Mexican	1 ounce	1/3 of 3.3-ounce tablet/disk; 2 1/2 wedges; 2 7/8 tablespoons powder
Chocolate mini chips	5 1/2 ounces	1 cup
Chocolate syrup	16-ounce jar	1 1/3 cups
Cinnamon/cassia	1 ounce	1/2 cup bark loosely packed; 1/4 cup ground
Cinnamon sticks	1 ounce	10 (4-inch) sticks
Citron/*cedro*, candied	6 1/2 ounces	1 cup
Citron, dried chopped	3 ounces	1 cup
Cloves, whole Ceylon	1 ounce	1/3 cup; 3 to 4 tablespoons ground
Cocoa/chocolate nibs	4 ounces	1 cup
Cocoa powder, Dutch processed unsweetened	2 1/2 ounces	1 cup sifted and leveled
	3 1/4 ounces	1 cup lightly spooned and leveled
	4 ounces	1 cup dipped and leveled
Cocoa powder, natural unsweetened	1 ounce	5 tablespoons plus 1 teaspoon lightly spooned and leveled
	2 2/3 ounces	1 cup sifted and leveled
	3 ounces	1 cup lightly spooned and leveled
	3 1/3 to 4 ounces	1 cup dipped and leveled
Coconut cream powder	4 1/2 ounces	1 cup
Coconut, desiccated	3 1/4 ounces	1 cup

Coconut, dried sweetened	7-ounce bag	2 2/3 cups flaked; 2 1/2 cups shredded
	1 pound	4 7/8 cups shredded or desiccated; 6 cups flaked
Coconut, dried unsweetened	3 ounces	1 1/2 cups wide-flake chips/shavings; 1 1/4 cups regular flaked; 1 cup shredded
	7-ounce bag	3 1/2 cups large coconut flakes/ shavings
	1 pound	5 1/3 to 6 2/3 cups grated, flaked, or shredded
Coconut, fresh	1 pound	5 3/4 to 6 cups grated or finely shredded, lightly spooned; 4 1/2 cups firmly packed
Coconut, fresh in shell	1 1/2 pounds	1 medium; 11 ounces nutmeat; 4 cups (about) grated or finely shredded; 1/2 to 1 cup liquid
Coconut milk, canned	13.5-ounce can	1 2/3 cups
Coconut milk powder	4 ounces	1 cup
Coconut nectar	1 ounce	2 tablespoons
Coconut oil	7 2/3 ounces	1 cup
Coconut puree	5 1/3 ounces	1 cup
Coconut shavings/chips	7 ounces	4 cups
Coffee beans, whole	3 ounces	1 cup
	1 pound	5 1/3 to 6 cups
Coffee, drip ground	1 pound	5 cups (about 80 tablespoons); 40–50 (6-ounce) cups prepared
Coffee, instant	4-ounce jar	2 1/2 cups; 120 (6-ounce) cups prepared
Condensed milk, sweetened	3 1/2-ounce can	1/4 cup plus 1 tablespoon
	10 3/4 ounces	1 cup
	14-ounce can	1 1/4 cups
Cookie crumbs	4 to 6 ounces	1 cup crushed crumbs
Cornbread (for stuffing)	1 pound	9 cups broken into 1 1/2- to 2-inch pieces; 6 cups coarsely chopped or cubed
Cornbread mix	13-ounce box	2 1/2 cups; 10 servings
Cornflakes cereal	1 pound	13 cups; 5 1/3 cups coarse crumbs; 4 cups fine crumbs
Corn flour, precooked	5 to 6 ounces	1 cup, yellow or white
Cornmeal, coarse-grind, stone-ground whole-grain	4 7/8 ounces	1 cup; 3 to 4 cups cooked
	1 pound	3 1/4 cups; 10 to 13 cups cooked
Cornmeal, fine/medium-grin	1 ounce	3 tablespoons

	4 1/4 ounces	1 cup; 3 to 4 cups cooked
	1 pound	3 3/4 cups; 10 to 13 cups cooked, depending upon consistency
Cornmeal, gluten-free	5 1/4 ounces	1 cup
Cornmeal, self-rising white	4 1/3 ounces	1 cup
Cornstarch	1/3 ounce	1 tablespoon dipped and leveled
	1 ounce	3 tablespoons unsifted; 1/4 cup sifted
	4 ounces	1 cup sifted and lightly spooned
	4 1/2 ounces	1 cup unsifted spooned and leveled
	1 pound	3 3/4 cups lightly spooned and leveled
Corn syrup, light or dark	1 ounce	1 tablespoon plus 1 teaspoon
	12 ounces	1 cup; 8 fluid ounces
Cottage cheese	8 ounces	1 cup (packed)
Crackers, gluten-free buttery	4 ounces	18 (1 cup fine crumbs)
Crackers, graham	4 ounces	17 (2 3/8-inch) squares; 1 cup fine crumbs
Crackers, matzo	4 ounces	6 (6 by 6-inch) sheets; 1 cup fine crumbs
Crackers, Ritz	3 ounces	24 to 26 crackers; 1 cup fine crumbs
Crackers, saltine	4 ounces	30 crackers; 1 cup fine crumbs
Crackers, stone-ground wheat	4 ounces	22 crackers, 1 cup fine crumbs
Crackers, whole-wheat	4 ounces	24 crackers; 1 cup fine crumbs
Cranberries, dried	3 3/4 ounces	1 cup
	1 pound	4 1/4 to 4 1/2 cups
Cranberries, fresh or frozen	12-ounce bag	3 to 3 1/2 cups; 2 1/2 cups chopped
	16-ounce bag	4 to 4 3/4 cups whole; 3 1/2 to 4 cups chopped;
Cranberry sauce, canned	16-ounce can	1 2/3 cups
Cream cheese	1 ounce	2 tablespoons
	3-ounce pkg.	6 tablespoons (1/3 cup plus 2 teaspoons)
	8-ounce pkg.	1 cup
Cream cheese, whipped	6 ounces	1 cup
Cream, heavy whipping	1/2 pint/8 ounce	1 cup; 2 cups whipped
Cream, light	1/2 pint/8 ounce	1 cup
Cream of coconut	10 ounces	1 cup; 8 fluid ounces
Cream of tartar	1 ounce	3 tablespoons
Crème fraîche	8 ounces	1 cup
Crisped rice cereal	1 pound	16 cups
Currants, black fresh	1 pound	4 cups; 3 1/3 cups stemmed
Currants, dried Zante	5 ounces	1 cup

	1 pound	3 1/4 cups
Currants, red fresh	1 pound	3 1/4 cups; 2 2/3 cups stemmed; 1 1/4 cups juice

D

Dates, Chinese red/jujube
See Jujubes

Dates, pitted	6 ounces	1 cup lightly packed
Dates, pitted chopped	5 1/3 ounces	1 cup (about 20 pitted whole dates)
	8 ounces	1 1/2 cups
Dates, pitted Medjool	1 pound	30 to 34 large
Dates, unpitted Deglet Noor	1 pound	60 to 75; 3 1/4 to 4 cups loosely packed; 2 1/2 cups pitted and chopped
Dates, unpitted Medjool	1 pound	24 to 30; 3 1/2 to 4 cups; 2 to 2 1/2 cups pitted and chopped
Dextrose	1 ounce	3 tablespoons
	5 2/3 ounces	1 cup
Diastatic malt powder	1 ounce	3 tablespoons plus 1 teaspoon
Duck eggs	1 pound	5 to 6
Dulce de leche	13.4-ounce can	1 1/4 cups

E

Eggs, dried pasteurized	8 ounces	26 eggs
Eggs, frozen	16 ounces	1 7/8 cups
Eggs, hard-cooked	1 dozen	3 1/2 cups peeled and chopped
Eggs, whole, shelled	1 dozen	3 cups extra-large; 2 1/3 cups large; 2 cups medium; 1 3/4 cups small
	1 pound	6 jumbo; 8 extra-large; 9 large; 10 medium; 12 small
	1 cup	4 jumbo or 4 extra-large; 5 large; 5 to 6 medium; 6 to 7 small; 8 fluid ounces
	1 extra-large	1.9 ounces; 4 tablespoons beaten egg; 2 fluid ounces
	1 large	1.7 ounces; 3 1/4 tablespoons beaten egg; 1 1/2 fluid ounces
	1/2 large	0.9 ounce; 1 1/2 tablespoons; 3/4 fluid ounce
	1/3 large	0.6 ounce; 1 tablespoon; 1/2 fluid ounce
	2 large	3.4 ounces; 1/3 cup + 1 1/2

	3 large	tablespoons; 3 fluid ounces 5 ounces; 1/2 cup + 1 1/2 tablespoons; 4.75 fluid ounces
	4 large	7 ounces; 3/4 cup; 6 fluid ounces
	5 large	8.7 ounces; 1 cup; 8 fluid ounces
	6 large	10.6 ounces; 1 cup + 3 1/4 tablespoons; 9.5 fluid ounces
	1 medium egg	1.8 ounces; 3 tablespoons; 1 1/2 fluid ounces
	1 small egg	1.3 ounces; 2 tablespoons + 1 teaspoon
Egg whites, dried pasteurized	8 ounces	2 1/2 cups; 40 egg whites
Egg whites, fresh	1 dozen	1 3/4 cups extra-large; 1 1/2 cups large; 1 1/3 cups medium; 1 1/4 cups small; 12 fluid ounces
	1 pound	12 extra-large; 13 to 14 large; 15 to 16 medium; 16 small
	1 cup	8.7 ounces; 5 jumbo; 6 to 7 extra-large; 7 to 8 large; 8 medium; 9 small; 8 fluid ounces
	1 extra-large	1.3 ounces; 2 3/4 tablespoons; 1.3 fluid ounces
	1 large	1 ounce; 2 tablespoons; 1 fluid ounce
	1/2 large	1/2 ounce; 1 tablespoon; 1/2 fluid ounce
	2 large	2 ounces; 1/4 cup; 2 fluid ounces
	3 large	3 ounces; 1/4 cup + 2 tablespoons; 3 fluid ounces
	4 large	4 ounces; 1/2 cup; 4 fluid ounces
	5 large	5 ounces; 1/2 cup + 2 tablespoons; 5 fluid ounces
	6 large	6 ounces; 3/4 cup; 6 fluid ounces
Egg yolks, dried pasteurized	8 ounces	45 egg yolks
Egg yolks, fresh	1 dozen	7.7 ounces; 1 cup extra-large; 7/8 cup large; 3/4 cup medium; 2/3 cup small; 7 fluid ounces
	1 pound	24 extra-large; 27 large; 30 medium
	1 cup	8.6 ounces; 12 to 13 extra-large; 14 large; 16 medium; 8 fluid ounces
	1 extra-large	0.7 ounce; 1 1/2 tablespoons;

		3/4 fluid ounce
	1 large	0.6 ounce; 1 1/4 tablespoons; 1/2 fluid ounce
	1/2 large	0.3 ounce; 1 3/4 teaspoons; 1/4 fluid ounce
	2 large	1.3 ounces; 2 tablespoons; 1 fluid ounce
	3 large	2 ounces; 3 1/2 tablespoons; 1.7 fluid ounces
	4 large	2.6 ounces; 1/4 cup; 2.2 fluid ounces
	5 large	3.3 ounces; 1/4 cup + 2 tablespoons; 3 fluid ounces
	6 large	4 ounces; 1/4 cup plus 3 tablespoons; 3.5 fluid ounces
Espresso powder	4 ounces	1 cup; 16 tablespoons

F

Farina, wheat	6.4 ounces	1 cup; 6 cups cooked
Feijoa/pineapple guava	1 pound	8 to 10 medium; 1 cup pulp
Fennel seeds	1 ounce	3 1/2 tablespoons
Figs, Black Mission, dried	1 pound	24 to 36 small to medium; 3 1/3 cups; 2 3/4 cups stemmed and cut into 1/2-inch pieces
Figs, Black Mission, fresh	1 pound	7 to 8 large; 9 to 16 medium; 17 to 21 small; 3 1/2 to 4 cups stemmed and sliced; 2 1/2 to 2 2/3 cups stemmed and chopped
Figs, Brown Turkey, fresh	1 pound	5 to 6 large; 12 to 14 medium; 16 small
Figs, Calimyrna, dried	1 pound	16 to 20 medium; 2 2/3 to 3 cups stemmed, thinly sliced or cut into 1/2-inch pieces
Figs, dried diced	1 pound	3 cups
Figs, canned	15-ounce can	12 to 16; 1 1/2 cups drained
Filberts *See* Hazelnuts		
Flaxseeds, black or golden	1 ounce	2 1/2 tablespoons; 1/4 cup ground
	5 1/2 ounces	1 cup; 1 3/4 cups ground
Flaxseed meal	4 ounces	1 cup
Flour, all-purpose enriched bleached and unbleached	1 ounce	3 level tablespoons unsifted dipped and leveled; 1/4 cup sifted spooned and leveled
	2 ounces	1/2 cup sifted; 2 1/2 ounces unsifted

	4 ounces	1 cup sifted into a cup and leveled
	4 1/4 ounces	1 cup stirred, spooned and leveled
	5 ounces	1 cup stirred, dipped and leveled
	1 pound	4 cups sifted; 3 1/2 cups spooned and leveled 3 1/4 cups dipped and leveled
Flour, almond, plain/raw	3 3/8 ounces	1 cup unsifted spooned and leveled
Flour, almond, toasted	3 5/8 ounces	1 cup unsifted spooned and leveled
Flour, amaranth	3 5/8 ounces	1 cup unsifted spooned and leveled
Flour, arepa, yellow	5 ounces	1 cup unsifted spooned and leveled
Flour, atta/chipati	4 1/8 ounces	1 cup unsifted spooned and leveled
Flour, barley malt	5 3/4 ounces	1 cup unsifted dipped and leveled
Flour, barley, King Arthur	3 ounces	1 cup unsifted spooned and leveled
Flour, barley, roasted	4 ounces	1 cup unsifted spooned and leveled
Flour, barley, stone-ground	5 1/4 ounces	1 cup unsifted dipped and leveled
Flour, bread, King Arthur	4 1/4 ounces	1 cup unsifted spooned and leveled
Flour, bread, national brands	4 1/2 ounces	1 cup unsifted spooned and leveled
	5 ounces	1 cup unsifted dipped and leveled
Flour, brown rice	5 1/3 ounces	1 cup unsifted spooned and leveled
	5 1/2 ounces	1 cup unsifted dipped and leveled
Flour, brown rice, extra fine	4.4 ounces	1 cup unsifted spooned and leveled
Flour, buckwheat	3 1/2 ounces	1 cup sifted spooned and leveled
	4 1/4 ounces	1 cup unsifted spooned and leveled
Flour, cake or pastry	3 1/2 ounces	1 cup sifted into the cup and leveled
	4 ounces	1 cup unsifted spooned and leveled
	4 1/4 ounces	1 cup unsifted dipped and leveled
	1 pound	4 1/2 cups sifted; 4 cups spooned and leveled; 3 1/2 cups dipped and leveled
Flour, cake, unbleached, King Arthur	4 1/4 ounces	1 cup unsifted spooned and leveled
Flour, chestnut	3 3/4 ounces	1 cup sifted spooned and leveled
	4 ounces	1 cup unsifted spooned and leveled
Flour, coconut	4 ounces	1 cup unsifted spooned and leveled
Flour, durum wheat	4 1/2 ounces	1 cup unsifted spooned and leveled
	5 ounces	1 cup unsifted dipped and leveled
Flour, flax	3 1/2 ounces	1 cup unsifted spooned or dipped
Flour, garbanzo bean (*besan*)	3 1/4 ounces	1 cup unsifted spooned and leveled
	3 3/4 ounces	1 cup unsifted dipped and leveled
Flour, gluten-free all-purpose, Gluten-Free Pantry brand	3 1/4 ounces	1 cup unsifted dipped and leveled
Flour, gluten-free all-purpose King Arthur brand	5 1/4 ounces	1 cup unsifted spooned and leveled
Flour, graham	5 1/2 ounces	1 cup unsifted dipped and leveled
Flour, Harvest Grains Blend		

King Arthur brand	5 1/4 ounces	1 cup unsifted spooned and leveled
Flour, hazelnut	3 1/8 ounces	1 cup unsifted spooned and leveled
Flour, high-extraction	4 1/2 ounces	1 cup unsifted spooned and leveled
Flour, high-gluten	4 1/4 ounces	1 cup unsifted spooned and leveled
Flour, high-maize	3 1/4 ounces	1 cup unsifted spooned and leveled
Flour, Irish-style, King Arthur brand	3 7/8 ounces	1 cup unsifted spooned and leveled
Flour, Italian-type 00	3 3/4 ounces	1 cup unsifted spooned and leveled
	4 1/2 ounces	1 cup unsifted dipped and leveled
Flour, Kamut	4 1/2 ounces	1 cup unsifted spooned and leveled
Flour, masa harina/corn	3 7/8 ounces	1 cup unsifted spooned and leveled
	4 ounces	1 cup unsifted dipped and leveled
Flour, oat	3 1/2 ounces	1 cup unsifted spooned and leveled
	4 ounces	1 cup unsifted dipped and leveled
Flour, Pastry Blend, King Arthur brand	4 ounces	1 cup unsifted spooned and leveled
Flour, pecan	4 ounces	1 cup unsifted, spooned, and leveled
Flour, potato	6 1/2 ounces	1 cup unsifted spooned and leveled
Flour, pumpernickel	3 3/4 ounces	1 cup unsifted spooned and leveled
Flour, quick-mixing	4 1/2 ounces	1 cup poured and leveled
Flour, quinoa	3 7/8 ounces	1 cup unsifted spooned and leveled
Flour, rice	4 1/2 ounces	1 cup unsifted spooned and leveled
Flour, rye, light or white	3 3/4 ounces	1 cup unsifted spooned and leveled
	4 ounces	1 cup sifted spooned and leveled
Flour, rye, medium	3 5/8 ounces	1 cup unsifted spooned and leveled
Flour, self-rising white	4 ounces	1 cup unsifted spooned and leveled
Flour, semolina fine-grind	5 3/4 ounces	1 cup sifted spooned and leveled
	6 ounces	1 cup unsifted spooned and leveled
	6 3/4 ounces	1 cup unsifted dipped and leveled
Flour, sesame seed	4 ounces	1 cup unsifted spooned and leveled
Flour, sorghum	4 7/8 cups	1 cup unsifted spooned and leveled
Flour, soybean, defatted	3 1/8 ounces	1 cup unsifted spooned and leveled
Flour, soybean, low-fat	3 1.8 ounces	1 cup unsifted spooned and leveled
Flour, soybean, roasted/kina	3 1/3 ounces	1 cup unsifted spooned and leveled
Flour, spelt	3 1/2 ounces	1 cup unsifted spooned and leveled
Flour, spelt whole grain	4 1/2 ounces	1 cup unsifted dipped and leveled
Flour, sprouted wheat	3 3/4 ounces	1 cup unsifted spooned and leveled
Flour, sunflower seed	4 ounces	1 cup unsifted spooned and leveled
Flour, sweet rice/glutinous	4 ounces	1 cup unsifted spooned and leveled
	4 1/2 ounces	1 cup unsifted dipped and leveled
Flour, teff whole-grain	4 3/4 ounces	1 cup unsifted spooned and leveled
	5 1/4 ounces	1 cup unsifted dipped and leveled
Flour, triticale whole-grain	4 1/4 ounces	1 cup unsifted spooned and leveled

Flour, white rice	5 ounces	1 cup unsifted spooned and leveled
Flour, whole spelt	4 1/2 ounces	1 cup unsifted spooned and leveled
Flour, whole-wheat	4 1/4 ounces	1 cup unsifted spooned and leveled
	5 to 5 1/2 ounce	1 cup unsifted dipped and leveled
Flour, whole-wheat, King Arthur brand	4 ounces	1 cup unsifted spooned and leveled
Flour, whole-wheat pastry	4 ounces	1 cup unsifted spooned and leveled
	4 1/2 ounces	1 cup unsifted dipped and leveled
Flour, whole-wheat pastry, King Arthur brand	3 3/8 ounces	1 cup unsifted spooned and leveled
Flour, whole-wheat white	4 ounces	1 cup unsifted spooned and leveled
Frosting, cake	3/4 to 1 cup	Covers 8-inch square or 9- or 10-inch round cake, top only
	1 to 1 1/2 cups	Covers 8- or 9-inch one-layer cake, top and sides only Covers 9 1/2 x 5 x 3-inch loaf cake, top and sides only Covers 12 (2- or 3-inch) cupcakes
	1 1/2 to 2 cups	Covers 8-inch square cake, top and sides only Covers 9 or 10-inch two-layer round cake, top and sides only Covers 13 x 9 x 2-inch sheet cake, top only
	3 cups	Covers 13 x 9 x 2-inch sheet cake, top and sides only Covers 8- or 9-inch two-layer round cake; top, sides, and filling Covers 8- or 9-inch three-layer round cake, top and sides only Covers 9- or 10-inch tube cake; top, sides, and center
	4 cups	Covers 8- or 9-inch three-layer round cake; top, sides, and filling
Fruit cocktail, canned	15-ounce can	1 3/4 cups; 1 1/4 to 1 1/2 cups drained
Fruit, dried	1 pound	3 cups (equivalent of 3 1/2 to 4 pounds fresh fruit)
Fruit glace and peels	6 ounces	1 cup
	1 pound	2 2/3 cups (about)
Fruit puree	8 ounces	1 cup

G

Gelatin, powdered	1/4 ounce	1 envelope; 2 1/2 teaspoons; to set 2 cups liquid
	1 ounce	1 (4 envelope) box
Gelatin sheets/leaves	1 ounce	11 (2.5-gram) silver-grade sheets
Ginger, crystallized	1 ounce	5 to 6 pieces; 3 to 4 tablespoons diced; 2 tablespoons finely chopped
	6 ounces	1 cup (1/4-inch) pieces firmly packed
Ginger, crystallized, soft	1 ounce	6 to 7 pieces
	5 ounces	1 cup; 30 pieces
Ginger, fresh young	4 ounces	1 cup peeled and thinly sliced
Ginger, ground/powdered	1 ounce	5 tablespoons
Ginger, juice	1/2 fluid ounce	1 1/2 to 2 ounces ginger grated, and pressed through a garlic press
	1 1/2 fluid ounce	1 cup minced ginger pressed through a sieve
Ginger, minced/grated	1 ounce	2 tablespoons
Ginger, stem, in syrup	4 ounces	1 cup drained
Gingersnaps/ginger cookies	4 ounces	14 to 16; 1 cup crumbs crushed fine
Glucose, liquid	1 ounce	1 1/2 tablespoons
	12 ounces	1 cup; 8 fluid ounces
Glucose, powdered	5 2/3 ounces	1 cup
Gluten, wheat	1 ounce	3 level tablespoons unsifted dipped and leveled
Goji berries, dried	4 ounces	1 (scant) cup
Golden syrup	1 ounce	1 tablespoon plus 1 teaspoon
	11 1/2 ounces	1 cup; 8 fluid ounces
Gooseberries, cape/physalis	1 pound	3 cups with husks removed
Gooseberries, hard green	1 pound	5 1/4 cups; 4 1/3 cups with tops and tails removed
Graham crackers *See* Crackers		
Granola	1 pound	4 to 5 1/3 cups
Grapefruit, canned	15-ounce can	1 3/4 cups drained
Grapefruit, fresh	1 pound	1 medium; 1 1/2 to 2 cups segments; 2/3 to 3/4 cup juice; 3 tablespoons zest
Grapes, canned	8-ounce can	1 cup drained
Grapes, fresh seedless	1 pound	75 medium; 2 2/3 to 3 cups; 2 cups halved
Guava, canned	17-ounce can	24 halves with syrup
Guava, fresh	4 ounces	1 medium; 1/3 to 1/2 cup sliced or pulp
	1 pound	2 to 3 large; 4 to 5 medium; 1 2/3 to 2 cups sliced;

		2 to 2 1/4 cups pulp; 1 1/2 cups pureed
Guava paste	4 ounces	1/2 cup cut into 1/4-inch cubes
Guava pulp/puree	8 ounces	1 1/3 cups

H

Half-and-half	1/2 pint	1 cup
Hazelnuts, shelled	1 ounce	18 to 22 nutmeats; 1/4 cup coarsely chopped
	4 ounces	1 cup finely chopped or ground
	5 ounces	1 cup whole; 3 1/2 tablespoons oil using an oil press
	1 pound	3 1/4 cups whole; 4 cups ground
Hazelnuts, unshelled	1 pound	1 1/2 cups shelled; 7 1/3 ounces
Hempseed	4 2/3 ounces	1 cup
Hibiscus, powdered	6 grams	1 tablespoon
High-maize natural fiber	4 1/2 ounces	1 cup
Honey	1 ounce	4 teaspoons
	8 ounces	2/3 cup; 5 fluid ounces
	12 ounces	1 cup; 8 fluid ounces
	1 pound	1 1/3 cups; 10 fluid ounces

I

Icing *See* Frosting, cake		
Invert sugar (Trimoline)	27 grams	1 tablespoon
	10 1/2 ounces	1 cup

J

Jaggery palm sugar	6 1/2 ounces	1 cup shaved, crushed, or chopped
Jam and preserves	1 ounce	1 1/2 tablespoons
	3–3 3/4 ounces	1/4 cup
	12–13 1/2 ounce	1 cup
Jam/Low-sugar spread	8 ounces	1 cup
Jujubes/Chinese dates, dried	1 ounce	15 (about)
Jujubes/Chinese dates, fresh	1 pound	12 (about)

K

Kanten	2/3 ounce	1 packet; 2 (10 x 1-inch) sticks
Kasha/roasted buckwheat	6 ounces	1 cup; 2 1/2 to 3 cups cooked
Kataifi dough	8 ounces	5 cups

Kiwi berry/cocktail kiwi	1 pound	10 to 12 medium
Kiwi fruit, green or gold	1 pound	3 to 4 large; 5 to 6 small to medium; 1 1/2 to 2 1/2 cups peeled, sliced, or cut into 1/4- or 1/2-inch cubes
Kudzu powder	1 ounce	2 tablespoons plus 1/2 teaspoon, crushed fine
Kumquats	1 pound	3 to 4 cups

L

Lactose	4 ounces	1 cup
Ladyfingers, large	1 pound	40 to 41 (3 1/4 x 2 3/8 x 1 1/8 inches)
Ladyfingers, cake-style	3-ounce pkg.	12
Lard, commercial	0.4 ounce	1 tablespoon
	7 to 1/3 ounce	1 cup
	1 pound	2 1/8 cups
Lavender, culinary, dried	1 ounce	1/2 cup plus 1 tablespoon
Lemon curd	1 pound	2 cups
Lemons, Eureka and Lisbon	2 2/3 to 4 ounces	1 small to medium; ends trimmed and cut into 8 paper-thin slices; 2 to 3 tablespoons juice; 1 to 1 1/2 teaspoons zest
	4 to 5 ounces	1 medium to large; 3 to 4 tablespoons juice; 2 to 3 teaspoons zest
	1 pound	4 to 5 medium; 3/4 to 7/8 cup juice; 1/4 to 1/3 cup zest
Lemon juice	8 1/2 ounces	1 cup; juice of 4 large or 5 to 6 medium lemons
Lemons, Meyer	5 to 6 ounces	1 medium; 1/4 to 1/3 cup juice; 1 1/2 to 3 tablespoons zest; 2 to 3 teaspoons dried zest
	1 pound	2 to 3 medium; 2/3 to 1 cup juice; 1/4 to 1/3 cup zest, packed
Limes, Bearss	5 ounces	1 medium; 1/4 to 1/3 cup juice; 1 1/2 to 3 tablespoons fresh zest; 2 to 3 teaspoons dried zest
	1 pound	2 large; 3 medium; 2/3 to 1 cup juice; 1/4 to 1/3 cup zest
Limes, Key/Mexican	1 to 1 1/2 ounce	1 medium; 1 1/2 to 2 teaspoons juice; 3/4 to 1 teaspoon zest
	1 pound	11 to 16 medium; 1/2 to 2/3 cup juice; 3 1/2 tablespoons to 1/3 cup zest

Limes, Omani dried	3-ounce pkg.	10 limes
Limes, Persian/Tahiti	2 to 3 ounces	1 medium; 1 1/2 to 2 tablespoons juice; 1 to 2 teaspoons zest
	1 pound	5 to 6 medium; 2/3 to 3/4 cup juice; 2 1/2 to 4 1/2 tablespoons zest
Longans, canned	20-ounce can	32 longans; 8.2 ounces drained
Loquats	1 pound	27 to 45; 2 1/2 cups halved or sliced
Lucuma flour/powder	4 ounces	1 cup
Lychees/litchis, canned	20-ounce can	20 pieces (1 1/4 cups fruit; 1 1/2 cups syrup)
Lychees/litchis, dried	1 ounce	11 to 12 pieces (about)
Lychees/litchis, fresh	1 pound	27 to 45; 2 1/2 cups peeled, pitted, sliced

M

Macadamia nuts	1 ounce	10 to 12 whole nutmeats
	1 pound	3 1/3 cups whole; 3 1/2 cups chopped or pieces
Macadamia paste	5.6 ounces	1 cup
Malted milk powder	5 ounces	1 cup
Malt powder, non-diastatic	4 ounces	1 cup
Maltodextrin powder	1/2 ounce	1 tablespoon
	3 1/8 ounces	1 cup
Malt syrup/barley malt syrup	3 ounces	1/4 cup
Mandarins, canned	15-ounce can	1 3/4 cups drained
Mandarins, fresh	1 pound	2 large; 3 to 4 medium; 4 small; 2 cups sections
Maple syrup	0.7 ounce	1 tablespoon; 1/2 fluid ounce
	11 ounces	1 cup; 8 fluid ounces
Margarine, stick *See* Butter		
Marshmallow crème	3 ounces	1 cup
	7 1/2-ounce jar	2 1/2 cups
	16-ounce jar	5 1/4 cups
Marshmallows, mini	2 ounces	1 cup; 80 marshmallows
Marshmallows, regular	1 1/2 ounces	1 cup; 10 to 11 marshmallows
	10-ounce bag	36 marshmallows; 6 to 7 cups
Marzipan	7 ounces	7/8 cup
Mascarpone	8.8 ounces	1 cup
Matzo meal	5 ounces	1 cup
Meringue powder	1 ounce	2 tablespoons
	6 ounces	1 cup

Milk, dry Baker's Special	5 ounces	1 cup
Milk, dry instant full-fat	3 2/3 ounces	1 cup powder; 1 quart reconstituted
	1 pound	4 1/3 cups powder; 4 quarts reconstituted
Milk, dry instant nonfat	3/4 ounce	1/3 cup powder; 1 cup reconstituted
	9.4 ounces	4 cups powder; 3 quarts reconstituted
Milk, dry regular full-fat	4 to 4.5 ounces	1 cup; 1 quart reconstituted
	1 pound	3 3/4 to 4 cups; 3 1/2 quarts reconstituted
Milk, dry regular nonfat	3 ounces	1 cup; 1 quart reconstituted
Milk, evaporated	5-ounce can	2/3 cup
	12-ounce can	1 1/2 cups
Milk, fresh	8.5 ounces	1 cup; 8 fluid ounces
Milk, soy	8.6 ounces	1 cup; 8 fluid ounces
Mizuame (rice starch syrup)	12 1/4 ounces	1 cup
Molasses, light or dark	1 ounce	1 1/2 tablespoons
	11 1/2 ounces	1 cup; 8 fluid ounces
Muffin mix	7-ounce box	1 1/4 cups; 5 muffins
Muffin mix, bran	7-ounce box	1 1/2 cups; 5 muffins
Muffin mix, corn	8 1/2-ounce box	1 1/2 cups; 6 muffins
Muffin mix, oat bran	14-ounce box	3 cups; 9 muffins

N

Nectarines, dried	1 pound	2 1/2 to 3 cups; 5 1/2 cups cooked
Nectarines, fresh	1 pound	3 to 4 medium; 2 to 2 1/2 cups sliced or chopped; 1 3/4 cups diced; 1 1/2 cups pureed
Nigella seeds	1 ounce	3 tablespoons
Nonstick cooking spray	0.17 ounce	1 teaspoon; 10- to 15-second spray
Nutmeg	1 whole pod	2 to 3 teaspoons grated
	1 ounce	5 to 6 medium pods; 3 to 4 tablespoons ground
Nutmeal	4 ounces	1 cup

O

Oat bran	2 tablespoons	1 ounce
	3 3/4 ounces	1 cup; 3 to 4 cups cooked
Oats, rolled	3 to 3 1/2 ounce	1 cup; 1 3/4 cups cooked
Oil, vegetable	1 ounce	2 tablespoons

	7 2/3 ounces	1 cup; 8 fluid ounces
Orange juice powder	4 ounces	1 cup
Orange, Seville/sour	4 to 5 ounces	1 medium; 1/3 to 1/2 cup segments; 2 to 3 tablespoons juice; 1 to 2 tablespoons zest
Oranges, fresh	5 1/3 ounces	1 medium; 1/2 to 3/4 cup segments; 1/4 to 12 cup juice; 2 to 3 tablespoons zest; 2 to 3 teaspoons dried zest
	1 pound	3 medium; 1 1/2 to 3 cups segments; 3/4 to 1 1/2 cups juice; 1/3 to 1/2 cup zest
	1 dozen	3 to 5 cups juice
Oranges, mandarin	11-ounce can	1 1/4 cups

P

Pancake mix	1 pound	3 1/2 cups
Passion fruit puree, frozen	14-ounce pack	1 1/2 cups
Passion fruit, purple fresh	1 pound	10 to 14 fruits; 1 (generous) cup pulp and juice; 1/2 to 3/4 cup strained juice
Passion fruit, yellow fresh	1 pound	5 to 7 fruits; 1 1/2 cups pulp and juice; 3/4 cup strained juice
Peaches, canned	15-ounce can	6 to 10 halves; 1 3/4 cups sliced
Peaches, dried	1 pound	31 to 35 medium halves; 2 3/4 to 3 cups; 5 1/2 to 6 cups cooked
Peaches, fresh	1 pound	3 to 4 medium; 2 1/2 cups peeled and sliced or roughly chopped; 1 1/2 cups pureed
Peaches, frozen	16-ounce bag	3 1/4 cups slices and juice, thawed
Peanut butter	1 ounce	2 scant tablespoons
	9 to 10 ounces	1 cup
Peanuts, shelled plain or salted dry-roasted	1 ounce	28 whole peanuts; 1/4 cup ground
	5 ounces	1 cup whole peanuts
	1 pound	3 1/4 to 4 cups whole or coarsely chopped; 4 cups ground nut meal
Peanuts, unshelled	1 pound	2 1/4 cups shelled; 10-11 ounces; 1/2 cup oil using an oil press
Pears, canned	15-ounce can	1 3/4 cups
Pears, dried	1 pound	26 halves; 2 1/2 to 2 3/4 cups; 5 to 5 1/2 cups cooked

Pears, fresh	4 to 5 ounces	1 medium; 1/2 to 3/4 cup peeled, cored, sliced, coarsely chopped, or cubed
	1 pound	3 to 4 medium; 2 to 2 1/2 cups peeled, cored, sliced, coarsely chopped, or cubed
		1 1/3 to 1 1/2 cups pureed
Pecans, shelled	1 ounce	10 large; 18 to 20 medium halves; 1/3 cup (about)
	4 ounces	1 cup halves; 1 1/4 cups chopped
	1 pound	4 cups halves; 3 3/4 cups chopped
Pecans, unshelled	1 pound	2 1/4 cups shelled; 8 1/2 to 9 ounces
Pectin, low-sugar powdered	1.75-ounce box	6 tablespoons
Persimmon pulp	8 1/2 ounces	1 cup
Persimmons, dried	1 pound	12 to 13 pieces
Persimmons, Fuyu, fresh	1 pound	3 medium firm-ripe; 2 1/4 to 2 2/3 cups sliced
Persimmons, Hachiya, fresh	1 pound	3 medium ripe; 1 1/4 to 1 3/4 cups pulp
Phyllo pastry sheets	1-pound package	20 to 25 sheets (12 x 16- or 17-inch)
Phyllo pastry shells	1.9-ounce box	15 mini baked shells
Piloncillo	8 ounces	1 cone; 1 cup minced or shaved, firmly packed
Pineapple, candied	8 ounces	55 chunks (about); 1 cup packed;
Pineapple chunks, canned	8-ounce can	3/4 cup drained
Pineapple, crushed, canned	8-ounce can	2/3 cup drained
	20-ounce can	2 1/4 cups undrained; 1 2/3 cups drained
Pineapple, dried	5 ounces	1 cup
Pineapple sliced, canned	20-ounce can	10 cored slices; 2 1/2 cups cubed
Pine nuts	1 ounce	3 1/3 tablespoons
	5 to 5 1/2 ounces	1 cup
Pistachio nuts, shelled	1 ounce	49 to 60; 1/4 scant cup
	1 pound	3 1/2 to 4 cups
Pistachio nuts, unshelled	1 pound	1 3/4 to 2 cups shelled; 8 ounces
Pistachio paste	10 ounces	1 cup

Plums, Angelino	1 pound	12 to 14; 2 cups pitted and halved
Plums, Damson, fresh	1 pound	8 large; 10 to 16 medium to small; 2 1/2 cups pitted, halved or quartered; 2 cups cooked
Plums, dried	5 ounces	1 cup
Plums, Italian/prune, fresh	1 pound	12 to 15 small ripe; 2 cups pitted and halved
Plums, Santa Rosa, fresh	1 pound	3 to 5 medium; 2 1/2 to 3 cups pitted and sliced; 2 cups cooked; 1 1/2 cups purée
Plums, sloe, fresh	1 pound	8 medium
Plums, whole, canned	16-ounce can	6 to 8 medium
Pluots, fresh	1 pound	4 to 5 large; 5 to 6 medium; 2 to 2 1/2 cups sliced
Pomegranate	7 ounces	1 medium; 1/2 to 3/4 cup pulpy seeds; 1/4 to 1/3 cup juice
Pomegranate seeds/arils, fresh	5 ounces	1 cup
Poppy seed, blue or white	1 ounce	3 3/4 tablespoons
	4 3/4 ounces	1 cup
Potato starch	5 1/4 ounces	1 cup lightly spooned and leveled
	1 pound	3 cups lightly spooned and leveled
Praline paste	11 ounces	1 cup
Preserves *See* Jam and preserves		
Prunes, Agen pitted	7 1/2 ounces	1 cup
Prunes, canned	16-ounce can	10 to 14 prunes
Prunes, dried pitted	6-ounce carton	15 to 20; 1 cup firmly packed
	1 pound	4 cups loosely packed; 2 2/3 cups firmly packed; 4 to 4 3/4 cups cooked
Prunes, dried, unpitted	1 pound	43 to 67; 2 1/2 to 3 1/4 cups; 4 to 4 1/2 cups cooked pitted; 2 1/3 cups puréed
Puff pastry, frozen	17.3-ounce box	2 ready-to-bake sheets (10.6 x 3.6 x 1.3 inches)
	14-ounce box	1 ready-to-bake all-butter sheet (9 x 15 x 1/2 inches)
Pumpkin, canned	15-ounce can	1 3/4 cups solid pack
	29-ounce can	3 1/2 cups solid pack
Pumpkin, fresh	1 pound	4 cups cut into 1-inch pieces; 2 cups cooked and drained; 3/4 to 1 1/4 cups cooked, mashed

Pumpkin puree	8 ounces	1 cup
Pumpkin seeds, shelled raw	1 ounce	3 1/2 tablespoons kernels
	4 1/2 to 5 ounces	1 cup kernels
Pumpkin seeds, unshelled	1 ounce	85 seeds (about)

Q

Quince	1 pound	3 or 4 medium; 1 1/2 to 2 cups peeled, cored, chopped; 1 1/2 cups pulp
Quinoa flakes	3 1/2 ounces	1 cup

R

Raisins, seedless black	2 ounces	1/3 cup firmly packed
	6 ounces	1 cup firmly packed
	15-ounces	2 1/2 cups firmly packed; 3 cups loosely packed
	1 pound	2 2/3 cups firmly packed; 3 1/8 cups loosely packed
Raisins, seedless large red	3 1/2 ounces	1 cup firmly packed
	1 pound	4 1/2 cups firmly packed
Raspberries, canned in syrup	16.5-ounce can	1 3/4 cups
Raspberries, fresh	4 1/2 ounces	1 cup whole berries; 1/4 cup pureed
	12 ounces	1 pint; 2 2/3 cups; 1 (scant) cup sieved
Raspberries, frozen	16-ounce bag	3 3/8 cups loose pack; 2 cups crushed; 7/8 (scant) cup pureed and strained juice
Raspberries, frozen in syrup	10-ounce box	1 3/4 cups
Rhubarb, fresh, red or green	1 pound	4 thick stalks, or 7 to 10 medium/thin stalks; 3 1/2 to 4 cups trimmed and cut into 1/2-inch pieces; 2 cups cooked; 1 cup cooked puree
Rhubarb, frozen	16-ounce bag	2 cups chopped or sliced
Rice bran	3 1/2 ounces	1 cup, 3 to 4 cups cooked
Rice, ground	6 ounces	1 cup
	1 pound	2 2/3 cups
Rice paper	16 ounces	30 (8 by 8-inch sheets)
Rice powder	4 ounces	1 cup
Ricotta	15 ounces	2 cups

Rose buds or petals, organic	1 ounce	2 cups
Rose hips, dried	1 ounce	1/2 cup
Rye berries, whole/cracked	7 ounces	1 cup; 3 cups cooked; 3 1/2 cups sprouts
Rye chops or flakes	4 1/2 ounces	1 cup

S

Salt, kosher (Diamond Crystal)	9 grams	1 tablespoon
	1 ounce	9 1/2 teaspoons
	5 ounces	1 cup
Salt, kosher (Morton)	14 grams	1 tablespoon
	1 ounce	2 tablespoons
	7.9 ounces	1 cup
Salt, kosher, coarse (Morton)	10.5 grams	1 tablespoon
	1 ounce	8 teaspoons
	7.7 ounces	1 cup
Salt, kosher (Redmond)	17 grams	1 tablespoon
	9.5 ounces	1 cup
Salt, Maldon or Welsh sea	18 grams	1 tablespoon
	1 ounce	4 1/2 teaspoons
Salt, Mediterranean or Pacific Sea, fine grind	16 grams	1 tablespoon
	1 ounce	5 teaspoons
Salt, Mediterranean or Pacific Sea, coarse grind	17 grams	1 tablespoon
	1 ounce	5 teaspoons
Salt, table (Morton)	10 ounces	1 cup
Salt, table, iodized or plain	pinch	1/16 teaspoon
	dash	1/8 teaspoon
	0.63 ounce	1 tablespoon
	1 ounce	4 1/2 teaspoons
	10 5/8 ounces	1 cup
Semolina, coarse See Farina, wheat		
Semolina, fine	6 ounces	1 cup
Sesame seeds, hulled	1 ounce	3 1/2 tablespoons; 2 (scant) tablespoons ground
Sesame seeds, unhulled	1 ounce	3 tablespoons
	5 ounces	1 cup
Shortening, vegetable	1/2 ounce	1 tablespoon
	1 ounce	2 tablespoons
	1 pound	2 1/4 cups

	20 ounces	3 sticks, 1 cup each
Sour cream	1 ounce	2 tablespoons
	8-ounce tub	1 cup
Sourdough starter, active	7 ounces	1 cup
Soy nuts	1 ounce	1/4 cup
Spices	1/8 ounce	1 to 1 1/2 teaspoons depending upon spice
	1/4 ounce	1 tablespoon
Splenda *See* Sucralose		
Star anise	1 ounce	10 whole; 5 teaspoons ground
Strawberries, dried	4 1/2 ounces	1 cup
Strawberries, fresh	12 ounces/1 pint	12 to 14 large berries; 20 to 25 small berries; 1 3/4 to 2 1/4 cups; 1 1/2 to 2 cups sliced; 1 to 1 1/4 cups pureed
	1 1/2 pounds	1 quart; 3 1/2 to 4 1/2 cups whole berries; 3 to 4 cups sliced or quartered; 2 cups pureed
Strawberries, frozen, sliced	10-ounce pkg.	1 1/4 cups packed in syrup; 1 cup drained
Strawberries, frozen, whole	20-ounce bag	4 cups; 2 1/4 cups pureed; 1 cup juice
Sucralose/Splenda/ Rapadura	7 ounces	1 cup
Suet, chopped or ground	8 ounces	1 cup packed
Suet, shredded/pregrated	5 ounces	1 cup
Sugar, black	5 1/3 ounces	1 cup firmly packed crushed sugar
Sugar, brown, dark	7 3/4 ounces	1 cup firmly packed
Sugar, brown, light	7 1/4 ounces	1 cup firmly packed
Sugar, Brownulated Light	6 1/4 ounces	1 cup poured
Sugar, Chinese yellow rock	1 2/3 ounces	1 cube; 2 crushed tablespoons
	1 pound	15 pieces
Sugar, confectioners'/ powdered/icing	3 1/2 ounces	1 cup sifted
	4 ounces	1 cup lightly spooned and leveled
	1 pound	3 3/4 cups unsifted; 4 1/2 cups sifted
Sugar, cubes/lumps-1/2-inch	5 1/3 ounces	1 cup; 60 cubes
	1 pound	180 cubes
Sugar, Demerara	7 3/4 ounces	1 cup
Sugar, granulated	4 grams	1 teaspoon
	1 ounce	2 1/3 tablespoons
	3 1/2 ounces	1/2 cup; 1/4 cup reduced to liquid caramel

	4 2/3 ounces	2/3 cup
	5 1/4 ounces	3/4 cup
	7 ounces	1 cup
	8 ounces	1 cup plus 2 1/3 tablespoons
	1 pound	2 1/4 cups poured or scooped
Sugar, invert *See* Invert sugar		
Sugar, lump	6 ounces	1 cup
Sugar, maple	1 ounce	1 (1 3/4 x 1 1/4 x 1/2-inch) piece
	5 1/2 ounces	1 cup granulated
Sugar, muscovado/Barbados	8 1/2 ounces	1 cup firmly packed
Sugar, palm	6 1/2 ounces	1 cup shaved or grated, packed
Sugar, rock	1 pound	16 (1-inch) pieces
Sugar, superfine/extra fine	6 1/2 ounces	1 cup poured or scooped
Sugar, turbinado cane	7 ounces	1 cup poured or scooped
Sultanas *See* Raisins		
Sunflower seeds, shelled	1 ounce	3 1/2 tablespoons kernels
	5 ounces	1 cup; 3/4 cup ground
Sunflower seeds, unshelled	1 pound	5 cups; 1 2/3 cups hulled kernels
Syrup, corn *See* Corn syrup		
Syrup, refiner's	12 ounces	1 cup

T

Tangerines and tangelos	1 pound	4 to 5 medium; 2 cups sections; 3/4 to 1 cup juice; 4 to 5 tablespoons zest
Tapioca, quick-cooking	1 ounce	3 tablespoons plus 1 teaspoon
	8-ounce pkg.	1 1/2 cups; 3 3/4 cups cooked
Tapioca starch	3 1/2 ounces	1 cup unsifted spooned and leveled
Tapioca starch, Expandex Modified	1 ounce	3 tablespoons
Tartaric acid	0.14 ounces	1 teaspoon
Treacle	1 ounce	1 tablespoon

U

Ugli/Uniq fruit	1 pound	2 small; 2 cups segments

V

Vanilla beans, grade B	1 ounce	7 to 8
Vanilla beans, Madagascar	1 ounce	7 to 12 beans
Vanilla beans, Tahitian	1 ounce	5 to 6 beans
Vinegar	1 fluid ounce	2 tablespoons

W

Walnuts, black	1 ounce	1/4 scant cup
Walnuts, English shelled	1 ounce	14 halves; 1/4 cup
	4 ounces	50 to 56 halves; 1 cup; 7/8 cup chopped
	1 pound	3 3/4 to 4 cups; 3 1/2 cups chopped
Walnuts, English unshelled	1 pound	1 3/4 to 2 cups shelled; 7 1/4 ounces
Wheat bran, toasted	1 ounce	1/3 cup
Wheat bran, unprocessed	1 ounce	1/2 cup
Wheat, cracked	5 1/2 ounces	1 cup
Wheat flakes, malted	4 ounces	1 cup
Wheat germ, toasted	1 ounce	4 3/4 tablespoons; 1/4 cup packed
	12-ounce jar	3 cups
Wheat starch	4 ounces	1 cup unsifted spooned and leveled
	4 1/2 ounces	1 cup unsifted dipped and leveled
Whipped topping mix	1.3-ounce pack	2 cups prepared whipped topping
Whipped topping, frozen	8-ounce tub	3 1/2 cups

X

Xanthan gum	12 grams	1 tablespoon

Y

Yeast, active dry	1/4-ounce pkg.	2 1/4 teaspoons
	1 ounce	3 tablespoons
Yeast, fresh compressed	0.6-ounce cake	1 tablespoon plus 1 teaspoon
	1 ounce	2 tablespoons plus 1/4 teaspoon firmly packed
Yogurt	8 to 8 1/2 ounce	1 cup
Yogurt, Greek-style	9 to 10 ounces	1 cup
Yogurt powder	1 ounce	3 tablespoons

Z

Zucchini	5 or 6 ounces	1 medium; 3/4 to 1 cup sliced or grated
	1 pound	3 medium; 3 to 3 1/2 cups sliced; 3 1/4 cups shredded or coarsely grated; 2 cups grated and squeezed or salted and drained

MEASURING METHODS AND WEIGHT EQUIVALENTS FOR FLOUR IN COOKBOOKS AND FOOD MAGAZINES

1 cup all-purpose flour, stirred, spooned, and leveled = 4 1/4 ounces
Better Homes and Gardens magazine and cookbooks
Betty Crocker cookbooks
Bon Appétit magazine and cookbooks
Cooking Light magazine and cookbooks
Fine Cooking magazine and cookbooks
Food Network Magazine
Good Housekeeping magazine and cookbooks
Gourmet cookbooks
King Arthur Flour cookbooks and articles
Joy of Cooking cookbooks
Martha Stewart Living magazines and cookbooks
Pillsbury cookbooks
Real Simple magazine
Rick Bayless's cookbooks
Saveur magazine and cookbooks
Southern Living magazine and cookbooks
Sunset magazine and cookbooks
The New York Times cookbooks

1 cup all-purpose flour, stirred, scooped, and leveled = 5 ounces
America's Test Kitchen cookbooks
Cook's Illustrated magazine and cookbooks
Cook's Country magazine and cookbooks
Dorie Greenspan's cookbooks
Eating Well magazine and cookbooks
Fannie Farmer cookbooks
Jeffrey Alford and Naomi Duguid's cookbooks
Jacques Pepín's cookbooks
Splendid Table cookbooks
The *Pioneer Woman* cookbooks
Williams-Sonoma cookbooks

1 cup all-purpose flour, no method or weight indicated
Family Circle magazine and cookbooks
Food and Wine magazine and cookbooks
Rachael Ray's magazine and cookbooks
Taste of Home magazine and cookbooks
Women's Day magazine and cookbooks
Vegetarian Times magazine and cookbooks

BAKING PAN EQUIVALENTS

When substituting one pan for another, use the following guidelines:

Bread: fill pans half full

Cakes: fill round pans half full, loaf and tube pans two-thirds full, fluted pans three-quarters full

Soufflés and casseroles: fill dishes to 3/4- to 1 inch below the top

Ovenproof glass pan: reduce the oven temperature by 25°F

Deeper pans or square pans: increase the baking time by one-eighth to one-quarter (although using the same depth as the original is best)

Shallower pans: reduce the baking time by one-eighth to one-quarter (although using the same depth as the original is best)

Baking Pans and Dishes
2 tablespoons (1/8 cup)
1 3/4 x 3/4-inch mini muffin cup or madeleine cup
1 7/8 x 3 3/4-inch barquette mold
2 1/2-inch scallop shell

3 tablespoons
1 7/8 x 2 3/4-inch financier mold

4 tablespoons (1/4 cup)
2 3/4 x 1 1/8-inch muffin cup

6 tablespoons
4 x 3/4-inch two-piece tart pan

1/2 cup
2 1/2-inch-high *baba au rhum* mold
2 2/3 x 1 3/8-inch muffin cup
3 x 1 1/2-inch ramekin
4 x 1-inch fluted round tartlet pan
4 x 1 1/4-inch round tart pan
3 1/4 x 2 x 1 1/4-inch mini loaf pan

2/3 cup to 3/4 cup
2 1/4 x 1 3/4 x 1/2-inch madeleine cup
3 x 1 1/4-inch jumbo muffin cup
3 x 2 1/2-inch popover cup
3 1/8 x 1 3/8-inch (5-fluid ounce) ovenproof ramekin
3 1/2 x 1 1/4-inch jumbo muffin cup
3 1/2 x 1 3/4-inch (6-fluid ounce) ovenproof ramekin
3 7/8 x 2 1/2 x 5/8-inch mini loaf pan
4 3/4 x 3/4-inch two-piece tart pan

1 cup
6 x 3 1/2 x 1 3/4-inch mini angel food cake pan

1 1/2 cups
4 1/2-inch deep-dish mini pie pan
5 1/2 x 1-inch two-piece tart pan

1 3/4 cups
5 3/4 x 3 1/4 x 2-inch mini disposable loaf pan
5 3/4 x 3 1/4 x 2 1/4-inch mini loaf pan

2 cups
5 x 3 x 2-inch loaf pan
5 1/2 x 3 x 2 1/2-inch loaf pan
5 3/4 x 3 1/4 x 2 1/2-inch loaf pan
5 5/8 x 3 1/8 x 2 1/4-inch loaf pan
7 x 1-inch pie pan
7 x 1 1/2-inch round cake pan

2 1/4 cups
5 3/4 x 3 1/2 x 2 1/4-inch loaf pan

3 cups to 3 1/2 cups

6-inch sapphire-style Bundt pan
6 x 1 3/4-inch heart-shaped cake pan
6 x 2-inch petal- or heart-shaped cake pan
6 x 3 1/2 x 2-inch loaf pan
6 x 4 1/2 x 3-inch loaf pan
6 1/4 x 2 1/2-inch ring mold
7 3/4 x 1-inch two-piece tart pan
8 x 1 1/4-inch pie pan

3 3/4 cups
6 x 2-inch round cake pan

4 cups to 4 1/2 cups
6 x 3-inch springform pan
7 1/2 x 3 3/4 x 2 1/4-inch loaf pan
7 3/4 x 3 5/8 x 2 1/4-inch loaf pan
8 x 1 1/2-inch pie pan
8 by 1 1/2-inch round cake pan
8 x 4 x 2 1/2-inch loaf pan
8 1/4 x 2 1/4-inch ring mold
8 1/2 x 2 1/4-inch ring mold
9 x 1 1/4-inch pie pan
9 1/2 x 1-inch two-piece tart pan
9 1/2 x 4 1/2 x 2 1/2-inch stoneware loaf pan
10 1/4 x 1 1/4-inch fluted *obsttortenform*

5 cups to 5 1/2 cups
6 1/2 x 3-inch Turk's head pan
6 1/2 x 3 1/2-inch small Bundt pan
7 x 2-inch round cake pan
7 x 2 1/2-inch springform pan
8 x 3 3/4 x 2-inch disposable loaf pan
8 x 3 3/4 x 2 3/4-inch brioche pan
8 x 4 x 2-inch loaf pan
8 1/4 x 4 1/4 x 2 1/2-inch ceramic savarin mold
9 x 1 1/2-inch pie pan
9 x 1 1/2-inch heart-shaped cake pan

9 1/2 x 1-inch tart pan
10 x 1-inch two-piece tart pan
10 x 1 1/2-inch fluted quiche mold

6 cups to 6 1/2 cups

7 x 3-inch brioche mold
7 x 5 1/2 x 4-inch oval melon mold
7 1/2 x 3-inch Bundt pan
8-inch bevel/fluted tube pan
8 x 2-inch round cake pan
8 x 3 1/4-inch Bundt pan
8 x 3 x 2-inch loaf pan
8 x 8 x 1 1/2-inch square pan
8 1/2 x 3 5/8 x 2-inch loaf pan
8 1/2 x 4 1/2 x 2 1/2-inch loaf pan
8 1/2 x 4 1/2 x 2 5/8-inch loaf pan
9 x 1 1/2-inch round cake pan
9 x 2-inch ceramic pie pan
9 1/4 x 8 1/2 x 2-inch heart-shaped cake pan
10 x 1 1/2-inch pie pan
10 x 6 x 1 3/4-inch rectangular pan

7 cups

8 1/2 x 3 1/2-inch kugelhopf pan
8 1/2 x 4 1/4 x 3 1/8-inch seamless loaf pan
9 1/2-inch Pyrex deep-dish pie pan
11 x 1-inch two-piece tart pan

7 1/2 cups

6 x 4 1/4-inch Charlotte mold
8 1/2 x 2 1/2-inch springform pan
9 x 2 3/4-inch ring mold

8 cups to 8 3/4 cups

8 x 8 x 2-inch square pan
9 x 2-inch deep-dish pie pan
9 x 2-inch round cake pan
9 x 3-inch fluted brioche pan
9 x 4 x 4-inch lidded/Pullman/*pain de mie* loaf pan
9 x 5 x 2 5/8-inch loaf pan

9 x 5 x 3-inch loaf pan
9 x 9 x 1 1/2-inch square pan
9 1/4 x 2 3/4-inch ring mold
9 1/2 x 3 1/4-inch glass kugelhopf mold
9 1/2 x 3 1/4-inch fluted brioche pan
9 5/8 x 5 1/2 x 2 3/4-inch loaf pan
10 x 2-inch two-piece tart pan
10 x 4 x 3-inch loaf pan
10 x 5 x 2 5/8-inch loaf pan
11 x 7 x 1 1/2-inch rectangular pan
11 x 7 x 2-inch rectangular pan (2 quarts)
12 x 4 x 2 1/2-inch tea loaf pan
13 x 4 x 4-inch lidded Pullman/*pain de mie* loaf pan
13 3/4 x 4 1/4-inch rectangular two-piece tart pan
14 x 4 1/2-inch rectangular two-piece tart pan

9 cups
8 x 3-inch tube pan
8 x 3 1/4-inch professional tube pan
9 x 3-inch Bundt pan
9 x 3 1/2-inch Bundt pan
12 1/2 x 1-inch two-piece tart pan

10 cups
8 x 3-inch round cake pan
8 x 3 1/4-inch round cake pan
9 x 2 1/2-inch springform pan
9 x 2 3/4-inch springform pan
9 x 3-inch tube pan
9 x 9 x 2-inch square pan
9 1/2 x 2 1/2-inch springform pan
11 x 6 1/2 x 3 1/4-inch baking pan
11 3/4 x 7 3/4 x 1 3/4-inch Pyrex baking dish
12 x 7 1/2 x 1-inch baking pan
15 x 10 x 1-inch jellyroll pan

10 3/4 cups to 11 cups
9 x 3-inch round cake pan

9 x 4-inch kugelhopf mold
9 x 4 1/2-inch fluted tube pan
10 x 2-inch round cake pan
15 1/2 x 10 1/2 x 1-inch jellyroll pan

12 cups

9 x 3 1/2-inch angel cake or tube pan
9 1/2 x 2 1/2-inch three-in-one springform pan
9 1/2 x 2 3/4-inch springform pan
9 3/4 x 4 1/4-inch kugelhopf mold
10 x 2 1/4-inch springform pan
10 x 2 1/2-inch springform pan
10 x 3 1/4-inch kugelhopf mold
10 x 3 1/2-inch Bundt pan
10 x 10 x 2-inch square pan
13 1/2 x 8 1/2 x 2-inch Pyrex baking dish

12 cups to 13 cups

10 x 4 1/4-inch kugelhopf mold

15 cups

10 x 4 1/4-inch Bundt pan
12 1/4 x 8 1/4 x 2-inch rectangular pan
13 x 9 x 2-inch rectangular pan
14 x 11 x 2-inch baking pan

16 cups

9 1/2 x 4-inch tube pan
9 1/2 x 13 x 2 1/2-inch rectangular pan
10 x 4-inch tube pan
10 x 5-inch nonstick tube pan
10 x 3-inch round cake pan
12 x 2-inch round cake pan

18 cups

17 x 12 x 1-inch rectangular pan
14 x 10 1/2 x 2 1/2-inch roasting pan

OVEN TEMPERATURE EQUIVALENTS

Fahrenheit	Oven Mark	Celsius	Heat of Oven
150°		66°	Lowest (used for dehydrating)
200°		93°	Warm oven
225°	Gas 1/4	110°	Very slow oven/very cool/very low
250°	Gas 1/2	120°	Very slow oven/cool/very low
275°	Gas 1	140°	Very slow oven/cool/very low
300°	Gas 2	150°	Slow oven/cool/low
325°	Gas 3	160°	Low oven/very moderate oven
350°	Gas 4	180°	Moderate oven
375°	Gas 5	190°	Moderately hot oven
400°	Gas 6	200°	Fairly hot oven
425°	Gas 7	220°	Hot oven
450°	Gas 8	230°	Hot oven
475°	Gas 9	240°	Very hot oven
500°	Gas 10	260°	Extremely hot oven

When using a convection/fan-assisted oven, lower the oven temperature by 25°F, reduce the cooking time by 25%, and use low-sided baking pans for best air circulation

Thank you for purchasing my book, dear reader.
I hope you will find it helpful.
                                    Jean B. MacLeod

BIBLIOGRAPHY

Allen, Darina. *Forgotten Skills of Cooking*. London: Kyle Books, 2009.

America's Test Kitchen eds. *The How Can It Be Gluten Free Cookbook*: *Revolutionary Techniques. Groundbreaking Recipes*. Brookline, MA: America's Test Kitchen, 2014.

Barham, Peter. *The Science of Cooking*. New York: Springer-Verlag, 2001.

Bartlett, Jonathan. *The Cook's Dictionary and Culinary Reference: A Comprehensive Definitive Guide to Cooking and Food*. Chicago: Contemporary Books, 1996.

Bender, David D. *Dictionary of Food and Nutrition*. 2nd ed. Oxford: Oxford University Press, 2005.

Beranbaum, Rose Levy. *The Bread Bible*. New York: W.W. Norton, 2003.

Boutenko, Serei. *Wild Edibles: A Practical Guide to Foraging, with Easy Identification of 60 Edible Plants and 67 Recipes*. Berkeley, CA: North Atlantic Books, 2013.

Boyce, Kim. *Good to the Grain: Baking with Whole-Grain Flours*. With Amy Scattergood. New York: Stewart, Tabori & Chang, 2010.

Braker, Flo. *The Simple Art of Perfect Baking*. New York: William Morrow, 1985.

Brill, Steve. *Identifying and Harvesting Edible and Medicinal Plants in Wild (and Not So Wild) Places*. With Evelyn Dean. New York: Hearst Books, 1994.

Clark, Melissa. *A Kitchen Primer*. New York: Berkley Books, 1997.

Corriher, Shirley O. *BakeWise: The Hows and Whys of Successful Baking with over 200 Magnificent Recipes*. New York: Scribner, 2008.

Crocker, Betty. *Betty Crocker Bisquick II Cookbook*. Hoboken, NJ: Wiley Publishing, 2004.

Culinary Institute of America. *The New Professional Chef*. 6th ed. New York: Van Nostrand Reinhold, 1996.

Cunningham, Marion. *The Fannie Farmer Cookbook*. 13th ed. New York: Alfred A. Knopf, 1996.

Daley, Regan. *In The Sweet Kitchen*. New York: Artisan Workman, 2001.

D'Aprix, David. *The Fearless International Foodie*. New York: Living Language, 2001.

David, Elizabeth. *English Bread and Yeast Cookery*. American Edition. New York: Viking Press, 1997.

Davidson, Alan. *The Oxford Companion to Food*. Oxford: Oxford University Press, 1999.

English, Camper. "The New Sweet." *Fine Cooking*, April-May, 2010, 37.

Field, Carol. *The Italian Baker*. rev. ed. Berkeley, CA: Ten Speed Press, 2011.

Figoni, Paula. *How Baking Works: Exploring the Fundamentals of Baking Science*. 3rd ed. Hoboken, NJ: John Wiley & Sons, 2011.

Forkish, Ken. *Flour Water Salt Yeast: The Fundamentals of Artisan Bread and Pizza*. Berkeley, CA: Ten Speed Press, 2012.

Fortin, François, ed. dir. *The Visual Food Encyclopedia*. New York: MacMillan, 1996.

Friberg, Bo. *The Professional Pastry Chef*. 2nd ed. New York: Van Nostrand Reinhold, 1990.

Gisslen, Wayne. *Professional Cooking*. 5th ed. New York: John Wiley & Sons, 2003.

Glezer, Maggie. *Artisan Baking*. New York: Artisan, 2005.

Green, Aliza. *Starting with Ingredients*. Philadelphia: Running Press, 2006.

Grigson, Jane. *Jane Grigson's British Cookery*. New York: Atheneum, 1985.

Grigson, Jane, and Charlotte Knox. *Exotic Fruits and Vegetables*. New York: Henry Holt, 1986.

Grigson, Sophie. *Gourmet Ingredients*. New York: Van Nostrand Reinhold, 1991.

Hamelman, Jeffrey. *Bread: A Baker's Book of Techniques and Recipes*. 2nd ed. Hoboken, NJ: John Wiley & Sons, 2013.

Harbutt, Juliet. Cheese: *A Complete Guide to Over 300 Cheeses of Distinction*. Minocqua, WI: Willow Creek Press, 1999.

Hibler, Janie. *The Berry Bible: With 175 Recipes Using Cultivated and Wild, Fresh and Frozen Berries*. New York: HarperCollins, 2004.

Imeson, Alan, ed. *Thickening and Gelling Agents for Food*. 2nd. ed. Gaithersburg, MD: Aspen Publishers, 1999.

Kallas, John. *Edible Wild Plants: Wild Foods from Dirt to Plate*. Layton, UT: Gibbs Smith, 2010.

Karousos, George, Bradley J. Ware, and Theodore H. Karousos. *The Patissier's Art*. Hoboken, NJ: John Wiley & Sons, 1994.

King Arthur Flour. *King Arthur Flour Whole Grain Baking*. Woodstock, VT: Countryman Press, 2006.

King Arthur Flour Master Weight Chart www.kingarthurflour.com/recipe/master-weight-chart.

Kipfer, Barbara Ann. *The Culinarian: A Kitchen Desk Reference*. Hoboken, NJ: John Wiley & Sons, 2011.

Kuntz, Bernie. *Whole Foods Kitchen Journal*. Redmond, WA: Elfin Cove Press, 1989.

Mackey, Leslie, and Sallie Morris. *Illustrated Cook's Book of Ingredients: 2,500 of the World's Best with Classic Recipes*. 1st. U.S. ed. New York: DK Publishing, 2010.

Madadian, Sacha. "Tasting Processed Egg Whites." *Cook's Country*. Feb/March, 2013, 23.

Malgieri, Nick. *Chocolate*. New York: HarperCollins, 1998.

——— . *Nick Malgieri's Bread: Over 60 Breads, Rolls and Cakes Plus Delicious Recipes Using Them*. Lanham, MD: Kyle Books, 2012.

Marks, Gil. *Encyclopedia of Jewish Food*. Hoboken, NJ: John Wiley & Sons, 2010.

Matsuoka Wong, Tama. *Foraged Flavor: Finding Fabulous Ingredients in Your Backyard or Farmer's Market*. With Eddy Leroux. New York: Clarkson Potter, 2012.

McGee, Harold. *Keys to Good Cooking: A Guide to Making the Best of Food and Recipes*. New York: The Penguin Press, 2010.

Medrich, Alice. *Bitter Sweet: Recipes and Tales from a Life in Chocolate*. New York: Artisan, 2003.

Nathan, Joan. *The New American Cooking*. New York: Alfred A. Knopf, 2005.

Netzer, Corinne T. *Encyclopedia of Food Values*. New York: Dell Publishing, 1992.

Nilsen, Angela, and Jeni Wright. *21st Century Cook: The Bible of Ingredients, Terms, Tools & Techniques*. London: Cassell Illustrated, 2006.

Page, Karen, and Andrew Dornenburg. *The Flavor Bible: The Essential Guide to Culinary Creativity, Based on the Wisdom of America's Most Imaginative Chefs*. New York: Little, Brown, 2008.

Pascal, Cybele. *The Allergen-Free Baker's Handbook*. Berkeley, CA: Celestial Arts, 2009.

Pennington, Jean, and Judith Spungen Douglass. *Bowes & Church's Food Values of Portions Commonly Used*. 18th ed. Baltimore: Lippincott Williams & Wilkins, 2005.

Quinn, Janie. *Essential Eating: Sprouted Baking with Whole Grain Flours That Digest as Vegetables*. Waverly, PA: Azure Moon Publishing, 2008.

Reinhart, Peter. *Peter Reinhart's Whole Grain Breads: New Techniques, Extraordinary Flavor*. Berkeley, CA: Ten Speed Press, 2007.

Resnik, Linda, and Dee Brock. *Food FAQs: Substitutions, Yields & Equivalents*. Tyler, Texas: FAQs Press, 2000.

Riely, Elizabeth. *The Chef's Companion: A Culinary Dictionary*. 3rd ed. Hoboken, NJ: John Wiley & Sons, 2003.

Robertson, Laurel, Carol Flinders, and Bronwen Godfrey. *The Laurel's Kitchen Bread Book: A Guide to Whole-Grain Breadmaking*. New York: Random House, 1984.

Rolland, Jacques L, and Carol Sherman. *The Food Encyclopedia*. Toronto: Robert Rose, 2006.

Schmidt, Arno. *Chef's Book of Formulas, Yields, and Sizes*. New York: Van Nostrand Reinhold, 1990.

Stagg, Camille. *The Cook's Advisor*. Brattleboro, VT: Stephen Greene Press, 1982.

Techamuanvivit, Pim. *The Foodie Handbook: The (Almost) Definitive Guide to Gastronomy*. San Francisco: Chronicle Books, 2009.

Thayer, Samuel. *Nature's Garden: A Guide to Identifying, Harvesting, and Preparing Edible Wild Plants*. Birchwood, WI: Forager's Harvest Press, 2010.

The Illustrated Cook's Book of Ingredients: 2,500 of the World's Best with Classic Recipes. 1st. U.S. ed. New York: DK Publishing, 2010.

Watt, Bernice K., and Annabel L. Merrill. Composition of Foods. Agriculture Handbook No. 8. Rev. ed. U.S. Department of Agriculture. Washington, DC: Government. Printing Office, 1963.

Weiss, Linda. *Kitchen Magic: Food Substitutions for the Allergic*. New Canaan, CT: Keats Publishing, 1994.

Other Books by Jean B. MacLeod

If I'd Only Listened to My Mom, I'd Know How to Do This: Hundreds of Household Remedies

The Waste-Wise Kitchen Companion: Hundreds of Practical Tips for Repairing, Reusing, and Repurposing Food

The Waste-Wise Gardener: Tips and Techniques to Save Time, Money, and Energy While Creating the Garden of Your Dreams

The Kitchen Paraphernalia Handbook: Hundreds of Substitutions for Common (and Not-So-Common) Utensils, Gadgets, Tools, and Techniques

Seasoning Substitutions: Swaps and Stand-ins for Sweet or Savory Condiments and Flavorings

Made in the USA
Coppell, TX
20 September 2020